MW01258310

THE PSYCHOANALYTIC VISION

Psychoanalytic therapy is distinguished by its immersion in the world of the experiencing subject. In *The Psychoanalytic Vision*, Frank Summers argues that analytic therapy and its unique epistemology is a worldview that stands in clear opposition to the hegemonic cultural value system of objectification, quantification, and materialism. *The Psychoanalytic Vision* situates psychoanalysis as a voice of the rebel, affirming the importance of the subjective in contrast to the culture of objectification.

Founded on phenomenological philosophy from which it derives its unique epistemology and ethical grounding, psychoanalytic therapy as a hermeneutic of the experiential world has no role for reified concepts. Consequently, fundamental analytic concepts such as "the unconscious" and "the intrapsychic" are reconceptualized to eliminate reifying elements.

The essence of *The Psychoanalytic Vision* is the freshness of its theoretical and clinical approach as a hermeneutic of the experiential world. Fundamental clinical phenomena, such as dreams, time, and the experience of the other, are reformulated, and these theoretical shifts are illustrated with a variety of vivid case descriptions.

The last part of the book is devoted to the surreptitious role beliefs and values of contemporary culture play in many forms of psychopathology.

For clinicians, *The Psychoanalytic Vision* offers a fresh clinical theory based on the consistent application of the subjectification of human experience, and for scholars, a worldview that provides the framework for a potentially fruitful cross-fertilization of ideas with cognate disciplines.

Frank Summers is a Professor of Clinical Psychiatry and the Behavioral Sciences at Northwestern University and a training and supervising analyst at the Chicago Institute for Psychoanalysis. Author of three previous books and numerous articles, he is currently President of the Division of Psychoanalysis of the American Psychological Association. He maintains a private practice of psychoanalytic therapy and psychoanalysis in Chicago, Illinois.

THE PSYCHOANALYTIC VISION

The Experiencing Subject, Transcendence, and the
Therapeutic Process

Frank Summers

Routledge
Taylor & Francis Group

NEW YORK AND LONDON

First published 2013
by Routledge
711 Third Avenue, New York, NY 10017

Simultaneously published in the UK
by Routledge
27 Church Road, Hove, East Sussex BN3 2FA

Routledge is an imprint of the Taylor & Francis Group, an informa business

© 2013 Taylor & Francis

Library of Congress Cataloging in Publication Data

Summers, Frank.
The psychoanalytic vision : the experiencing subject, transcendence, and
    the therapeutic process / authored by Frank Summers. — First edition.
        pages cm
    1. Psychotherapy.   2. Psychotherapist and patient.   3. Transcendence
(Philosophy)   I. Title.
    RC480.5.S82 2013
    616.89'14—dc23
    2012037264

ISBN: 978-0-415-51939-7 (hbk)
ISBN: 978-0-415-51940-3 (pbk)
ISBN: 978-0-203-56916-0 (ebk)

Typeset in Garamond
by Apex CoVantage, LLC

TO ALANA

CONTENTS

ACKNOWLEDGEMENTS

I wish to express my gratitude to the staff of Routledge who worked on this project: Kris Spring, who first suggested the idea, Kate Hawes, Kirsten Buchanan; and Denise File at Apex. All were very helpful and supportive. And I owe a special debt of gratitude to two colleagues who gave generously of their time to read and comment on some of the chapters: Dr. John Riker and Dr. Kris Yi. Their invaluable comments and suggestions were of great help to me in composing final drafts.

I would like to thank the following who have given permission to use my previously published work in this book:

Chapter 2:
Summers, F. (2011) "Psychoanalysis, the Tyranny of Objectivism, and the Rebellion of the Subjective," *International Journal of Applied Psychoanalytic Studies*, 9 (1) pp. 35–47.

Chapter Four:
Summers, F. (2011) Psychoanalysis: Romantic, Not Wild, *Psychoanalytic Psychology*, 28 (1) pp. 13–32.

Chapter Seven:
Summers, F. (2012) The Transcendent Experience of the Other, *Journal of Theoretical and Philosophical Psychology*, 32 (4) pp. 236–245.

Part I

THEORY

1

THE SUBJECT OF PSYCHOANALYSIS

In commenting on the Hegelian system, Kierkegaard once said that it was perfectly elegant and complete, except for one minor point—which was, of course, the existing subject. Psychoanalysis, while never as desubjectified as the Hegelian system, has, in its history, a trend of favoring abstract theoretical concepts over patient experience, as one finds, for example, in some forms of classical ego theory (e.g., Hartmann, Kris, & Loewenstein, 1946, 1949). But, in recent years, in opposition to this reliance on abstract concepts, the experiencing subject has become the focal point of psychoanalytic discourse and practice, often pushing theory into the background. This historical transformation of the field has received impetus from relational theory, but the movement toward subjectification of analytic thought and practice can be found in most major analytic schools (e.g., Gray, 1973, 1982; Kohut, 1984; Winnicott, 1971; Bollas, 1987; Williams, 2010). The plea to give pride of place to the analysand's experience can be heard among analysts of a variety of persuasions, many of whom disagree with each other, but all of whom want to return the analytic enterprise to its origins in the experience of the analysand. This book is an exploration of what it means for psychoanalysis to see itself as a process of illumination, engagement, and transformation of the experiencing subject.

It may seem puzzling that more than one hundred years after the first analytic cases lay on Freud's couch, analysts are still debating the very nature of psychoanalysis. However, if one looks at the psychoanalytic undertaking in the context of Western culture, especially American culture, dominated by materialism, objectification, and quantification, the very concept of psychoanalysis is controversial because its subject matter is the experiencing subject who is neither material, objectifiable, nor quantifiable. When one attempts to explore subjective life in the Anglo-American world, controversy soon follows. Not being immune to the culture in which it is embedded, psychoanalysis has come under the influence of values and beliefs antithetical to its purpose, and the result is confusion about the ontological status of psychoanalysis (e.g., Beland, 1994).

Freud had two conflicting, perhaps contradictory, views of the analytic enterprise. From his first analytic publications, his data consisted of case studies in which the patient's experience was the only evidence for the treatment approach and research conclusions (Breuer & Freud, 1895). For each patient, Freud showed that the patient's symptoms could be understood and removed through understanding their unconscious origin. The subject of analysis here was the experiencing subject, which was both source and arbiter of analytic inquiry.

The analytic strategy was to allow the patient's associations and experience to lead the process. Freud analogized the analytic stance to the telephone receiver of a transmitting microphone. In his papers on technique he advocated an open-ended listening in which the analyst must be in a position to "make use of all he is told." Freud (1912) inveighed that the analyst "turns his own unconscious like a receptive organ toward the transmitting unconscious of the patient." Irrespective of whether such an attitude is possible in the pure way Freud depicted it, in this statement he made openness to all the patient's material in an "evenly hovering" attitude central to his technical approach. The analyst's role is to uncover and interpret the patient's unconscious experience, and therefore in his analytic work Freud used a hermeneutic method. Such an analytic stance would appear to make the essence of the field a specialized process of inquiry, rather than a particular content.

Nonetheless, in the same year as the publication of his first volume of case studies, *Studies on Hysteria* (Breuer & Freud, 1895), Freud wrote *The Project for a Scientific Psychology* in which the subject disappears (Freud, 1895a). In the latter he attempted to account for the psyche solely by neurological excitations and discharges, and this somatic view of the psyche was not jettisoned by Freud's later theoretical innovations. On the contrary, it was reaffirmed in *Instincts and Their Vicissitudes*, which founded the psyche on drives that have biological origin but psychological manifestation (Freud, 1915) and in his latest writing, in which the psychical apparatus is described in terms of organized energies (Freud, 1938).

It was the somatic nature of the psyche, Freud believed, that made psychoanalysis "a science like any other" (Freud, 1938, p.158–9). He was consistent in his contention throughout his career that it is the somatic nature of the psyche, extended in space, which makes psychology a natural science (p.196–7). He believed that the laws of the psyche are as discoverable as those of any natural science. Science was equated with somatic processes, and because Freud was committed to including psychoanalysis among the sciences, he regarded biological phenomena, such as energy discharge and instinctual forces, as the essence of the psyche. This way of viewing the psyche eliminated the subject. In this theoretical work, we see a "biological Freud," as opposed to the "hermeneutic Freud" who engaged the individual patient's experience.

The juxtaposition of *Studies on Hysteria* (Breuer & Freud, 1895) and *The Project for a Scientific Psychology* (Freud, 1895a) written in close temporal proximity demonstrates the split within Freud who advocated a method of openness to the experience of the subject while holding to a neurological model of tension discharge that eliminated the experiencing subject. Freud's method was hermeneutic while the theory on which he attempted to found the field was neurological.

Given Freud's (1938) belief that the task of psychoanalysis as a natural science is to understand the somatic processes that form the psychological organization, Freud (1912) the biologist was focused on showing that psychoanalysis had a knowledge base on which the field could rely. The discoveries made in exploring unconscious mental phenomena led him to conclusions regarding the etiology of neurosis (e.g., Freud, 1895b, 1896, 1916–17, 1924, 1926). The cause was first believed to be the repression of sexual trauma, later changed to sexual fantasies and wishes, and finally the Oedipal Complex, the discovery of which was regarded as a major contribution of psychoanalysis to science. Although *Studies on Hysteria* is a hermeneutic work, even then Freud held the sexual seduction theory of neurosis. The purpose here is not to assess that etiological theory, but to highlight the fact that from the beginning of the field Freud had a conclusion which the analytic process was expected to reach despite his advocacy of complete openness to the patient's experience.

An analytic stance that presumes repressed Oedipal conflicts are the core of all neurosis is in direct conflict with the open-ended technical strategy Freud was advocating as the essence of the analytic method. The telephone receiver attitude was the essential instrument of analytic technique, but it is difficult to see how the analyst can be open to all "transmissions" while assuming that the Oedipal conflict was at the core of the neurosis. Nonetheless, these two attitudes permeate Freud's theoretical and clinical writing. Insofar as he assumed a conclusion he was not following the precepts of his open-ended technique and the experiencing subject was no longer the source and arbiter of analytic inquiry. The analyst's theory held sway as a ready-to-hand tool standing between the patient's experience and analytic listening. To this degree Freud displaced the existing subject from her preeminent position at the center of the analytic process. Nonetheless, Freud never abandoned his view that the clinician should adopt a stance of openness like a human telephone receiver to all patient transmissions.

The upshot is a legacy of two conflicting ways of viewing the psychoanalytic method, each of which gave rise to a paradigmatic way of conceptualizing the nature of the analytic enterprise. While developmental and clinical theories have garnered the lion's share of attention in analytic debates, here we see another decisive cleavage in analytic thought that cuts across theoretical differences and has critical clinical implications. We will now trace the historical evolution of both paradigms in order to arrive at an interpretation of the nature of contemporary psychoanalysis.

"The Deductivists"

On one side, those who insist on the "scientific" status of analysis see the field as a body of established scientific principles to be applied in the clinical arena. The subject's experience is sought and recognized in order to see how one can apply the knowledge base of psychoanalysis to the patient's symptoms and psychic deficits. Theory is applied deductively, and the individual patient's situation is an instance of this theoretical knowledge. The analyst adopts a clinical stance that seeks indications of a presupposed theory and interprets the patient's material in terms of the theory when such evidence appears. This deductive imposition of theoretical ideas on the patient's experience is a product of the belief that a scientific body of psychoanalytic knowledge has been established and is applicable to the individual case. In this sense, the deductive approach is a derivative of "scientism," the claim to be a science based on an effort to imitate the scientific method without regard for whether the method fits the subject matter (e.g., Ricouer, 1950; Maslow, 1969; Putnam, 1990). Although theoretical imposition is not technically what is meant by "scientism," it is a product of the scientistic belief that scientifically established truths can be applied to the individual instance.

One can see, then, that the epistemological stance of the analyst has a direct and highly significant impact on clinical strategy. The scientistic attitude has given rise to a long tradition of deductive interpretation. For analysts who adhere to the classical drive theory, there was, and continues to be, a presumed truth which it is the task of analysis to uncover. Ego psychology added the importance of analyzing the ego, but in its classical form the aim of analysis continued to be the uncovering of repressed Oedipal conflicts (e.g., A. Freud, 1936; Hartmann, Kris, & Loewenstein, 1946; Loewenstein, 1950; Rapaport, 1951, 1957). This presupposed conclusion directs the analytic inquiry, thus compromising the therapist's openness to the patient's experience. That this analytic posture is not a "straw man" nor an antiquated approach no longer practiced, one need only consider the following case reported by senior well-respected, well-published analysts in the esteemed *Journal of the American Psychoanalytic Association* (Busch et al., 1999).

Mr. J., a successful and highly competitive 30-year-old professional, came for treatment for panic episodes. Both parents were emotionally volatile, and his father was especially temperamental and abusive, both physically and verbally. He reported that he was by far his father's favorite among four children. His father attended all his athletic events while ignoring the other children. Mr. J. recalled "throwing" sports contests because he became "tired" of pursuing them and feeling anxiety and guilt when telling his father of the losses. The father had political and athletic aspirations for Mr. J., and wanted his son to work part-time for him. When Mr. J. refused, his father responded angrily: "You've ruined our relationship." This threw Mr. J. into an anxious, angry, and guilty state during which he had an altercation with a police officer.

In the analysis, Mr. J. realized that all three of his panic episodes had occurred after successes. He had a dream in which he drove a truck over a bridge because he did not make adequate preparation. In association to the dream, Mr. J. commented that he felt unable to care for himself. The therapist interpreted that belief as a fantasy that he needed to make himself a nonthreatening figure for his father. Mr. J. responded that he believed that if he asserted his independence, he would hurt and enrage his father who would then withdraw his love and support. The therapist suggested that this was the reason he had to undo his successes by panicking. His "throwing" athletic events in his youth and provoking the police officer were interpreted as further examples of self-sabotage and punishment seeking. The authors concluded that Mr. J. feared his desire for independence would cause castration and the loss of his father's love and that for Mr. J. "being successful and powerful represented a guilty oedipal triumph." Although they acknowledge that his father had narcissistic wishes for Mr. J. to be an athletic champion and political hero, they do not fit that fact into their formulation of the case.

Mr. J's neurosis is conceptualized as an "Oedipal triumph" despite the absence of any evidence that Mr. J. feared his father's castration or retaliation in any way were he to be successful. There was abundant evidence that the father was threatened by his son's *autonomy*, but the authors equate that fear with fear of his son's success, a gargantuan and unjustifiable leap. The clinical evidence indicated to the contrary that Mr. J.'s father was narcissistically invested in his favorite child's achievements, including having political aspirations for him. In fact, the son was overcome with guilt and anxiety when telling his father of his losses, not his successes. The father's rage at the son's refusal to work for him makes sense only if the father was threatened by his son's autonomy, not his success. In fact, success in which the father took part was what the father most desired. He had political aspirations for his son, was enraged when the younger man did not follow them, and furious when his son refused to work for him. The father did not fear his son's success as long as he participated in it. In fact, the father was overly invested in his son being successful in the way the father chose. The older man was threatened by success only if it was achieved *without him*. Mr. J.'s father was virtually demanding that his son be an achiever in a manner from which the older man could derive narcissistic gratification. The evidence strongly suggests that Mr. J.'s sabotage was a way to retaliate against his father's effort to exploit him, rather than self-punishment. While it is always difficult to draw definitive conclusions from clinical reports, this alternative formulation fits the published evidence better than the Oedipal interpretation.

The authors' formulation is representative of the all-too-common tendency in the analytic tradition to impose preconceived theory on the analysand's experience. In their zeal to arrive at the Oedipal conclusion their theory predicts, the authors of this paper overlook some of the patient's most significant and painful experiences, such as his anxiety over any exercise of autonomy and his fear of disappointing his father by failing. Such decisive distinctions cannot be made when the analyst uses theory as a presupposition and the patient's experience is bypassed in favor of theoretical dogma. Instead of a heuristic, theory became a Procrustean bed into which the patient's experience was forced.

The fact that the paper was published in a prestigious journal is significant because it demonstrates that not only the authors, but also the editors of a preeminent analytic journal did not find fault with the analytic reasoning. Clearly, neither the authors nor editors were concerned about the inferences made, which suggests that the theoretical imposition in this case is representative of common analytic thinking.

It would not be difficult to argue that another theory would be a better fit for the clinical data of the case, but to leave the critique at that point would miss the deeper and more far-reaching epistemological flaw. The most serious problem with the authors' analysis of this case is not that the Oedipal theory was used, but *how* it was used. The authors' reasoning represents a common misuse of theory in approaching clinical material. If the problematic relationship of theory to technique is not grasped, one would expect the same error to be repeated by proponents of any analytic theory. And the history of psychoanalysis provides abundant evidence that this is the case. Institutional psychoanalysis has cemented the self-confirmation of the classical theory. Brenner (1971) argued that the fact that analysts have long believed in the existence of the aggressive drive is sufficient evidence of its legitimacy. This claim, of course, has no more validity than the contention that the sun travels around the Earth because astronomers once believed it to be so. Moreover, any analyst from the American Psychoanalytic Association who openly opposed the drive theory at the time Brenner wrote did so at the risk of jeopardizing her career. So, for survival, analysts were conjoined to accept the drive theory, often without question, and that coerced belief was used as evidence in favor of the theory.

Melanie Klein (1957) shifted the origin of pathology from Oedipal dynamics to excessive aggressivity and envy in unresolved paranoid-schizoid or depressive position dynamics, but she shared with ego psychology the epistemological position that the analyst has a body of knowledge that is to be applied to the patient when the clinical material is suggestive of the assumed dynamics.

For example, Klein reports the case of a patient who missed two analytic sessions due to shoulder pain and upon her return complained of the pain and others' lack of interest in her, and wished to have someone cover her shoulder, warm her, and then go away. She dreamed that no one served her in a restaurant but a "determined" woman took two or three cakes and then the patient did the same. Klein interpreted the shoulder pain as unsatisfactory breast experiences; the cakes, the missed sessions; the determined woman, the analyst who is assumed to be an object of both identification and projection of her greed. There is scant evidence for any of this, especially the envy, not a hint of which appears in the clinical material. Such leaps of interpretive inference are likely to lead the content in a direction that fits the analyst's theory rather than the patient's experience. Furthermore, even if it does capture some aspect of the patient's dynamics, it is so far removed from the patient's experience as to be of questionable value. Despite her decisive differences from ego psychology, Klein adopted the epistemological stance of ego psychology by assuming dynamic explanations to which the analysis is to arrive.

Despite some significant modifications in Kleinian theory, many contemporary Kleinians make the same assumption about analytic outcome (e.g., Grotstein, 1977; Segal, 1983; Joseph, 1992; Steiner, 1993). For example, Joseph (1971) reported a case of perversion in which after she made what she regarded as a helpful interpretation, the patient would typically go into a deep silence often with heavy breathing. The session, and with it the entire analysis, had a flat, verbose feel. Joseph believed it was "clear" that the patient was making her work sterile and obliterating analytic feeding and creativity out of envy. As with the Klein example, there is no indication of envy in the reported clinical material. Nonetheless, she offered this understanding not as a possibility, but as a foregone conclusion. The inference that envy laid at the root of his problems was presupposed, not derived from the clinical material. The presupposition that aggressivity and envy are the source of pathology pulls for the deductive use of theory commonly seen in Kleinian case reports.

Neo-Kleinians follow suit. Kernberg's et al., (1989) contention that splitting of good and bad objects is the pathogenic root of the borderline, narcissistic, and other personality disorders is another example of deductive clinical inference. He offers examples of patients who, when confronted with their presumed split off aggression, become increasingly mistrustful, angry, and often act out (Kernberg, 1975, p.95–6.). In one case Kernberg insisted that the interpretation was accurate *because* the patient went on a substance abuse binge and needed to be rehospitalized. One wonders what reaction would cause Kernberg to question his theory. Irrespective of what the patient's clinical picture was or her reaction to interpretations of splitting, in each case he defined the pathology as splitting and the treatment as the integration of the two "contradictory attitudes." His conclusion that splitting was the essence of the pathology is misrepresented as a "theoretical frame."

For example, one woman could not have orgasm except by fantasizing mutilation of her and her partners' genitals. The only principle Kernberg reported was the fear of confusing sexuality and warmth with aggression despite the fact that they were already fused in her belief that only in hatred and death could "true love" be found. The problem was to *undo* the inextricable entanglement of warmth and love with aggression, not to fuse them. Furthermore, the patient's fears of orgasm emerged as fear of personality dissolution into uncontrollable fragments and fears of "uncontrollable wetness." The fact that she feared disintegration in orgasm did not enter Kernberg's formulation of her sexual inhibition. His focus on splitting so dominated his thinking that he invoked it even when it had little relevance to the symptoms. Kernberg's formulations, like those of the Kleinians, tend to be presupposed explanations triggered by any data that have even a slight resemblance to the awaiting formula.

Similarly, it is not uncommon for self psychologists to conclude that any particular transference fits the self psychological mold. For example, any indication that the patient feels a need to be close to, is disappointed in, or is disrupted by an analytic error is sufficient evidence to label the transference "idealizing" (e.g., Shapiro, 1985; Ornstein, 1990; Lachmann & Beebe, 1992). At times this interpretation is made without any justification beyond the patient's disappointment or dependence, as though these experiences, in themselves, are sufficient evidence to infer an idealizing transference.

For example, Lachmann and Beebe (1992) report a case of a woman who was disrupted by the analyst's interpretation that she might need to be cared for, but found herself repeatedly in the self-sacrificing role of caring for others. This dynamic was traced to a shift in her relationship with her father beginning in puberty when she realized that he needed her. She felt he had been "daring" but as he began to decline, she used her competence to make him feel strong and effective, which made her feel valuable and needed. Her father was proud of her and his bragging about her made her feel "really good." It was concluded that the young woman was held together by the support of her father, which made her feel proud and competent.

The authors believe that the patient, through her efforts, had restored her father to an idealized position, and, therefore, saw fit to characterize the patient's relationship with her father as "idealized." The problem with this formulation is that if the father's self-esteem was dependent on his daughter's bolstering, it strains credulity that she would idealize him. And there is no evidence that she did. She wanted to restore him to the "daring" man he once was and clearly needed him to be effective, but all that militates against idealization. One does not idealize figures whose stature one has to sustain. When fathers are idealized, the idealizing figure does not see the father as needing her to boost him into the idealized position.

An illustrative self psychological case is the report of a man who feared becoming attached to and dependent on the analyst due to fears of helplessness and vulnerability (Shapiro, 1985). He felt safe when he was close to the analyst, but felt pressure to sense the analyst's needs and please him, fearing that if he did not, his analyst would lose interest in him and withdraw. Separations from the analyst hurt, making him feel weak and helpless. Again, the transference was labeled "idealizing," but to depend on another and fear withdrawal and abandonment is not idealization; it is a relationship of fragile dependence and anxiety over abandonment. The patient feels that anyone who is helpful to him is on the precipice of abandoning him unless he extends himself by pleasing that person. That dynamic is very different from the patient who basks in the glow of the analyst's majestic presence. The patient's connection to the analyst is much better captured by the attachment theorists' concept of the "anxiously attached" child than by idealization (Bowlby, 1988). This critical clinical difference is lost if the patient's transference is encapsulated under the rubric "idealizing transference."

Similarly, Ornstein (1990) reports a case of a man who was said to form an idealizing transference in the second year of treatment based on his strong reactions to disruptions in the analytic relationship. The analyst was late once, and he took a week to recover. When Ornstein disappointed him, the patient felt she was taking advantage of his "needy, vulnerable position." While Ornstein correctly notes that she had become important to him, importance is not tantamount to an idealization. The transference consisted of a growing attachment suffused with anxiety and paranoia. As with the above-mentioned cases, the specific clinical experience of the patient is obfuscated, perhaps even dismissed, by the global attribution of "idealization" for which there is little evidence. By conceptualizing the transference as "idealization" the patient's experience is fit into a category that drains it of its unique emotional meaning. Theory trumps the patient's lived experience.

All of these examples from a variety of theoretical models illustrate that the epistemological problem of using theory deductively rather than as a heuristic is both common and widely accepted in analytic theory and practice across theoretical divisions (Fonagy, 2000). Utilizing analytic theory in this way represents the strand of psychoanalytic thinking that issues from Freud's "scientistic" side. While theoretical prejudice is not technically equivalent to scientism, each of the theories reviewed conceives of itself as a body of knowledge applicable to the clinical process, and that viewpoint issues from the scientistic belief that invariant principles are applicable to the individual case. The pressure to fit into the natural sciences has led these analysts to believe that psychoanalysis possesses definitive knowledge of human functioning applicable to the individual case. The mistake in this approach is not simply one of theoretical prejudice, but of assuming that psychoanalysis possesses a body of knowledge for which evidence will be found in the clinical material. As we can see from these routine examples, adherents of each school regard their ideas as established knowledge, and, as a result, the analytic material was selectively organized to fit preconceived theory. And that is inevitable if the analyst assumes he possesses a set of psychic laws that hold the key to each case. The mistake of deductive thinkers is not in adopting a theory, but in the presumption that their "knowledge" must apply in each case, and under those conditions, the patient's experience is going to be misread.

As has been noted, this deductive approach represents only one prong of the Freudian epistemological legacy. Freud also advocated the adoption of an open-minded receptiveness to the clinical material. Many analysts have opted for this posture, even if they belong to a theoretical school, and those analysts form a second and rapidly growing tradition that builds on Freud's hermeneutic clinical technique.

The Hermeneutic Analysts

The second group of analysts, representatives of which may be found in every analytic theory, shape their primary clinical stance from Freud's advocacy of open-minded receptiveness. Analysts who conduct themselves in this way believe the patient's experience should lead the process. The experiencing subject trumps other considerations, including theory, and the analyst's job is to respond to the patient, rather than wait for opportunities to apply theoretical presuppositions. As we saw in our discussion of deductivism, the latter stance is not a straw man, but a historically common analytic practice. This second group of theorists focuses on the process of inquiry, rather than content, and therefore may be properly termed hermeneutic (Dilthey, 1900). The emphasis is on the revelation of individual meaning by employing rules of interpretation, rather than searching for any particular content. In this interpretation of analytic inquiry, theory is a heuristic, used to facilitate the understanding of the patient's experience, rather than a preset body of knowledge.

Some early analytic clinicians emphasized responsiveness to the patient's experience above theory. Ferenczi (1932/1945), for example, adopted Freud's libido theory, but interpreted it so broadly that he experimented with responding to the desires of patients whose issues were not at the Oedipal level and thought to be unanalyzable. Balint (1968) also interpreted the analytic task as a way to reach the patient's deepest experience, no matter how primitive it might be. Both held that the analytic relationship resulting from this responsiveness is a powerful component of therapeutic action, and in some cases, the decisive clinical moment. However, this approach of leaving the direction of the analytic process to the patient's experience without preconception of where it should go remained peripheral to mainstream psychoanalysis for the first half of the twentieth century.

A pivotal turn in analytic attitude was taken by Winnicott's (1965, 1971) conceptual shift to the maturational process and facilitating environment as the fundamentals of analytic theory. By introducing the idea that analysis is about the resumption of an arrested maturational process, Winnicott shifted the analytic aim to the realization of the unique potential of each individual. Winnicott's view was that each person is born with a tendency to grow in a particular direction that cannot be changed, but can be impinged upon or facilitated. Impingements interfere with the "going on being" leading to defenses to protect the self and derailing the unfolding of development. The purpose of the analytic process, from this point of view, is not to achieve any preconceived aim of health, but to help the patient resume the maturational process that guides her unique life trajectory according to her experience. Analysis then becomes open-ended, directed by the patient's experience and the analyst's response to it. That is why for Winnicott the analytic space is a potential space, a bounded formlessness, and interpretations are not bits of information to be consumed, but offerings to be shaped, developed, and utilized according to the patient's experience.

Winnicottian-influenced analysts have tended to build on the idea of open space in the analytic process. Bollas (1987) has elaborated Winnicott's ideas with his concept of a personal idiom, a unique grammar that lies at the core of each individual. This analytic theorist distinguishes destiny, the inner purpose of one's life, from fate, the imposition from without (Bollas, 1989). Bollas argues that the analyst cannot be simply a "decoder of symbols," but must expand his role to offer a "culture of relatedness" in which the patient's destiny can be brought to fruition. He calls the path to this end "unconscious freedom," the opening up of the psyche to expand its awareness and possibilities (Bollas, 1992).

For Mashud Khan (1974) the essence of the analytic process is the openness that allows the articulation of the previously unsayable. Similarly, for Margaret Little (1977), focusing on characterologically disturbed individuals, theoretical content recedes in importance as the process of translating action discharge into symbolic discourse takes center stage. The essence of therapeutic action, for Little, is the provision of space in which discharge can become symbolic discourse.

Little and Khan believed the countertransference could be used to reach the patient's experience, and that idea formed a bridge between the Winnicottians and Kleinian theory. Bion (1962), the undisputed leader of this movement, went beyond conceptual shifts to thinking of analysis as an interpersonal process the therapeutic action of which is built upon the freshness of each clinical encounter. Bion's (1970) famous statement that the analyst should enter every session "without memory or desire" is a clarion call to jettison theory in favor of analytic openness to the immediacy of the clinical encounter.

Despite the fact that this trend away from theoretical hegemony toward the experiencing subject has pervaded theoretical divisions, this movement has not received the attention nor codification enjoyed by other contemporary developments, such as the relational turn and the shift from ego to self. To set this trend into high relief, we may consider the remarkably similar journeys of two preeminent analysts, Heinz Kohut and Herbert Rosenfeld, working thousands of miles apart from distinct theoretical positions.

Kohut's (1971) experience with one patient, Miss F., was key to transforming his analytic model. Utilizing a classical perspective, Kohut first thought Miss F. was engaging in self analysis, and she responded positively to his summaries of her material, but he noticed that when he was silent or attempted to go beyond her associations, she felt disrupted, became enraged, and accused him of ruining the analysis.

After struggling against these reactions, which he initially regarded as resistance, Kohut came to the conclusion that her reproaches were correct, that he was ruining the analysis by attempting to interfere with the mobilization of her childhood needs. Kohut believed that the analysis began to make progress when he saw her demands as a positive effort to integrate her grandiosity, rather than a resistance, and he began to recognize and appreciate Miss F.'s strivings even if she disagreed with his interpretations. Kohut dramatically shifted his analytic stance by relinquishing his theory to make the patient's experience the determinative feature of his analytic interventions. He adopted the stance that all was to be understood from the patient's point of view (Kohut, 1984).

Only a few years later on the other side of the Atlantic, Herbert Rosenfeld, a devoted Kleinian, was in a stalemate with a multiply traumatized borderline patient who, after two and one-half years of analysis, attacked Rosenfeld viciously for being critical of him (Rosenfeld, 1987). The vituperative assaults, which made Rosenfeld feel like a helpless child filled with futile rage, led to a therapeutic stalemate, and the patient decided on termination within two weeks. Rosenfeld asked the man to sit up and go over all his criticisms. Instead of interpreting as usual, Rosenfeld (1987, p.221) "adopted an entirely receptive, empathic, listening attitude to him." The man decided to remain and Rosenfeld shifted his clinical technique from a singular emphasis on interpretation to holding the patient's projective identifications for a sustained period. He even suggested that the analytic relationship should replicate a good mother-infant relationship and that interpretations are often effective due to their soothing and gratifying effect, similar to physical holding, rather than their content. Needless to say, such a clinical strategy was apostasy to the Kleinian community of his day.

These examples represent the fact that changes in Kleinian analysis and the creation of self psychology were both motivated by therapeutic dilemmas in which the analyst's theoretical agenda conflicted with the patient's experience. While both analysts attributed their patients' improvements to their new theory, in Kohut's case the mobilization of a mirror transference, and for Rosenfeld, the containment of projective identification, they share a striking similarity in the way they responded to their patients. In both cases, the analyst listened to the patient and decided that the conflict was due not to the patient's resistance, but to the analyst's failure to recognize the needs of the patient. Rather than insisting on deploying theoretical constructs, both Kohut and Rosenfeld adapted their clinical technique in accordance with what they heard from the patient. By giving primacy to the patient's experience, both Kohut and Rosenfeld were willing to adapt their clinical strategy in remarkably similar ways. So, while both analysts believed their new theory was responsible for unlocking the therapeutic stalemate, neither considered that the patients may well have been freed by the analyst's willingness to shift his approach in response to the patient's experience of the analytic process.

Other Kleinians or Kleinian-influenced analysts, although continuing to use Klein's basic concepts, have similarly made their clinical target the depths of the patient's experience while relegating theory to a secondary role. They use Kleininan theory as a heuristic for exploration of the patient's inner world, rather than as an established body of knowledge (e.g., Williams, 2010).

Foremost among non-Kleinians using Kleinian concepts is Thomas Ogden (1994) for whom psychoanalysis is differentiated from other interactions by the creation of the *analytic third*, a form of experiencing subjectivity, or I-ness in which both analyst and patient participate. Ogden (2001) sees unconscious states as lying on the "frontier of dreaming," and the analytic work is about the opening up of space for the creation of new psychic reality, from the "frontier of dreaming" to the creation of a new dream. The essence of the analytic process, for Ogden, is not drawing conclusions about the patient's experience, but in abetting the patient's creation of new experience.

Eigen (1993a, 2005) uses Bion's work to develop a theory of analysis as a powerful affective exchange between patient and analyst. The role of the analyst for Eigen is not to provide information, but to be evocative, to rouse the patient from her somnolence. Eigen's considerable corpus is about ways to reach the psychic depths of even the most disturbed patients by stimulating and bringing to life the dormant within. The essence of the analyst's contribution, for Eigen, is not knowledge conveyed, but a mode of inquiry.

Ego psychology has undergone changes in theoretical and clinical theory for very similar reasons (Gray, 1995; Busch, 1995). Contemporary structural theory aims to uncover defensive layering by responding from the surface to depth. The key therapeutic ingredient consists of working with each level of defense as it can be experienced, as opposed to interpreting directly to deep unconscious material.

Significant developments within self psychology have continued the trend of fealty to the patient's experience. Goldberg (1988) believes the analyst is as locked in by his convictions as the patient is in his. The analyst then aims to negotiate these differences by understanding the patient's world. One can see here a conscious theoretical effort to refrain from imposing theory more than is necessary given our all-too-real humanness. Moreover, contemporary self psychology tends to view therapeutic action as optimal responsiveness to patients, a mixture of gratification and deprivation that is designed to stimulate arrested growth (Bacal, 1985, 1988). This type of thinking puts the analytic emphasis on the mode of relating to the patient, rather than conveying any particular content.

Another way of looking at analytic process is suggested by Modell (2003) who has developed Winnicott's ideas about the inherent creativity of the mind in a similar, but slightly different, direction. What makes us uniquely human, Modell argues, is our ability to use metaphor, that is, to shift from one domain to another. Unconscious memories exist as potential categories that require imagination to be brought to form and become conscious. Trauma freezes memory, stifling the imagination. So, the analytic process consists of the opening up of the ability to use metaphor, to shift levels of consciousness in freedom.

While these changes constitute a movement toward engaging the experiencing subject, the subjective does not appear *de novo*. Although motivated by a need to respond to the patient's experience, the relational sensibility added a crucial element. The child and patient can bring to fruition their potential as beings only if there is an other, recognized as a subject, who sees the child as subject (e.g., Benjamin, 1995).

The shift to an intersubjective sensibility is built on the awareness that the experience of patient and analyst create the analytic process rather than the analyst's theory (Mitchell, 1988; Aron, 1996). In this way, analysis has evolved into a process between two people who engage each other for the express purpose of transforming and expanding the subjectivity of one party.

Placing the greatest emphasis on the analytic relationship and the mutual engagement of patient and analyst virtually defines relational theory, which is perhaps the only analytic theoretical approach other than the Winnicottian movement to codify a theory without concretizing content. Analysis consists of an evolving relationship between analyst and patient in which both participate and the outcome of which is undetermined (e.g., Mitchell, 1988; Aron, 1996). The analyst does not have privileged knowledge as much as a different perspective, but not necessarily a superior viewpoint. Mitchell (1993) was explicit in his belief that psychoanalytic knowledge is not a set of enduring truths, but a collection of theories that might be useful in making sense of the patient's life and helping deepen his relationships and experience. From this viewpoint, imposition is theoretically minimized, although it can still take place. Hoffman (2002) has elaborated the epistemological position of this theory with his view that the immersion of the analyst makes any opinion he possesses as subject to prejudice as the patient's viewpoint.

While relational theory offers a theoretical openness to the patient's experience, the caveat is that the emphasis on the use of the therapist's experience creates the possibility that such disclosure and active participation in general have a greater chance of interfering with the patient's self expression than is true of other theoretical stances. The danger is not theoretical imposition as in other theories, but an intrusion of the therapist's experience.

The work of neo-Winnicottians such as Bollas and Eigen, some Kleinians, a group of contemporary self psychologists, and relational theorists all combine to define psychoanalytic therapy by its open-ended mode of inquiry rather than a specialized body of knowledge. Lear (1998) has highlighted the fact that what epitomizes the analytic way of knowing is its open-mindedness, the attitude of receptiveness to ever new experience. He argues that the tragedy of Oedipus was not any wish he had, but his hubris, the self certainty that closed his mind so that he could not think about what he was doing. The result was that he performed the acts he most feared: killing his father and marrying his mother. In contrast, the genius of psychoanalysis, according to Lear, is its willingness to keep the mind open and question what appears to be known. The analytic attitude is skepticism, the insistence on questioning even presumptively established truths. In this way, contemporary hermeneutic psychoanalysis is the present-day Socratic icon: asking the questions the interlocutor (read patient) does not ask and may not want to be asked. In addition, in recent years there has been a slow, but growing resurgence of interest among some analysts in asking such questions of the culture.

An open-minded approach means no theory can foreclose where the inquiry may go. The subject of analysis, then, is experiencing at every level: not only in the immediate sense of present experience, but also to include what is not conscious and what might be possible. The analyst's role is to respond to, illuminate, expand, and enrich that experience. Knowledge of psychic functioning is important, but that understanding is most effective when it responds to the patient's experience. The uniqueness of the analytic approach is its ability to pursue psychic depth and open avenues of exploration in accordance with the elaboration of the patient's experience. The presupposition of any particular content toward which that voyage is expected to land would limit the routes to be taken and constrict the analytic process. In short, theoretical imposition is anti-analytic.

As we have seen, from the inception of the field it has been known that the patient must be able to experience any offered insight if it is to have a chance of success. To impose preconceived knowledge pulls for compliance or opposition, both of which interfere with the patient's elaboration of experience, the goal of analytic inquiry. The hermeneutic approach is an effort to define analysis in a way that provides maximum opportunity for the patient to have an affective response to the analyst's understanding. This analytic attitude is more consonant with the psychoanalytic spirit of inquiry than the deductive approach because its fealty is to the patient's experience, rather than a supposed body of truths.

The hermeneutic clinical approach is also consistent with the developmental evidence on the growth of the self. The child does not internalize the parent as much as use the parent to develop her own means of coping (Demos, 1991). The child is helped to master negative affects by parental responses to the pain and the offering of a different viewpoint. As a result, the optimal conditions for the child are both mutual and self regulation (Beebe & Lachmann, 2002), so the analogue for the patient would be analytic ministrations that help the patient regulate her affects and a space to create her own means of coping.

The hermeneutic theorists in any analytic school are those who keep their theory "ready-to-hand," to borrow a term from Heidegger, available if needed and used only to enrich and expand the patient's experience. Those of every analytic persuasion who deploy theory as a heuristic give priority to the patient's experience as the criterion for analytic investigation, and, in this way, have the greatest chance of transforming the patient's historical patterns.

Theory in the Analytic Process

These considerations raise the question of the role of theory in analytic practice. The time-honored rejoinder to the critique of theoretical imposition is that the analyst cannot operate without theory (e.g., Wallerstein, 1992). Popper's (1962) dictum that all observation includes theory is often used to justify theoretical imposition, but there is a decisive difference between the heuristic use of theory and the imposition of theory on experience. Popper was clear that theory informs observation, but the theory must be testable, and that testing prevents theoretical dogma from taking hold. Examples of theoretical imposition, as we have seen in Kernberg (1984), for example, tend to be defended with the truism that all observations require a theoretical frame. But, as we have seen, deductive analytic theorists, such as Kernberg, mask preconceived conclusions behind the concept of "theoretical frame." What tends to be missed in such discussions is that not all use of theory is the same. To prejudge outcome, as Kernberg does, is not a "theoretical frame," but a preconceived conclusion.

The use of theory in the service of understanding, that is to say, the heuristic use of theory, guides an open inquiry that can go in a variety of directions. In our review of deductive theories we saw that the mistake there is not that theory is used, but that it is misused as a presupposed conclusion. Theory does not imply the use of presuppositions; it means we must adopt a *position. Positions* are stances we take toward the world, an inevitability for living and a requisite for analytic work. Positions, by their nature, are subject to scrutiny and justification, and in the case of the analyst's position, such self-observation is a requirement. But, Kernberg and other deductive theorists confuse *position* with *presupposition.* The latter lack evidential foundation and are not subject to confirmation by analytic data because they presuppose conclusions. It is an unjustifiable leap to suggest that any analyst has knowledge of the patient's psyche without ever seeing her, and, therefore, there is no rationale for presupposing analytic conclusions. Analytic knowledge lacks validity when it uses theory as presupposition. Assumed and not subject to scrutiny, presuppositions become traps that can lead us in directions we cannot control even if they are wide of the mark.

But, analytic hypotheses are *suppositions.* Derived from positions, they are hypotheses about concrete clinical situations based on analytic data, and are subject to the evolution of analytic evidence. Presuppositions can never be invalidated or validated, but suppositions are judgments that are modified, accepted, or rejected depending on the evolution of the clinical data.

It is therefore imperative that the analyst understands what position he adopts, see his ideas as suppositions, and, above all, is vigilant about any presuppositions he may be tempted to assume. Analytic self scrutiny tends to be cast as the analyst's observation of her own psychodynamic issues that may be influencing the process. Less attention has been paid to the analyst's theoretical presuppositions, which can be equally dangerous when mistaken for a "theoretical frame." Analysts' statement of their theory tends to be accepted at face value, thus blinding the analytic community to the misuse of theory.

Conclusion: The Subject of Analysis

The subject of analysis, then, is the experiencing subject where experience is understood as including all levels of consciousness and unconsciousness. Any offered insight, from whatever theoretical perspective, can be justified only on the grounds of the patient's experience; and judgments of efficacy, only on the patient's further experience in response to the offered understanding. It follows that the experiencing subject is both source and arbiter of analytic truth. While it may seem obvious to some to say that analysis is about the experiencing subject, we have seen in our review of deductivism that theoretical presuppositions have often been privileged over the patient's experience. The scientist model has led to the assumption that psychoanalysis must possess a body of truths, but no matter how carefully such knowledge is qualified, the resulting deductive reasoning inevitably becomes a frame into which experience must fit, thus constricting and molding rather than expanding the patient's experience. We have seen that this often subtle pressuring of the patient's experience to fit the analyst's preconceptions is not uncommon across a variety of theoretical viewpoints.

For analysis to be effective, the concentrated focus of analytic therapy must be a consistent recognition and illumination of the experiencing subject in its ever expanding varieties of experience. That is why any attempt to fit psychoanalysis into the model of the natural sciences by giving it a somatic basis is doomed to fail. It is not by accident that Freud gave up the *Project* (Freud, 1895a) and never published it. The hermeneutic interpretation of analysis wins out over its deductivist rival by virtue of its fealty to the experiencing subject, the very subject of analysis.

This model of engaging the subjective has evolved almost imperceptibly to become a widely deployed but little articulated analytic way of thinking. This lack of notice is due partly to the extraordinary attention given to the two-person model, but in addition the shift to the lessened influence of theory has been a gradual evolution that has not had an epiphanic moment and does not fit any particular psychoanalytic viewpoint. Nonetheless, it is the thesis of this book that the implications of consistent engagement and illumination of the experiential world with all its unconscious and conscious vicissitudes has far-reaching implications for psychoanalytic theory and therapy that have not yet been fully realized. The deceptively simple premise that psychoanalytic therapy is a concentration on the experiencing subject demarcates a field of investigation and transformation that has implications for the model of mind, analytic strategy and conduct, the experience of the other, and the nature of a variety of mental phenomena, many of which will be articulated in subsequent chapters. As a discipline of the subjective, of the depth exploration of experiencing, psychoanalytic therapy requires its own epistemology and standards for truth and efficacy that have yet to be fully articulated. It is the purpose of this book to delineate the epistemological, theoretical, and clinical basis for the unique science of the subjective that is psychoanalysis.

From concentration on the experiencing subject in all her complexity emanates a mode of engaging human experience that defines a distinct psychoanalytic vision. And it is this vision that will be elaborated in the chapters to follow. Exploration of the experiencing subject can appear deceptively simple, but the inclusion of unconscious levels, the complex connections among experiences, past and present, real and potential, makes the concrete experience of the moment a complex phenomenon that is only glimpsed, but never captured, in the immediacy of experience. This is to say, the essential feature of the analytic subject is the potential to open worlds of experiential possibility that can be explored, but neither predicted nor deduced. The opening of new worlds that transcend the immediacy of experience is the psychoanalytic vision.

From the premise that inquiry into the experiencing subject, understood as including both conscious and unconscious experience, is uniquely psychoanalytic and defines the psychoanalytic project, contemporary psychoanalysis becomes a science with its own subject and method derivative of that unique subject of inquiry. Such a discipline raises many theoretical and clinical questions that will be addressed in the chapters that follow. Conceptually prior to the clinical issues is the fundamental question: If psychoanalysis is a unique inquiry into the experiencing subject, of what type of knowledge does it admit? Or, we may ask: What is unique about the psycho-analytic way of knowing and how are its claims justified? And that is the subject of the next chapter.

2

PSYCHOANALYSIS, THE TYRANNY OF OBJECTIVISM, AND THE REBELLION OF THE SUBJECTIVE

We have seen that the subject of psychoanalytic therapy is not behavior, nor any observed indicators of behavior, but the experience of the subject. Inquiry into how people experience themselves and their worlds is a different thematic and form of inquiry from the observable behavior studied by traditional social science and the program of empirical psychology. This qualitative difference has resulted in a conflict between psychoanalytic claims to knowledge and the canons of empirical psychology. Psychoanalytic insights into human experience have been attacked as invalidated speculations by adherents of the empirical method (e.g., Hook, 1960; Scriven, 1962; Popper, 1963; Grunbaum, 1984, 1993). The time-honored contention from the scientistic community that analytic thought and therapy lack objective evidence for their claims has now taken hold in the clinical world via the advocacy for "evidence based treatment" (e.g., Spring, 2007; Wampold, 2007). Rapid technological advances and societal change, including the burgeoning of neuroscience, have accelerated and widened this assault on analytic claims to knowledge.

In this chapter the basis of this scathing indictment of psychoanalytic knowing will be examined in order to demonstrate that the uniqueness of psychoanalytic inquiry requires its own epistemological underpinning. This critique will be the launching point for a psychoanalytic epistemology derived from the subject matter of the discipline, rather than imposed from an area of inquiry with a different purpose.

Objectivist Epistemology

Psychology texts are unanimous in dismissing psychoanalytic ideas as empirically unverified (e.g., Munn et al., 1969; Morgan et al., 1985; Kalat, 2007). It need be mentioned only briefly that while some analytic conceptions have not been supported by experimental research, others have, and the claim of the effectiveness of the analytic process has held up well to empirical scrutiny (e.g., Seligman, 1995; Shedler, 2010). Not only does meta-analysis of research show that analytic therapy leads to greater improvement than other forms of therapeutic intervention, but the effects of its popular rival, cognitive behavioral therapy (CBT), may well come from its tendency to mimic analytic techniques. Those who claim to oppose psychoanalysis due to its lack of scientific support ignore the substantial body of evidence demonstrating its effectiveness and then draw unfounded and unscientific conclusions regarding its supposed lack of success. While the data may be debated, to dismiss or ignore them is to substitute ideology for evidence under the guise of making an evidence-based argument.

The uncompromising dismissal of analysis is not based on research findings but on the fact that psychoanalysis fails to fit into the dominant objectivist ideology of the social science culture. While the objectivist method has undoubtedly reaped great benefits in the natural sciences, its application to the human sciences is based on the epistemological stance elucidated by E. L. Thorndike (1918): "Whatever exists, exists in some amount, and whatever exists in some amount can be measured" (p.16). This concept of reality has been accepted uncritically by academic psychology for almost 100 years despite the failure of its adherents to provide any justification for it. That is to say, objectivism is a dogma, a tyrannical imposition on human inquiry.

In accordance with the objectivist stance that only the measureable exists, psychology texts define the field as the study not of the psyche, but of the behavior of living organisms (e.g., Munn et al., 1969; Morgan et al., 1985; Kalat, 2007). One highly representative example in an introductory textbook makes clear that this definition is determined by method rather than content: "Behavior, rather than mind, thoughts, and feelings, is the subject of psychology because it alone can be observed, recorded, and studied" Morgan et al. (2005). There can be no clearer statement that academic psychology defines the field not by its subject matter, but by a preconceived method the relevance of which to psychological functioning remains unestablished.

It is unnecessary to enumerate all the problems with the objectivist position, so I will briefly state only its most obvious and egregious flaws. First, the contention that reality is quantity cannot hold up on its own terms because that statement itself is not measureable. According to objectivism, the very statement of objectivism does not exist. Those who hold this position insist on consistency in their scientific method, but ignore the self-contradictory nature of their own viewpoint. The fact that not all reality is measurable is demonstrated in the very statement of objectivism. Neither Thorndike nor any scientistic theorist after him has provided any justification for the view of reality on which they base their method.

In addition, no discipline can be defined by a method, much less a preconceived method, rather than by the subject of study. Defining psychology by a method is equivalent to defining economics by statistics, cultural anthropology by fieldwork, or archeology by digging. As many have pointed out, Thorndike's definition of reality is equivalent to looking for a lost watch under a street lamp even though it was lost in a dark alley a block away. It should not be necessary to state that an area of study is definable only by its content and the methods must be chosen for their suitability to the subject matter. Unfortunately, academic psychologists are so enamored of objectivism that they presuppose the method, which forces them to redefine the discipline in a way that expunges its very nature.

Moreover, objectivism fails to recognize that objects in the sense of things as points of mass governed by laws in homogeneous space do not relate to each other in space, they occupy space, whereas human beings reside in their space, relate to space in a variety of ways. The application of objectivist space to humans is a theoretical prejudice that ignores the distinctively human quality of being in the world.

Finally, the nature of psychic experience militates against the use of objectivist methods for psychological inquiry. As Bergson (1910/2010) demonstrated over a century ago, there is no magnitude in psychic states. What we refer to as quantitative differences in psychological experience are actually qualitatively different states for which we lack distinct names. When we speak in terms of magnitude of psychic states, such as saying we are "very" angry, we are in fact speaking metaphorically and oversimplifying a shift in psychic quality. The "very" refers to a state different from mild anger, which is again distinct from "a little angry." Whatever names are used for these states, they are qualitatively distinct. Because psychic states are not quantitative, measurement does not apply to them.

Instead of investigating the very nature of its subject matter, the psyche, and developing a method suitable to it, the academic form of psychology has without any argument, justification, or reflection, adopted the hegemonic objectivist ideology of the culture at the cost of its subject. While academic psychology did not invent objectivism, its uncritical acceptance of it for psychology makes the objectivist stance an unfounded imposition on the subjective, that is to say, a tyranny.

This elimination of the psychical in the definition of psychology used in academia has considerable influence because a conservative estimate is that more than one million undergraduates take introductory psychology each year. These students are taught that the experiencing subject, the psychical, is not a matter to be investigated, explored, or understood. In this way, psychology not only complies with objectivism, but also spreads its influence to the wider culture.

Objectivism in the Culture

The tyranny of objectivism in psychology raises the question of why such a clearly self-contradictory and misplaced ideology enjoys such unquestioned dominance over psychological inquiry. Absolute control over the content and method of a domain can be achieved by a belief system only if the ideas embedded in it conform to the ideology and needs of the larger culture. Objectivism is embraced by the Anglo-American world, and, correlatively, confirms and strengthens that Zeitgeist. The Industrial Revolution begun in the eighteenth century and the assembly line in the nineteenth crystallized a view of the human as a commodity, human capital, analogous to any other type of resource. The human became a "factor" to be studied in human factors research; the industrial worker an atomized commodity physically with others but without any human connection. This instrumentalization results in the objectification of human being that completes the circle of a materialist worldview. That is to say, the dominance of objectivist ideology results in the objectification of human being.

In the American world, value is quantitative. The dominance of quantity in the American value system is easily seen in the tendency to quantify virtually all human activity. It is difficult to find any area of American life that has not been assessed on a scale of quantification. The media report the health or illness of the nation largely by the most quantifiable of measures, economic data, most prominently GDP. Companies are valued solely by their most quantifiable measures, such as profits and price/earnings ratios, whereas other criteria, such as innovation, contribution to society, creativity, and ethical conduct are given no mention (Arvidsson, Bauwens, & Peitersen, 2008). The fortunes of political leaders follow the Dow-Jones because the Dow is supposed to tell us how satisfied the citizenry is with its lot. Not only companies, but professionals, such as lawyers and doctors, are commonly ranked, as well as musicians, athletes, universities and professional schools, cities and towns, just to name a small number. The coverage of political campaigns is dominated by a plethora of polls which quantify a variety of variables. Political campaigns are reported as races, much like sports events, with popularity percentages as the score keeping. Far less attention is given to the substance of the issues than is devoted to breaking down polls of various demographic groups to show who is ahead and who is behind in the race.

Valuation by quantification is the essence of a materialist society, and materialism is rapidly increasing (Schumacher, 2001). The 5% of the world population that is American now consumes more than 30% of nonrenewable resources. More than 90% of 13-year-old American girls identify shopping as their favorite activity; the average 8-year-old can list 30 popular brand names. In 1968 children between 4 and 12 years of age spent about $2 billion, now the figure is about $30 billion. In 1970 80% of American college students had a "meaningful life" as a goal; by 1989 the figure had dropped to 41%, whereas the number aiming to be "very well off financially" increased in that period from 39% to 75%. Simultaneously, 85% said a six-figure income was required for their lifestyle, while only 30% of those earning that amount felt it was doing the job (Gellner, 2005). Since 1950 the average house size has doubled while family size decreased during that period. Americans spend more on shoes, jewelry, and watches than on higher education (de Graaf, Waan, & Naylor, 2005). Perhaps the values of American culture are well captured by a suburban shopping mall that has three boutiques selling clothing, diet supplements, and confections—for dogs.

The logical conclusion of value by quantification is placing a price tag on human life, and in this regard American society does not disappoint. That "net worth" places a dollar amount not just on assets but on life is demonstrated by assiduous economists and bioethicists who debate a variety of sophisticated formulae to determine the dollar value of a life (e.g., Beauchamp & Childress, 2001). One method is the Discounted Future Earnings (DFE) determined by what an individual would earn if continuing to live. The unemployed, prisoners, the mentally ill, and others have a negative DFE. A more sophisticated, and, to some, ethically defensible method is Willingness to Pay (WTP), calculated by how much an individual is willing to pay to reduce the risk of death. According to one economist, Dr. Orley Ashenfelter, "They say you can't put a value on life, but we do it all the time." This dollar valuation of individual lives is the logical conclusion of a culture that objectifies human experience.

One would think that the natural opposition to the hegemony of objectification of the human process would come from psychology as the study of the human subject, but by adopting the dominant cultural ideology, academic psychology has eradicated any possibility that it might provide a counterpoint to objectification. The erasure of the subject from psychology has collaborated with objectification in the wider culture to strengthen a societal reductionism that promotes the treatment of people as commodities to be utilized as means to ends imposed upon them. As a means not an end, the person as commodity is fair game to be manipulated, cheated, and mistreated in a variety of ways.

The Phenomenological Alternative

The alternative is to begin with the nature of being human. As Husserl (1913) demonstrated to his eternal credit approximately 100 years ago, every act of consciousness is consciousness of *something*. There can be no consciousness without the world, and we have no awareness of the world without consciousness. Husserl undercut Cartesian dualism by showing that experience and the world are co-given, neither can be thought of without the other. Husserl demonstrated that in every act of consciousness the world is endowed with meaning. In this way, Husserl showed what it is to be a human subject: It means endowing the world with meaning. So, when, in psychoanalysis, we say that we are exploring the human subject, we are immersing ourselves in the patients' meaning creations, which cannot be differentiated from his relationship to the world.

Heidegger (1962/1927) built from Husserl's foundation the understanding of human being as Being-in-the-world. As we saw in Chapter One, what makes human beings distinct from objects in homogenized space is that people do not simply occupy space; they relate to the world. Even the hermit is relating to the world in his withdrawal from the community of others. Heidegger's term for the distinctly human way of being is *Da-sein*, or *Being-there*. The human way of being is to relate to the world, and this fundamental quality defines the difference between human beings and objects in homogenized space. In this way, Husserl and Heidegger returned us to the ontological stance of the pre-Cartesian world.

Da-sein, "being there," means an openness that encounters the world. It is this releasement to the world, the openness to perceiving/receiving, that determines the fundamental nature of Being-there, human being. To be human is to dwell in the world, not just occupy space as does a material object. The person sees the chair in a particular way, relates to it whether by viewing it as an aesthetic object, a place to rest, or a means for climbing to get a book high on a shelf. While the human endows the chair with meaning, the desk has no such relationship to the chair. This distinctively human way of being is precisely what makes us human and is eliminated in the ideology of objectivism. In opposition to the Cartesian *cogito* cut off from the world, "Da" in *Da-sein* means an openness to what is given. This openness to experiencing what is given, as opposed to occupying space as in the material world, means that we are always and already both "of" and "in" the world (Heidegger, 1962/1926, p.20–1).

The phenomenological understanding of the relationship between person and world, based on the nature of human experiencing rather than the eighteenth-century natural science standpoint, constitutes the philosophical foundation for psychoanalytic theory because, as we have seen, the uniqueness of psychoanalysis lies precisely in its inquiry into the experiencing subject. But, if the nature of human being is to relate to the world, the time-honored psychoanalytic way of construing the very nature of the psyche becomes questionable. The distinction psychoanalysis makes between "internal" and "external" experience is now set into question. It is commonly overlooked in psychoanalytic theoretical writing that these terms are metaphors. One cannot observe a wish or thought "inside" nor can we look "outside" to find an experience. Rather than being treated as metaphors, "inside" and "outside" are given reality status, as when the analyst writes, "at the intrapsychic level" or "the patient's intrapsychic world." Such common analytic phrases reify metaphors.

And then we can ask the further question: Are these good metaphors for different categories of experience? I suggest they are not. The routine use of these metaphors has obfuscated the fact that they are a historical creation of Cartesian thinking. The ontological revolution that Descartes initiated and that gathered powerful momentum with the scientific revolution split the person from the world. As Foucault (1980), Heidegger (1977), and others have demonstrated, the language of "inside" and "outside" is a product of the creation of the natural science worldview. Once "objects" were created as points in homogenized space, it became possible to refer to them as "outside" as though external to experience, and other psychic events, such as fantasies and dreams, as "inside." Descartes's *cogito* is perhaps the first intrapsychic concept in the Western World.

Nonetheless, since Aristotle, it has been recognized that community is essential to the very nature of being human. When Aristotle wrote that "man is a political animal" he meant that what defines the distinctively human animal is our life in the polity. Without a community, there can be no self; and no community can sustain itself unless individual members can realize a self within it. The ancient world recognized that the self can come to fruition only within a community, so the idea of "intrapsychic" and "extrapsychic" did not exist. One does not become a Greek or Indian, an intellectual, or a shoemaker, a businessman or a merchant, without a community in which such identities have meaning. One cannot be a computer programmer in Ancient Greece, nor a dandy, nor a "deadhead" because those roles did not exist in the Greek community.

Once the presuppositions of the Cartesian worldview are suspended, it becomes evident that we have a variety of forms of consciousness, each of which has distinct qualities and a unique type of object. A dream is different from a perception, which again is different from a fantasy, and doing mathematics is another type of experiencing, or, as Heidegger called them, "ways of being in the world." So, fantasies, dreams, and speculations are distinct ways of being in the world, but it is a prejudice to call them "intrapsychic." The object of perception can be touched, felt, looked at from different perspectives, and that is how it differs from fantasies and dreams.

Freud, of course, was a man of the science of his time and a modernist, so his assumption was that the person has an "internal" world separated from the "external" environment. The two make contact because the nature of human instinct is such that the bestial impulses of our animal heritage must be controlled via the superego for the survival of the species and the development of civilization. Whereas for Freud civilization was needed to rein in our animal nature, for Aristotle, the community is necessary to realize our inborn potential as human beings. No frustration is needed to create civilization for Aristotle because it is in the nature of the human animal to find self in community. Winnicott (1965) brought psychoanalysis closer to this Greek way of thinking by broadening the primary analytic concept of development to the maturational process, which can be realized with the aid of a facilitating environment. In so doing, he explicitly made the environment a key to self development.

Once we recognize that the focus of psychoanalysis is the experiencing subject and that inquiry is founded on the phenomenology of the human subject, we are in a position to effect a critique of the person-world split. When this bifurcation is presupposed, experience becomes divided between "internal" and "external," the exclusion of experiential context becomes a crucial gap, and psychoanalysis expends a great deal of intellectual capital attempting to integrate person and world. But, as Husserl, Heidegger, and other philosophers have demonstrated, this split is based on reifications that have no ontological basis. Rather than reifying the metaphorical sundering of person and world and then trying to show their connection, we are better served to jettison those reifications and adopt the phenomenological rallying cry: "Back to the things themselves!" When we do so, we find the world is inherent in all experience; never having been separated, person and world do not need a rejoining.

Lost to the present age is the fact that the natural science conception of homogenized space in which objects are points of mass governed by laws is a relatively recent creation. In ancient Greece there was no "object" in this sense, and, therefore, objectification was not possible. After science invented the "object" as a point in homogenized space, the human became a "subject" in the Cartesian sense, separated from the world. The next step was the application of the objectification to human being, and in that step the very nature of being human was lost.

Based on this ontological understanding of human being, the way to study the human process is to immerse oneself in the being one hopes to know, the very opposite of objectification. Understanding human experience means grasping ways of being in the world and that requires immersing oneself in the experiencing subject. The other's ways of being cannot be studied from afar; they can only be grasped by entering into the other's ways of being and relating. Is this not an apt description of contemporary hermeneutic psychoanalysis as the study of the experiencing subject?

When one views the changes in psychoanalytic therapy as making the patient's experience the source and arbiter of analytic truth, it becomes apparent that the biggest winner in the break from the past is not any particular analytic theory or approach, no recent mode of analytic thinking, not even new technical strategies. An overwhelming victory has been won by the experiencing subject in the form of the analysand whose demand to be heard has called forth a responsiveness from the analytic world that has changed the field, most likely permanently. We saw concrete examples of such patient victories in our discussion of Kohut and Rosenfeld in Chapter One. This primacy of experience in knowing the other is precisely the approach to the human condition that follows from the phenomenology of Husserl and Heidegger.

The Rebellion of the Psychoanalytic Worldview

In practicing his craft, the analyst attends persistently to the patient's experience, including what is embedded in it that the patient does not see, and his own experience of the interaction. Even that simple outline describes a way of being that conflicts with the concept of reality of the hegemonic culture. The effort to articulate the unsayable and the awareness of the analyst's own experience of the patient are designed to bring forth meaning and motivation that have not previously been known to either party. The path for this achievement is the patient's spontaneous mental activity and the analytic therapist's immersion in it. This relationship of what Winnicott (1971) called "overlapping subjectivities" is not measureable. A consistent application of objectivism cannot recognize the reality of any of this.

A successful moment in any analysis is the emergence of truth from the patient-analyst interaction. Both the purpose of the process, which might look like madness to an experimental scientist, and its unfolding defy any effort to measure. The analytic procedure uses a criterion of subjective truth; if the analyst believes some understanding to be accurate, she must remain skeptical if the patient does not experience it. But, if the patient feels the analyst has hit the mark, that something previously unknown has now been articulated, if a powerful affective response says "yes" to what was previously unsaid, and the insight fits the developing narrative of the patient's experience, the criteria for analytic truth are met. Thus, the analytic interaction conducted to discover meaning by articulating the previously unsayable as well as the criterion for truth conflict with the culture of objectivism and quantification.

The analyst, by adopting a stance toward the patient that says "all is meaningful, and much meaning is hidden, but detectable, and new forms of meaning are possible" is not only conducting a treatment, she is adopting what we have called the psychoanalytic worldview. In engaging the patient's experience in an analysis, the analyst is refusing to genuflect to the view of reality held by the dominant culture. That is to say, the psychoanalytic craft expresses a worldview that stands in stark opposition to the Zeitgeist that defines reality by quantification.

By virtue of practicing analysis in today's America, the analyst is refusing to be reduced to the societal conditions in which he finds himself. Willingly or not, he is cast in the role of rebel, to borrow Camus's (1951/1992) concept of the individual who refuses to be objectified by historical conditions. For Camus, the rebel affirms the value of human life by a steadfast refusal to reduce herself to the demands of any particular culture. "Rebellion, in man, is the refusal to be treated as an object and to be reduced to simple historical terms. But man, by rebelling, imposes in his turn a limit to history, and at this limit the promise of a value is born" (p.250). For Camus, to be an existing human is to rebel because in the refusal to be reduced to objective conditions one's humanity is found. The alternative is to not *be*, but to fall into the desires and expectation of others, a "falling" that Heidegger called "das Man," or everyman. Thus, for Camus, the rebel is a subject who affirms his own existence. By adopting the analytic stance, the analyst is refusing to be reduced to the historical circumstances of the time, and, instead, affirming a way of being that does not fit the cultural norm.

In a culture that valorizes quantification, the analytic way of being is inherently social criticism. The analytic stance of opposition to the tyranny of objectivism accounts for the vitriolic attacks leveled against it by those committed to the ideology of quantification. Analysis confronts the American value system with a science of the subjective, an oxymoron in a culture that defines reality by quantity. The analytic concept of truth conflicts with the objectivist concept of reality and the materialist culture on which it is based. The practice of psychoanalysis represents an alternative worldview based on the belief that human experience can only be understood by engagement with it and that engagement cannot be assessed by the methods of objectivism. Analysis has become a guerilla warrior attempting to affirm itself against a dominant and imposing enemy determined to destroy its very being.

Effects of the Culture of Quantification

Both the individual and society have suffered from the effort to erase the experiencing subject. Peltz (2005) has aptly described the excessive consumerism she calls the manic society that results from an environment that does not facilitate the growth of the experiencing subject. Such a culture is a logical outgrowth of an objectivist/materialist value system and its debilitating consequences. To Peltz's formulation it may be added that in such a society persons are routinely treated as means, not ends. Splitting and demonizing the other grow rapidly in a soil fertilized by consumerism and objectification. Since Kant, ethics have been predicated on treating others as subjects in their own right, but that is not possible if the other is reducible to behavior. That is to say, the tyranny of the objective eliminates the human process in which ethics are rooted.

The unethical can be expected to flourish in such a culture, and the data do not disappoint expectations. Approximately 25% of women and 7.6% of men are raped or physically assaulted by the partner of an intimate relationship at some point in their lives. More than 1,000 women in the United States are murdered by an intimate each year, and more than 2,000,000 injured. In 2007 alone there were 248,300 rapes and sexual assaults reported against women, an increase of 23% in only two years. In addition to sexual violence, more than 18,000 homicides are documented annually, or an average of approximately 50 per day. Fifteen million five hundred thousand children live in homes in which partner violence has taken place. In a single day in 2008, 16,458 children were living in a domestic violence shelter or transitional housing facility.

While cheating has always been part of American life, it has increased manifold in the last three decades (Callahan, 2004). No one needs to be reminded of the Wall Street, Anderson, and Enron scandals, and, of course, Bernard Madoff cheating his investors, some of them charities, out of approximately $50 billion. Less well known are the Sears auto repair fraud which bilked car owners out of approximately $40 billion, an estimated overbilling of the Federal Deposit Insurance Corporation by $100 million, the routine padding of hours by lawyers, and the lavish trips and gifts given by drug companies to doctors who then prescribe drugs for unapproved uses and sell health supplements worth $200 million per year out of their offices. But, cheating is not the exclusive province of the wealthy. It is estimated that up to half of all resumes include lies. After 9/11, one of the oldest credit unions in America, the Municipal Credit Union of New York, many of whose members are police and firefighters, lost its ability to monitor transactions, and 4,000 members overdrew their accounts.

Whatever complex factors are responsible for the pervasiveness of cheating in contemporary American life, it is made possible by the objectification of fellow human beings. The mistreatment of others whether by physical assault or cheating flourishes in a culture of objectification. By adopting the dominant view that persons can be objectified, psychology abdicates any position of opposition to the objectivist culture.

In addition, the objectified person is a poor candidate for a democratic society. Democracy requires the citizen to possess the ability to feel, think, and imagine in order to contemplate alternatives and make decisions (Krause, 2008). Totalitarian regimes seek to abolish spontaneity and the imagination, the very capacities denied to reality by the objectivist position (Nafisi, 2003; Arendt, 1959). The deterioration of society into dehumanized entities characterizes the pretotalitarian state (Arendt, 1959). Those who implemented Hitler's policies did not think of themselves as destroying human beings, but as routinely following social codes (Arendt, 1963). Disavowal and the cessation of autonomous mental functioning allowed such individuals to commit some of the most horrendous crimes in human history without any conscious awareness of so doing. Arendt (1963) described Eichmann this way: ". . . what he said was always the same. . . . The longer one listened to him the more obvious it became that his inability to speak was closely connected with an inability to think, namely to think from the standpoint of someone else" (p.49). Here we see the connection between objectification, the lack of autonomous thinking, and the inability to empathize. The objectification of human being creates a culture in which instrumentalism, manipulation, and even violence grow, and in their ultimate form can become totalitarianism, mass murder, and even genocide.

Conclusion

Psychoanalysis assumes a lonely stance as a beacon of opposition to the objectivist culture and the manic society it creates. Inherent in the analytic worldview is the belief in and search for meaning and empathic recognition of the other as a subject on which self development relies. It is not by accident that psychoanalytic psychologists were the most numerous and visible group opposing the complicity of the American Psychological Association in torture (Summers, 2007; Soldz, 2010). Mistreatment of the other is a violation of the psychoanalytic worldview.

While any area of public policy or discourse can benefit from an understanding of the meaning and the motivation provided by a psychoanalytic perspective, the uniquely psychoanalytic way of knowing is most needed in areas where objectification is most destructive. Since World War II the United States has suffered almost 1,500,000 war casualties, and inflicted many times that number on Laotians, Vietnamese, and Iraqis. This type of destructiveness perpetrated without ethical or political basis can be understood from an analytic perspective. The analytic understanding of objectification can shed light not only on those who were directly responsible for the killings, but also on the American people who required little justification to acquiesce in these invasions (Summers, 2010). The country prefers to disavow the killings for which it is responsible in each such war under the guise of "looking forward," which means denial of the crimes and guilt. To be convinced that such denial serves to ensure the repetition of the destructive pattern, one need only see the similarity between the wars in Vietnam and Iraq. The analytic worldview insists on uncovering the meaning of such disastrous societal behavior.

So, psychoanalysis fills a cultural lacuna not only because people need to be understood and have their experience responded to when they seek help. In addition, analysis is a counterpoint, albeit a lonely one, to a culture bent on squeezing subjectivity and meaning out of the world. The uniqueness of human relating and the ethic on which it is based have been lost in the hegemonic culture that has eroded the foundation for treating people differently from objects. To transform this suffocation of human subjectivity requires an alternative built on the human way of being. And that is what the psychoanalytic worldview offers: a way of responding to and expanding human subjectivity. That is the position of the rebel in the American materialist/objectivist culture; a voice for the discovery and creation of meaning, a voice, that is, for the assertion of human experiencing in opposition to the cultural pressure to objectify human being. That is the psychoanalytic vision.

In that valorization of the experiencing subject a standard for the treatment of others is implied. That is to say, the psychoanalytic worldview contains an implicit ethic. And it is to the ethical basis of human relating that we now turn.

3

THE EMERGING PSYCHOANALYTIC ETHIC

The most immediate and common objection to any clinical theory that aims for the expansion of subjectivity is that it encourages licentiousness. Is a concept of analysis that valorizes affective experience and opens up the world of passion and subjectivity not a carte blanch for permissiveness? Does this type of analysis not constitute an endorsement for unbridled human passion that in the hands of at least some would become irrational, unethical, and could even be used to justify dictatorial behavior? The vision of analysis as the exploration of human subjectivity can work only if it can be shown that there is an ethic built into the heart of the desire the psychoanalyst seeks to liberate.

This question is not at issue in the classical model because the superego is internalized as heir to the Oedipus complex. Thus, the representative of societal restriction is a counterforce to potentially uncivilized passions from an early age. Ego psychology is not simply a theory of liberating psychosexual and aggressive wishes and passions; it is a model that seeks a rapprochement among the competing needs of id, reality, anxiety, and superego (e.g., Rapaport, 1951, 1957; Arlow & Brenner, 1964; Brenner, 1976; Gray, 1990). The ego has the central seat at the table of psychological organization. With regard to the superego, the analyst aims not for its overthrow, but for a benign form of internalized ethical principle. The analysis may aim for a less restrictive structure in cases of harsh, punishing superego demands, and a more solidified, inhibitory superego in cases that lack sufficient moral restriction. The purpose of an ego analysis is to form a new balance among these forces that allows for a sufficient degree of gratification while accepting the demands of reality and morality. A good analysis, from this viewpoint, loosens the grip of a harsh superego, but sustains the superego as the internalized representation of societal restrictions on desire.

For the classical model, then, the healthy structure toward which the analysis aims includes an ethic imposed by societal forces and internalized by the child through familial relationships. Each person, according to this view, must adopt the prohibitions required by the family and society at large (e.g., Freud, 1923, 1930). Therefore, personal morality results from the imposition of an authoritarian structure. Freud was not an advocate of authoritarianism; he simply believed that civilization is made possible by the imposition of an authoritarian morality that tames the passions and channels them into productive uses that we call civilization (Freud, 1930). This theory of moral development, referred to by Erich Fromm as "authoritarian conscience," is an imposition morality.

By contrast, for those who hold to a conception of the analytic process as a way of elucidating and expanding human subjectivity, the establishment of individual morality is not as easily explained. If the purpose of analytic therapy is to expand the arena of desire and passion, it would appear that imposition of stricture would be the type of restraint that it is the purpose of analysis to loosen, or perhaps overcome completely. If the therapeutic process is aimed to overthrow societal and familial imposed injunctions, what limits does it encounter?

Given that the structural model does not provide the form of psychic organization in the new psychoanalytic vision, if, indeed, the new vision has no defined form for how the mind should function, but constitutes a method for unleashing dormant potential, is there any constraint on where self expression may lead? Is the new vision not an endorsement of the narcissism analytic thought regards as pathological and from which the contemporary world already suffers too much? These fundamental questions must be answered definitively if the emerging psychoanalytic vision is to be a viable stance toward patients seeking relief from distress as well as the wider society.

Empathy and Ethics

The question of unbridled licentiousness raises the question of the very nature of the self. Questioning whether unethical, impulsive, unrestrained, and even destructive behavior would be the outcome of self realization, even though framed as an interrogatory, makes the assumption that the self develops and sustains itself apart from the interpersonal world. The self implied in the question is a Hobbesian self, developing and existing apart from the experience of others. Whatever truth there may be in the belief that Freud saw the human organism in these terms, the contemporary analytic view of the self stands in clear opposition to such a view.

Analytic theory and the findings of developmental research are in agreement that the child becomes a self only if seen as a subjective being by an other (e.g., Winnicott, 1971; Kohut, 1977; Beebe & Lachmann, 2002; Stern, 1985). Affective dispositions appear to be inborn (Tomkins, 1962), but the child needs a similar response from the caretaker to develop these inborn states into affective experiences that can eventually be formed into a self. Without such a response, affect, and consequently self development, withers (e.g., Demos, 1991). The finding in contemporary psychoanalytic thought and research that the self develops and sustains itself only with the affective immersion of an other demonstrates the interdependent relationship between self and world and has brought empathy into the heart of analytic discourse (e.g., Kohut, 1984; Levy, 1985; Basch, 1988; Feiner & Kiersky, 1994; Reiser, 1999; Bolognini, 2001, 2009). Relying on empathy for its nurturance, the self is not an isolated entity that may engage the world as one of its contingencies, but is, in its very essence, a way of relating to the world. It is this insight into the nature of the person-world relationship that provides a basis to found a new psychoanalytic ethic on empathy, an ethic based not on the superego, but on the kind of relationship between people that forms and sustains the very sense of self.

The crucial role of empathy in current analytic thought has stimulated the philosopher John Riker (2010) to conclude that psychoanalysis has within it the ethical foundation for the modern world. While this is undoubtedly a bold claim, Riker makes a strong case that contemporary psychoanalysis can achieve what religion and philosophy have no longer been able to sustain. Riker's theoretical elucidation is of such pivotal importance that it must be a launching point for any consideration of the relationship between psychoanalytic theory and ethics.

Riker (2010) has provided a dual foundation for ethics in the modern world by using the conceptual tools of self psychology. The philosopher's first connecting link between self psychology and the ethical groundwork of modern life is the need for selfobjects. The argument is that because we need selfobjects for the evolution of the self, we are constrained to be empathic to others so they will treat us in kind. If we do not treat others empathically, we will lack the selfobjects necessary for our own self love. We are and should be good to others because we need them and we need them to be good to us.

Riker has made the most significant breakthrough in using analytic thought as a foundation for ethical behavior since Erich Fromm (1947). His analysis demonstrates the intimate connection between the construction of the self, empathy, and an ethical life. Nonetheless, there are difficulties with the particulars of Riker's analysis. First, one may question whether the child, the mother, or adult others are empathic in order to invest for a later return. Is it credible to believe that the mother is empathic with her baby so the child will possess the selfobjects necessary for the mother's self love? It would seem to attribute a calculation to the caretaker or any subject of empathy to regard empathic resonance as an investment in future goods.

Second, and perhaps more important, Riker's ethic is founded on an instrumentalist view of the other who is experienced only as a source of gratification or frustration. The other as a selfobject is not seen as a subject of experience of her own, but only for her effect on the subject. We are empathic, for Riker, only out of a calculated desire to receive the other's empathy. The other is not seen as a subject in her own right, but as a potential source of empathy for the self.

Because a selfobject, by definition, is an object that fulfills functions, the self-selfobject relationship does not include seeing the subjectivity of the selfobject (Kohut, 1971, 1984). For example, in childhood the mirroring selfobject functions to recognize the child's states, but nowhere in Kohut's description, nor in later self psychological formulations, is there a role for the child's recognition of the experience of the mirroring selfobject. Such an object is not seen as a subject, but fulfills the crucial role of recognizing the child's affective states, whether in development or in the mirroring transference. While the function of the mirroring selfobject is to provide empathy, the source of the empathy is not an other seen as a subject, but an object who provides functions.

In a similar way, the child relieves tension states by attaching himself to an idealized object seen as possessing exceptional qualities (Kohut, 1971). What the idealized object actually experiences is not a component of the idealization process, and it does not enter into the relationship or function of the idealization either in development or analytic therapy. The analysand idealizes without knowing anything about the experience of the person whom he idealizes, and the empathy of the mirroring object is felt without any sense of the experience of the object doing the mirroring. That is why Fosshage (1991) has characterized self psychology as a "one and half person psychology."

The same analysis is applicable to every type of selfobject, including the selfobject functions enumerated after Kohut's main texts, such as the validation of affective states, soothing tension states, the recognition of uniqueness, and organizing affective experience (Kohut & Wolf, 1978; Bacal & Newman, 1990). Selfobjects serve functions, but empathy, because it means contacting the subjectivity of the other, is outside the purview of the self-selfobject relationship. In self psychology, empathy is provided by certain types of selfobjects, but it is not a part of the self's relationship to its selfobjects. The child is the recipient of selfobject functions, but does not recognize the selfobject as a subject, so the relationship to the selfobject can neither create nor sustain a sense of subjectivity. Therefore, a self-selfobject relationship as conceptualized by self psychology can never fulfill the requirements of self development and so the gaze of the selfobject does not issue in a sense of ownership.

So, while Riker has achieved a breakthrough in the effort to build a foundation for ethics from analytic theory, his instrumentalist reasoning built on the selfobject concept falls short of achieving its goal. The notion that a child, mother, father, or any other acquaintance or relationship, is empathic as a way of purchasing insurance for one's own empathic needs in the future makes the other a function for one's benefit. Such a view sustains an objectivist treatment of the other. According to this line of thinking, empathy becomes a benign and perhaps even a seductive form of treating the other as a means for one's own eventual benefit. Here we encounter the inherent problem in any attempt to establish an ethic on the basis of the selfoject concept. By taking this concept as far as it can be taken toward an ethic, Riker's work has shown its limitations. An ethic of seeing the other as an end in herself, as accorded the rights and respect of a separate person, requires a move beyond the self-selfobject relationship. Therefore, a conceptualization of the child-caretaker relationship limited by the selfobject concept cannot provide a foundation for the ethical treatment of others. So, while I agree with Riker that the self needs the gaze of the other to develop its potential, to account for the ethical sense we need to move beyond the concept of the selfobject.

The Development of the Self

The child's first affective experiences are nascent psychic states that seek a response from the other. What the child sees when she sees the mother responding to her is critical to how the child feels about herself in relation to others (e.g., Sander, 1975, 2000; Sroufe, 2000). As Winnicott (1971, p.112) wrote, "When the baby looks at the mother, what the baby sees is related to what the mother sees there." The baby knows herself first by finding herself in the eyes of the mother. Benjamin (1995, 1997, 2004) provides the pivotal insight that if the mother is not seen as a subject, her gaze cannot

34

help the child become a subject. For the baby to find her self in the mother's gaze, she must see the mother as a subject of experience. It is, then, contact with the other's subjectivity that brings the child alive as an experiencing subject. At this point, the child can experience her affective states as belonging to her.

Benjamin (1995) has outlined the recognition process as passing through several key developmental steps. It begins with the mother's confirming response that says to the infant: "We have created meaning together!" The recognition is, then, essentially mutual. However, beginning at the developmental crisis of six to nine months which Mahler et al. (1975) call the "differentiation" subphase of separation-individuation, the child becomes aware that she cannot control the mother's comings and goings, and so the baby is forced to the realization that the mother has a mind of her own. In the mother's movement away from the child, in her assertion of a self not under the child's control, there is a negation of the child's desire that affirms the mother as a separate person (Benjamin, 2004). This very negation, the limitation placed upon the child, enforces the boundaries of the self, which is to say, helps shape the self.

At this point the child has shifted from "we created meaning together" to "you, as an other, share the feeling." But, in the rapprochement subphase, as the child moves back to reconnect with the mothering figure, a power struggle ensues as the child realizes that she does not feel the same as her mother. The battle cry of the two-year-old striving for separation while still dependent on the caretaker is "I want my way! And your feeling is a coercion!" At this point, the child's recognition of the mother is directed to a subject seen as an other who, in turn, affirms the boundaries of the self.

An emotional identification with the other's position is then possible. This ability to assume the other's viewpoint becomes "You know what I feel even when I feel the opposite of you." This move is the culmination of the development of recognition, a process that ends in the ability to empathize with the other, even if the other's experience is different from or opposite to one's own. In the development of the capacity for empathy, the self learns to adopt a variety of viewpoints. In Winnicottian terms, the relationship with others has become a play space, a space for the experimentation with a variety of identifications and roles. Defining empathy as the recognition and appreciation of the other's experiential viewpoint, even if different from one's own, we can see that empathy and the growth of the self are not simply in synchrony; they are mutually enhancing processes.

For these reasons, the recognition of and respect for the other's experience is an imperative for the self to become who he can be. It is not sufficient for the child to be empathized *with*, her empathy for the other allows the other to be seen as a subject, and then the gaze of the other helps the baby come alive as a subject. Key to the child becoming a subject is her empathy for the caretaker's experience. That is why self realization does not result in an unbridled licentiousness that pays no heed to the other. The birth and growth of the self is inherently a function of both experiencing empathy and being empathic toward the other. But, this process is not just about the growth of the self; it is simultaneously, the foundation for a psychoanalytic ethic based on the recognition and appreciation of the subjectivity of the other, that is to say, an ethic founded on empathy. As the child realizes her potential in the mutuality of empathy, she simultaneously is living an ethic of respect for others. In this way, contemporary psychoanalysis shifts the foundation of ethical principles from the superego, an ethic of imposition, to empathy, the recognition of the other as subject, an ethic of inclination.

We may now consider what happens if this empathic connection is lacking. If, when the child seeks a response to her affective states, none is forthcoming, the baby will continue to pursue the other for a response, but if no response can be elicited, the child will eventually withdraw in what may be called a shame reaction (Beebe & Lachmann, 2002). Affective development is then arrested, and the self loses a significant component of its potential to function (Demos, 1992), thus weakening the self and creating a feeling of vulnerability. A desperate, but not uncommon, reaction to this lack of visibility is the erection of a grandiose defense that needs constant adulation. The self absorbed personality that draws so much attention under the label of the "narcissistic personality organization" is not a developed self, but a product of arrested self development. The entitlement one finds in such a personality is a product not of empathy, as defined here, but of its absence. A defensive illusion of being able to control uncontrollable events and satisfy every whim serves to deny the painful reality of deprivation, emptiness, vulnerability, and invisibility.

Thus, narcissistic exploitation, manipulation, or dismissal of the other are not symptoms of a self without constraints, but of the vulnerability of some aspect of the self to develop. Grandiosity serves to defend against anxieties and vulnerabilities, but it renders empathic contact impossible. From the lofty perch of grandiosity, there can be no empathy for others, and so the gaze of the other's subjectivity required for self development cannot take place. In this way, grandiosity is both a product of arrest and an assurance of its continuation.

In essence, the distinction between the other experienced as a subject and the other seen as a selfobject is decisive for a psychoanalytic ethic. Benjamin's expansion of the ideas of Winnicott and Kohut along with overwhelming developmental findings demonstrates that the child becomes a self by recognizing the other as a subject. The development and experience of the self are inextricably linked to contacting the subjectivity of the other seen as separate. The self is born from the intersubjective world and so has the stamp of that world in the fiber of its being. Continued contact with the experiences of others is necessary to nourish and sustain the self.

This view of morality is strongly, although indirectly, supported by Kohlberg's (1981) research on children's moral development, research that debunks the belief that morality issues from superego demands. Of particular importance to our concerns is the difference in children who operate on a moral basis of "conventionality" and the group Kohlberg called "principled children." Those in the former group see morality in stereotypical, simplistic terms that seem to be based on conventional phrases easily repeated without any moral reasoning. Such children will say cheating is wrong because "it is wrong," "you should do your work," or similar brief catch phrases without explanation or meaning. By contrast, those Kohlberg calls "principled" children use moral reasoning to justify behavior with principles. This group sees morality as a function of the rights of all humans to be respected, equality of treatment, and contractual obligations that are the basis of a community.

The details of this work need not concern us here. Suffice it to say that when children are given the opportunity to cheat on a test with no apparent concern by the experimenters, the second group is less likely to do so, but not because their superego demands were any more severe. The noncheaters did not have stronger, more solidified superegos than those likely to cheat. In fact, the "principled" children were no more opposed to cheating than "conventional" children, so it was not that they possessed any greater aversion to conventional rules about cheating. Once the experimenters' attitude was established, the "conventional" children had no reason not to cheat because the social environment did not support their "reasons." The conventional children had only vague ideas of why cheating was wrong, so when the situation permitted, they disregarded those beliefs and cheated. These children did not include the rights of others in their concept of morality. However, the "principled" children believed that taking the test in an honest way was the fulfillment of their social contract, and they "defined the issue as one of inequality, of taking advantage of others, of deceptively obtaining unequal opportunity" (p.186).

While Kohlberg saw the important difference in the two groups to be that the "principled" group saw the issue as one of justice, the essence of their concept of justice was awareness of the impact of cheating on other children and even the culture at large. The concept of justice that Kohlberg found crucial to ethical conduct is, in essence, an adherence to the principle that others have rights equal to oneself; it is wrong to give oneself an unfair advantage over others. As Kohlberg himself concludes: "The motivational power of principled morality does not come from rigid commitment to a concept or a phrase. Rather, it is motivated by awareness of the feelings and claims of other people in the moral situation" (p.188). Kohlberg's study shows that morality derives not from superego strictures directed against immoral impulses, but from the awareness of others as separate subjectivities and the impact of one's behavior on other people and the wider society. That is to say, Kohlberg's studies of children's moral development confirm the contemporary psychoanalytic view that empathy for others regarded as equal subjects is the basis of adherence to moral principles.

Because contact with other minds is inherently enriching and stimulates affective life and the growth of the self, empathy is typically not a strategic offering for an expected return. The recognition of the other as a separate source of experience is inherently pleasurable and promotes the growth of the self. Those who are unable to achieve this level of experience remain in an omnipotent world unable to benefit from others as subjects, and, as a consequence, are unable to develop a sense of themselves as subjects in a world of other subjects. Their self withers as they objectify others and become objectified themselves as a result.

The psychoanalytic basis of ethical behavior is rooted in the mutuality between empathy and the growth of the self. One finds in the experience of the other as a separate subject the gaze of a subject who can enhance one's own experience. This benefit of empathic recognition is experienced by the baby with an attuned mother in the first months of life. Without this recognition, we are lost in a narcissistic enclosure that stifles any potential self development. In Benjamin's words, we need a place for "waste disposal," and if we do not get it, we remain ensconced in a grandiosity that remains static, and the self runs the danger of atrophying. Only by grasping the subjective states of caretaking figures can the child become most uniquely himself. Empathy is not just for others, but it is not an instrumentalist investment; in finding others, we find ourselves.

Ethics and the Integrity of the Self

Riker's second contention is that the realization of the self cannot take place if the self is split; so disavowed behavior is antithetical to the growth of the self. The argument is that to stray from what one knows to be right militates a disavowal that splits the self and damages the ability of the self to function. The need for integrity, therefore, ties self development to the maintenance of ethical principles. To act on ethical precepts is to sustain the integrity of the self, and, therefore, to make possible the actualization of its potential, whereas to act in opposition to one's ethical beliefs requires a disavowal that erodes the integrity of the self. That is the meaning of Fromm's (1947) contention that virtue is the realization of one's powers.

Riker makes an invaluable point that an ethical breach has to be disavowed, split off from the part of the self that engages the interpersonal world. We may extend Riker's idea by noting that this split has profound implications. The need to defend against awareness of ethical violation becomes an organizing feature of the personality. As the self needs to deploy defenses such as denial and rationalization, any interaction, or potential interaction, that may threaten the revelation of the disavowed part of the self must be avoided. Because many self experiences must be kept in a separate, disavowed state, the self organization becomes locked in a "vertical split" (Goldberg, 1999). As new defenses are added to fortify existing self protective maneuvers, possibilities are occluded, and other potential ways of being are not brought to fruition. The result is a weakened self that has difficulty using its full resources.

For example, the academic cheater may feel the immediate relief of getting a good grade, but then has to construct a defensive system to rationalize the acceptability of cheating. His mind may become occupied with rationalizations to justify the unjustifiable in an effort that can never be completely successful. The grade does not feel valid, and the result is a feeling of emptiness and lack of accomplishment, thus adding to his preoccupation with self-justification. Not being able to convince himself of his rationalizations, he fears being discovered as a fraud. The result is an impoverishment of his sense of self, leading to an ever more frantic effort to enhance his feelings of worth with manipulative and defensive strategies. Unable to accept any approbation or admiration for the degree acquired by fraudulent means, the guilt and sense of fraudulence result in an emptiness that is often covered by substance abuse and other symptoms that do not appear to be related to his cheating.

Cheaters frequently convince themselves of their rationalizations, but rarely do they connect their malfeasance with the emptiness in their lives, and it is even less common for them to see that any derivative symptoms, such as substance abuse, may be rooted in their ethical transgressions. While the perpetrator may feel he is successfully avoiding consequences due to his stealth and cleverness, in fact, he does not see the cost in the ultimate stagnation of the self.

From the viewpoint of any psychoanalysis of the self, ethical transgressions constitute a sense of betrayal that is repressed or disavowed, but cannot be easily vanquished. The disloyalty to the principles of the self results in one of a variety of self weakening experiences, such as the conviction that one has no right to positive experiences or even to exist at all, or the feeling that one's existence is unjustified. The latter is not simply a superego phenomenon, but a symptom of a crime against the self. As Freud (1923) saw long ago, unconscious guilt and the disavowal of its content result in a need to create external reasons for its justification. So, the patient performs an unethical deed in an effort to rationalize the guilt and thereby avoid awareness of self betrayal, which is far more painful and shameful.

Guilt dreams, self-defeating behavior, the need to fail, anxiety over success, and the enactment of ethical transgressions are only a few of the symptomatic expressions of self betrayal. Rather than isolated eruptions, these symptoms reflect a self whose development is occluded by a gnawing preoccupation with its own betrayal. Actions taken against one's moral precepts, however disavowed they may be, compromise the integrity of the self and so constrict its potential that symptoms are likely to follow. Although the form may differ widely, the self tends to pay a price for betrayal, even though the cost may be hidden.

Clinical Illustration

John, a young single man in his late twenties entered analysis complaining of lack of motivation and success in his life. While he found his current job boring and lacking in challenge, he acknowledged that he had never worked at anything. But, he also had not found any activity, whether gainful employment or avocation, worth strong emotional or intellectual investment. After he had been in analysis for a number of months, he revealed that he was engaging in unethical and illegal activities. None of his ethical transgressions were violent or abusive, but typically scams he had concocted to cheat companies for which he had worked or with which he had some business contact. He claimed to feel little guilt over his malfeasance, justifying his behavior on the basis that the companies were corrupt and "anyway, everyone cheats if they can."

To summarize a lengthy analytic exploration, the details of which need not concern us here, he was chronically fearful that others were going to abuse and take advantage of him. In an effort to protect his vulnerability, he thought of ways of cheating others to reassure himself that people whom he believed to be more powerful were not shaming him. While in the midst of a scam, he came alive, became excited, and entered a state of stimulation in dramatic contrast to his default state of boredom. Only at these times did he feel powerful, in control of his life. The extent of the criminal and unethical activity had been kept from me for the first year of the analysis, and he acknowledged a fear of telling me. His past was replete with petty criminal behavior for which he had escaped punishment. He had been leading two lives, one a common worker unhappy with his lot and facing a long uphill battle to advance, and the other, a petty thief and con man always on the lookout for the next deceptive intrigue. All the excitement in his life going into the scams, he had little emotional investment in his "above ground" legitimate life. While he would acknowledge neither guilt nor shame over his ethical and legal malfeasance, he kept all that activity disavowed, sequestered off, and he had little interest in the respectable life he was leading on the surface. He complained of an empty feeling and a life without direction or purpose. His restlessness only intensified his desire to violate moral and legal codes in order to inject excitement into his life, and the more he did that, the deeper the split and sense of emptiness. His life was a vicious cycle from which he could see no escape.

When we were able to understand the origins and nature of the paranoia in a volatile and unavailable mother, John expressed his dissatisfaction with his underground life and hoped to end it. His paranoia was appreciably reduced, but he continued to express dissatisfaction with the lack of excitement in his life and his questionable activity persisted, although at a reduced pace. He wished to give it up completely, but his illegal activity was his only source of enjoyment, short-lived though it was. What matters in the current context is that much of the analytic work consisted in his gradual acceptance of the fact that his unethical behavior was the cause of his emptiness, not a symptom of it. By splitting off the only source of gratification he received in order to disavow his corruption, John was left with a cavern of emptiness where a self should have been. The need for moral malfeasance had sundered the self, and he could not quit the dangerously unethical breaches completely until he found a worthy substitute in the world of social propriety.

After a lengthy period of self exploration in which he came to confront his guilt and shame over his behavior, John began to use the analysis to search for alternatives. In one session he came to the realization that the rare times he felt good were instances of helping others. Determined that he would pursue a life of commitment to bettering the lot of the less fortunate, he sought and found a job with a charitable organization. His life then became a reflection of deeply held precepts, and thus, his daily life was more integrated with his values. Overcoming the disavowal led to the integration of the self and a great enough degree of life satisfaction that he was able to relinquish the need for criminal behavior. The case of John demonstrates that the split self can be both a source of ethical transgression as well as a product of living an ethically compromised life.

Ethics and Splitting

John rationalized cheating companies by declaring that they were cheating their customers and workers. Like many patients who commit ethical violations, John could admit no positive characteristics of these companies because that would interfere with the demonization that he used as a justification. Even if the object is seen as "all bad" before the abusive treatment, the ethical transgression solidifies that perception. Once the other is reduced to a representation of badness or evil, mistreatment becomes justifiable.

The embezzler will rationalize thievery by devaluing the company from which he stole as exploitive. The man who has an extramarital affair will justify himself on the basis of his wife's neglect or possession of negative character traits. Recently, a man murdered several people in a Missouri city council meeting and gave as the reason his mistreatment by a racist and unfair government. To be sure, the objects of such wrath must already be demonized for the act to occur, but unethical conduct fortifies and crystallizes splitting by creating the need to organize the personality on the basis of a simplistic reduction of others to "all good" or "all bad."

To perpetrate the maltreatment, the abuser has to maintain the rigidity of the split. The recruiting and manipulation of experience to fit this preconceived pattern becomes an organizing principle of the self, which is then reduced to assuming the obverse role of the targeted object. The object world being hardened into solidified split representations, the self is "all good" and any negative traits are disavowed in an effort to split off the guilt while positive traits of the object are denied. Thus, splitting constricts experience into rigid, narrow categories. In John's case, this dynamic became paranoid, but it need not reach this level in every instance of ethical malfeasance.

Seeing the other's subjectivity becomes a threat to this defensive system, so interpersonal experience is hardened against the recognition of the other's experience. The self is then reduced to categorizing others as objectified part objects, thereby losing its ability to see itself in the other. Because the other's experience is not contacted, the gaze of recognition cannot enrich the self. Such solidified splitting not only objectifies the other, but also arrests the growth of the self.

But, certainly, one might object: Is it not the case that those who commit ethical transgressions are at least on some occasions reacting to real deeds, unethical behavior directed to them or others? If the perpetrator is harming another person, is it not justifiable to ascribe "badness" to that person? The answer to this question is key to understanding the depth of the proposed ethic.

Here again Benjamin's (2004) work provides the direction for an answer. In concert with her emphasis on recognition of the other, Benjamin notes that a common response to unethical and unjustifiable behavior is to victimize the perpetrator as a bad object. The result is to lock both victim and perpetrator into a binary of "doer and done to." This is true at the societal level in response to national tragedy, as in the events of 9/11 or conflicts between ethnic and religious groups, but it is also applicable to the clinical context. The patient who demands that the clinician meet impossible demands tends to make the therapist feel victimized, and the result is that both parties in the dyad feel victimized by the other. The patient may well feel the analyst is unresponsive and abusive to her continual requests, but as long as the therapist feels abused and regards the patient as the abuser, there is no escaping the binary of "doer and done to." Such a response perpetuates splitting the dyad into victim and perpetrator. The road out of this binary is to transcend the splitting not by avoiding one's own responsibility, but by assuming it.

Benjamin argues that when the therapist is willing to acknowledge her role in the interactional stalemate by accepting her hatred and guilt, the patient is freed to do the same, that is, to take ownership of her role and destructive desires. Then, and only then, can the way out be discerned. A mutual recognition of responsibility and guilt transcends the binary of perpetrator/victim. This is what Benjamin calls the "moral third," the third that transcends the splitting of "doer and done to." By taking responsibility for one's destructive desires and guilt, splitting of the self is obviated. So, the willingness to take ownership over one's desires to destroy, even kill, makes it possible for the other to do the same, as in the therapeutic relationship. When both parties are able to assume ownership over their negative, devaluing emotions, the relationship shifts.

It is now possible to construct a third, which does not deny desires but obviates the need to act on them, because they are experienced in the potential space of mutual recognition. The moral third is the space in which destructive, hateful desires can be felt and avowed, not defended against, and in this space, they transcend the splitting that makes them so dangerous. Furthermore, in the assumption of responsibility for one's own anger, even hatred, and guilt, the need for disavowal is obviated, and the self becomes unified.

So, the key to understanding the depth and implications of a psychoanalytic ethic can be found in the response to unethical conduct. To victimize the perpetrator is to repeat and even strengthen the cycle of "doer and done to." The ethic of recognition means that one does not split the object, even if its conduct is reprehensible, but recognizes one's own destructive, immoral desires. The ownership of one's dark side makes possible a dialogue with those who do not respect the rights and values of others. Rather than demonizing such a person by splitting her into a bad object, one engages the perpetrator, but that is possible only from the vantage point of one's own potential for ethical transgression. Ultimately, it is this dialogue, this articulation of the range of experiences, good and bad, which is the road out of the trap of "doer and done to," victim and perpetrator, good and bad objects. An ethic of recognition, an ethic built on empathy, flows seamlessly from experiencing oneself and others as fully responsible subjects of a range of experience along the ethical continuum. The new psychoanalytic ethic is fundamentally a dialogue, that is, it consists of the ability to have discourse among persons who may clash sharply in their positions and views. Empathy cannot be expunged at the moment of the unethical act. Indeed, that is when it gets its most telling test.

Conclusion: The Reason to Be Good

Transgressions of ethical principles cost the self a great deal. It is tempting to compromise ethical principles, and the price paid is not immediately visible because it is paid indirectly and well after the moment of malfeasance. It is easy for the immoralist to rationalize unethical behavior and deny there is any cost when the transgression brings immediate gratification paid for with a psychic credit card. This lack of visibility makes denial easy, but the cost is borne by a crippled self that cannot easily be repaired. As the battle is won and the war lost, it is difficult indeed to convince those who pursue desire and pleasure that cutting ethical corners is not in their interest.

The ultimate conflict is not between self-interest and a higher principle, but between self-interest narrowly conceived, and the ultimate self-interest of becoming who one can be, the only long-term self-interest that can be meaningful.

As we have seen, analysis is about the experiencing subject, but the development of human subjectivity requires the engagement of the other. Fulfilling the capacities of the self requires the maintenance of integrity, a position that mandates the recognition and appreciation of the other. Breaks in empathy and objectification of the other tend to rob the self of experiences that can foster its growth, thus stimulating self protective responses, such as grandiosity, envy, and greed. On the other hand, with consistent experiences of mutual empathy and the maintenance of integrity, the self becomes who she can be. This fully functioning self both receives and gives empathy as an inherent part of the realization of her capabilities.

Thus, contemporary psychoanalysis breaks down the distinction between self development and ethics. The self who realizes his capabilities is a source of empathy for others and integrity. In this sense, the psychoanalytic model of ethics fits with Charles Taylor's (1989) concept that the "expressivist turn" in the Romantic period was decisive for Western identity. By using this term Taylor was drawing attention to the shift in sources of identity in Western civilization from the external, such as Plato's ideas or religious dictums, to the feelings, passions, and experience unique to each individual. Once that pivotal event took place, Taylor argues, the sources of morality also shifted from the imposition of religious or theoretical ideas to concrete experience. There was no appeal to religion or monarchy for what was right. The ethical emerged from growth of the self. Contemporary psychoanalysis represents and continues the expressivist turn by founding ethics in the experience of empathic mutual recognition, what we have called an ethic of inclination, as opposed to the ethic of imposition represented by the superego.

In this interpretation of the analytic worldview, no other principles, injunctions, or higher causes must be imposed to account for ethics. Conduct motivated by respect for others is implicated in the very process of achieving selfhood. And that is why it is good to be good.

With these considerations we have defined the ethical basis of the psychoanalytic vision of the human condition. The relationship that inheres between the recognition of the other and the subjectivity of the self forms the foundation of the psychoanalytic ethic. As the understanding of subjectivity requires its own epistemological basis, so the realization of the self has become the foundation of a uniquely psychoanalytic ethic. The purpose of this vision is ultimately to help in the process by which the self can realize its potential. We are now in a position to see how the analytic vision becomes a clinical strategy.

Part II

CLINICAL

4

THE ROMANTIC INTERPRETATION
OF PSYCHOANALYSIS

In Part One, we followed the historical battle between the legacies of the "two Freuds," the scientistic group who are prone to theoretical primacy and the hermeneuticists who favor an open-ended inquiry. In concluding that the latter is the most viable approach to the uniqueness of each patient's experience, we have defined psychoanalysis as a unique method for the engagement and expansion of the subjective. In terms of the concrete clinical encounter this definition means that the purpose of analysis is to help the patient realize potential ways of being that have been arrested in the developmental process. The fealty of the analyst is to the patient's experience rather than theoretical conceptualization. However, the patient's potential having been arrested, the analytic engagement goes beyond the meaning and motivation of the patient's immediate experience to the stimulation and facilitation of potential ways of being and relating, the occlusion of which stifles the growth of the self (Summers, 1999). In this chapter I will apply this model of the subjective to a conceptualization of analytic therapy to show how the hermeneutic, open-ended approach to the patient's experience results in therapeutic change.

Nietzsche once said, "We all must simply become who we are." This imperative for the human purpose, consonant with the aims of contemporary psychoanalysis, sounds straightforward, but given the complexity of the philosopher's work and the painful struggles of his life, we may safely conclude the "simply" refers to the concept, not its execution. A sober appraisal of Nietzsche's injunction came from Herman Hesse's (1919/1999) character Demian who lamented the difficulty of living a life that expressed his authentic beliefs and feelings. The simplicity of Nietzsche's statement and the Herculean task of carrying it out over which Demian agonized seem to capture well the dilemma of so many contemporary analytic patients. Indeed, as we have seen, patients' insistence on self articulation has motivated prioritizing the uniqueness of the patient's experience over theoretical principles and norms of human functioning. Because in analysis the patient's experience has to be the source and arbiter of analytic truth, psychoanalysis is not defined by any theoretical content, but by its unique method of psychological inquiry. This shift from content to process is a decisive break with the past.

While others have advocated defining analysis by its mode of inquiry rather than content (e.g., Lear, 1998; Schwaber, 1992; Ghent, 2002), I propose to extend this definition to a process that includes the expansion of the subjective, the realization of dormant potential, in accordance with authentic experience. That is to say, an analytic engagement with the experiencing subject includes its transcendental possibilities. The concept of transcendent experience in the analytic encounter codifies a method for the creation of new ways of being and relating from dispositions buried under trauma and defense.

In elucidating the implications of this unique analytic responsiveness, I will show that this transformation in analytic stance is closely linked to one of the great intellectual movements in the history of Western thought. The Romantic Movement of the late eighteenth and early nineteenth centuries was motivated by concerns remarkably concordant with those of contemporary psychoanalytic thought, and I believe that the conceptual overlap between these two movements has much to offer today's analytic therapist. The application of the Romantic sensibility to analysis results in a profound shift in the way the analysand is engaged, and the therapeutic action unfolds. The result is psychoanalytic therapy conducted in a new key.

Neoclassicism and Romanticism

This decisive transformation of the analytic Zeitgeist parallels a powerful paradigm shift in the humanities from a time before analysis existed. In the seventeenth and most of the eighteenth century, literature was dominated by the neoclassicist position that order and reason must be imposed on the inherent sinfulness of human nature. The need for constraints on human freedom led neoclassicists, such as Samuel Johnson and Alexander Pope, to seek a return to the classical Greek and Roman era for the model of literature, the arts, and human living. The iconic work of this movement was Pope's (1709/2008) *Essay on Criticism*, which advocated the Greek and Roman ideal as the standard for all artistic creation. Typifying the period was Johnson's (1738) poem *London*, an imitation of the Roman poet Juvenal.

As we saw in Chapter One, analytic orthodoxy of any theoretical persuasion tends to share the neoclassical view of a preconceived form toward which the process aims. The most powerful reaction against the neoclassical position was the Romantic Movement, a powerful and passionate intellectual force that regarded the neoclassical assumption of a given form for artistic expression and life as oppressive of freedom, creativity, and passion. According to Romantic theorists, such as Friedrich Schlegel (1798–1801/1991) and Novalis (1797–1799/1997), the highest good was not to be found in adopting an external form but in the full realization of individual human capacities, or *Bildung*, a term roughly translatable as "formation, implying the development of something potential, inchoate, and implicit into something actual, organized, and explicit" (Beiser, 2003, p.26). For the Romantics the most complete human life was not to be found in adopting a norm, whether classical or modern, but in the development of the unique powers of the individual including intellect, passions, and creativity. Schlegel (1798–1801/1991) made this point most dramatically, ". . . to be human, to cultivate oneself are expressions that mean the same thing" (p.55).

The Romantic Movement was above all else a return to the experiencing subject in an effort to realize the unique potential of each individual. The poets, literary figures, and philosophers inspired by the Romantic sensibility sought truth not in the outside world or the scientific method, but in the experience of the individual (Stoljar, 1997), which is why no less a figure than Thomas Mann (1941) called Freud a romantic. The realization of individual potential, for the Romantics, was not simply a right, but an imperative, an ethic, the calling of each person, what Fichte (1848) called the vocation of man.

Although the ideas of Romantic theorists emerged from the Enlightenment belief in individual rights, the Romantic Movement opposed two principal components of that movement, both of which have direct relevance for psychoanalysis. First, the Romantics departed from the Enlightenment view of the isolated individual who forms interpersonal bonds by agreeing to a social contract. Greatly influenced by Hegel, the Romantics believed that the self can only achieve its full potential if recognized by the other who must be experienced as a subject in her own right. Because self realization requires the other to be experienced as a subject, the Romantics saw individual development as inseparable from a network of social relations. The self owes its existence to the subjectivity of others; as a consequence, self and community are interdependent. No agreement is needed to connect the individual to the rest of humanity because they are not separated.

In the Romantic view, we are born as seeds requiring education and nourishment to grow to full flower. *Bildung* implies pedagogy, the education of human potential that can only be provided by other human beings (e.g., Schlegel, 1799, p.131). This process comes to fruition only in love because love inspires creativity and growth (Schlegel, 1798–1801/1991). So, for the humanities scholars who composed the Romantic Movement, the destiny of each individual was intimately related to the "selfless love of community" because the nourishment for the self was love and the community of others (Stoljar, 1997). This inextricable bond results in an ethic of inclination, as opposed to the ethic of imposition.

The Romantics returned to the Aristotelian concept of self as inherently formed through community in opposition to Locke's Enlightenment notion of a "social contract" that assumed an originally self-sufficient individual who agrees to form bonds with others. Novalis (1798, p.45) was disdainful of Locke's social contract theory according to which the self-sufficient individual forms bond with community out of mutual self-interest. For Novalis, the pursuit of raw self-interest could lead only to the "fleeting happiness of the gambler. Enduring happiness, by contrast, results only from acting justly in a just state. So, human happiness is dependent on the nature of the state as well as one's actions within it. And that just state is bound by "selfless love in the heart and maxims in the head" (p.46).

Second, the Romantics objected to what they regarded as the overemphasis on reason characteristic of the Enlightenment. The self cannot realize its potential without the full exercise of all human capacities, including the emotions, for it is passion that moves people. That is why love was the nourishment for the growth of the self. Nonetheless, they believed in the expression of all emotions, positive and negative, and saw the human psyche as both "creative and limited, a doer and done to, and a sufferer, infinite in spirit and finite in action" (Barzun, 1943, p.26). No human feeling was to be avoided, no matter how much anguish it might bring. Even the darkest suffering is to be embraced in order to utilize its potential for growth. As Wordsworth (1843/2010) put it: "We will grieve not, rather find Strength in what remains behind . . . in the soothing thoughts that spring out of human suffering."

The Romantics did possess an optimistic conception of the human ability to create the self, to find new potential in pain and suffering, and, in essence, to bring to fruition many of the infinite human capacities within an individual life. But, for that very reason, all negative emotions must be experienced to their fullest so that their potential can be realized. The danger for the Romantics was not in the painful experiences, but in the refusal to experience them, in which case their potential cannot be realized. As Novalis (1797–1799/1997) put it, "life must not be a novel that is given to us, but one that is made by us" (p.66). Correlatively, in opposition to the neoclassical conformity to a preexisting norm, the Romantics favored the individual's ability to affect and shape the world as well as being affected by it.

Shelley's (1820) Prometheus, who combated seemingly overwhelming powers to sustain authentically held principles, was the prototypical Romantic hero. Unlike Aeschylus's version of the play, Shelley's Prometheus made no accommodation to Zeus, defying omnipotent power, not for his self-aggrandizement or envy, but because he believed what he did was right. In contemporary terms, Shelley's Prometheus valued authenticity, the calling of his most authentic values, over immediate self-gratification and conformity to any power, no matter how strong.

The highest good, *Bildung*, could be achieved only with the deployment of imagination to create the self and affect the world. The Romantics saw this powerful human ability not as a separate human faculty, but as a necessary component of all meaningful experience (e.g., Larmore, 1996). They did not substitute the imagination for reality, as some have charged, but they did believe one could maximize the potential of the world only by imbuing the mundane with the imaginative. The imagination was essential to life not because it opposed reality, but because it brings out its full possibilities. As Novalis (1797–1799/1997) so proudly remarked: "insofar as I give the commonplace a higher meaning, the ordinary a mysterious appearance, the familiar the dignity of the unfamiliar . . . I romanticize it" (p.60). In Wordsworth's poem "Michael—A Pastoral," a heap of stones unnoticed by passersby contains the story of a father's love for his son and their forced separation. In typical Romantic fashion, Wordsworth saw poetry as a way to use the imagination to counter received opinion, to remake the very perception of the world. The revolution, for Shelley and Wordsworth, was to be initiated from within, with a new culture of subjectivity founded on the imagination (Turner, 1988).

In this way, the Romantic Movement initiated what Charles Taylor (1989) calls the "expressivist turn" in the Western concept of identity. With the advent of the romantic mode of thought, identity and meaning in life are no longer to be found in religion or the world of ideas, nor in any other source outside of the person. The pivotal move, for Taylor, is the shift to the experience of the individual. Although

Taylor acknowledges that the Romantic Movement itself was short-lived, he has demonstrated that the legacy of that intellectual movement has been the emphasis on feelings and the meaning of ordinary activity for the sense of identity. The Romantic Movement opposed any normative concept for human life in favor of the flowering of the individual uniqueness.

All of these Romantic tenets are of the greatest relevance for the contemporary analytic sensibility. The importance of passion as a human motivation has always been at the core of analytic thought. In fact, it is what motivated Freud to create his theory. He once told his young friend Ludwig Binswanger, "Man has always known he has spirit; I had to show him he has instinct" (as quoted in Binswanger, 1957, p.81). Each of the other core ideas of the Romantic Movement represents a break from the past. The inherent link between self and appreciation for the other has become the way contemporary analytic thought views self development. The goal of self realization is a virtual renaming of *Bildung*, and that new and exciting analytic aim requires movement beyond understanding who the patient is now to whom she may become in the future. The imagination then becomes integrated into the analytic theory of change. The highest good for both the Romantic Movement and contemporary psychoanalysis is the full functioning of the unique capacities of each individual. Because the self can be realized only if recognized by other subjects, these two viewpoints eschew normative content in favor of an ethical standard: the appreciation and respect for the other. In this way, contemporary psychoanalytic thought is developing a Romantic sensibility, albeit without clarifying its application to the theory of technique. To codify these Romantic tenets into the analytic theory of therapeutic action is to conduct psychoanalytic therapy in a new key.

The Romantic Interpretation of Psychoanalysis

The movement toward an anormative psychoanalysis with the aim of realizing the unique potential of each individual weds contemporary psychoanalysis to the fundamental Romantic principle that fealty to one's experience leads to the most fulfilling life. Without any external standard that can justifiably be imposed, the analytic purpose has become building the self from its dispositional potential, a psychoanalytic form of *Bildung*, reflected in concepts such as true self, destiny, the nuclear program of the self, and authenticity. This interpretation of the analytic project goes beyond engagement and understanding of the patient's patterns to the evocation of new possibilities that cannot typically be foreseen. The analytic therapist hopes the process stimulates the release of potential that has never before come to fruition.

In adopting this stance, the analyst returns to the etymological roots of therapy as he assumes the posture of the *Therapeutis*, the attendant, who immerses himself in the patient's experience and the potential sedimented in it. If successful, the patient will see the unrealized parts of himself, what strivings and dispositions that have not developed, and then struggle to bring them to fruition. It is in this creation of new form, the realization of what was once dormant, that the analytic process most closely lives out its Romantic heritage.

Despite the diatribes sometimes directed to the Romantic Movement, it has remained a major influence in Western thought and art, albeit sometimes in opposition to the dominant culture. The Romantic sensibility, despite its adherence to the Enlightenment, was designed to counteract the overemphasis on reason characteristic of that movement as well as the normative thinking and rigidity of the neoclassicists (e.g., Barzun, 1943; Taylor, 1989). Freud was an heir to this tradition when he showed that much of human motivation was irrational, or passion driven. As we saw in Chapter Two, the tyranny of objectivism has infiltrated psychoanalysis in the form of a normative psychological endpoint. To presuppose dynamics or outcome based on a theory is, in essence, Freud's (1910) concept of wild analysis, whether or not he was guilty of practicing it himself. In admonishing a physician who told a patient her anxiety neurosis was caused by insufficient orgasms, Freud stressed that analytic insight can be experienced only if the patient's awareness is in the "neighborhood" of the repressed material and the transference has evolved to the point that the patient is attached to the analyst. In his critique of the "wild analysis" physician, Freud committed himself once again to the principle that the patient's experience and its uncovering are the essence of analysis. Because the only viable criteria for analytic intervention are resonance with and expansion of the patient's subjective world, to deploy theory in a way that does not meet these criteria is to be guilty of wild analysis. Any view of analysis that presupposes a norm may justifiably be labeled wild analysis, irrespective of theoretical content. This usage may appear to be idiosyncratic, but when the analytic criterion of effectiveness is the patient's experience, the deductive use of theory to conceptualize experience violates the most fundamental analytic rule.

The Romantic Movement shares the contemporary psychoanalytic view that the self requires contact with others as subjects and therefore has what we have called an ethic of inclination, rather than an ethic of imposition. As we saw in Chapter Three, the mutual dependence of self development and recognition of the other's subjectivity lays to rest any concern that self realization could legitimately ever be used to rationalize unethical, even evil behavior. The analytic view is an application of the Romantic concept that recognition of the other and self development are interdependent phenomena. The appreciation of the other being inherent in the psychoanalytic ethic, any denigration or objectification of the other reflects an incomplete analysis. Failure to recognize the subjectivity of the other is not an expression of self development, but a symptom of its derailment, what Kohut (1977) called a "breakdown product" and Novalis, "raw self-interest." Immorality is predicated on just such an objectification of the other. Fromm's (1947) view that ethical motivation is not in conflict with the need for self realization, but inherent in it, is a quintessential Romantic position.

Similarly, it was a tenet of Romantic thinking that the individual could only realize her full capacities, and therefore become fully human, through the community of others. Given the goal of self realization, psychopathology becomes psychic interference in the realization of the self's capacities (Summers, 1999). For example, a conflict between the child's potentially aggressive affect and the caretaker injunction to inhibit energetic expressions will typically issue in a disavowal of aggression, thus occluding the aggressive potential of the self. The resultant failure to deploy assertiveness and confront conflict is pathological by virtue of the inability to create aggressive ways of being and relating. Affects so crippled are in a dis-positional state, not yet in position to assume a form and become real. The analysand is then not able to transform potential aggressivity into a way of being. If, however, the analysis stimulates the aggressive disposition, it may come to fruition as anger, joy, rage, play, a striving for social justice, sexual excitement, or ambition, among many other possible forms.

The key clinical implication is that to elicit unconscious affect is to evoke new possibilities, the eventual form of which cannot be foreseen. To realize psychic potential, effective interpretation must stimulate feelings and thoughts that go beyond the analyst's formulation. Eigen (2005), whose thinking represents well the Romantic sensibility in psychoanalysis, sees the analyst as more of an agent who evokes new experience than an instrument for understanding what is. Similarly, Lacan has suggested that the purpose of interpretations is to "make waves" (Eisenstein, 2007). Openness to traveling the emerging pathway, what Casement (1985) calls "learning from the patient," is a sine qua non of an analytic process that seeks to expand the patient's ways of being (Summers, 2005a; 2012). It follows that the analyst must adopt a technical stance of not knowing. The tempting desire for omniscience among those who sit in the analytic chair runs the underappreciated danger of suffocating the openness required for self formation (Eigen, 1993a). Interference with the analytic space can be subtle, but the consequences may impair the patient's freedom to explore the unknown. It can be seductive for both parties to enact the roles of knower and known, but the more the analyst is able to sustain the openness of the analytic space, the greater is the opportunity for the analysand to uncover new possibilities.

Although Bion's admonition to greet every analytic hour without desire or memory is fanciful on its face, one can appreciate the spirit of Bion's interpretation of the analytic stance as openness to the unknown. Eigen (1993a) interprets Bion's dictum as an injunction to "opt for the primary of perception and attention over memory and knowledge" (p.125) and cautions that attempting to control where the truth goes risks imposing on the emerging truth of the patient's experience. And here we come to a fundamental shift in the analytic stance. We have now reconceptualized the analytic task from knowing the patient to *engaging her being*, an analytic attitude suggestive of Heidegger's (1968/1954) concept of openness to Being. When the analyst adopts this way of attending to the patient, he has shifted his top priority from discovering new knowledge to receiving the being of the other. This interpretation of the analytic task does not obviate the role of understanding; it sees the value of insight in its ability to make contact with and expand the patient's experience. In this sense, contemporary analysis accords with the Romantic value system articulated by Fichte's (1848) statement that Being is prior to knowledge. Knowledge, or self awareness, subserves the creation of new ways of being and relating.

A major advance toward a clinical technique organized around openness to the patient's experience has been the deployment of the concept of empathy initiated by self psychology (e.g., Kohut, 1984; Basch, 1983; Beebe & Lachmann, 2002).

Attunement, or affective synchrony analogous to musical harmony, captures an affective resonance with the analysand's experience that is invaluable in bringing unconscious patterns to light and helping patients feel deeply understood. Here we have the analytic love of which Freud (1906) wrote. Bettelheim (1984) defined analytic technique as the "cure through love" by which he meant the willingness to engage, appreciate, and understand the patient's experience, however painful or ugly it might be. Some analysts are so moved by the power of empathic experience that they equate it with therapeutic action (e.g., Schwaber, 1990, 1992, 2005). However, this clinical strategy, being limited to engagement of the patient's affective states, lacks a concept for creating new form, a necessity if the analytic goal is to be the creation of new ways of being and relating. This consideration motivated Loewald's (1962b) belief that analysts cannot treat a patient unless they have a vision of her that goes beyond her current condition. Analytic love is an appreciation of the patient's experience, but to help the patient out of her suffering and dysfunction, faith that the patient can transcend her current ways of being is required. That is why Loewald (1960) concluded that there is a spiritual dimension to the analytic process. As Bettelheim (1950) famously said, "Love is not enough." A concept of transcendence must be added to analytic love.

Interpretation is necessary to bring to awareness the patient's patterns as they are enacted in the analytic relationship. But, this awareness in itself rarely contains sufficient transformational power for the creation of new form. Here we confront a gap between the aims of contemporary analysis and clinical technique. To facilitate the formation of the self, a strategy is required that goes beyond making unconscious states conscious and beyond even engaging what is dissociated, even beyond the awareness of relational patterns, to the creation of new ways of being and relating. To fulfill the goal of self realization, analysis must become a theory of creation, a means for creating ways of being and relating that transcend historical patterns. What *is* must be transcended for *what may be* to appear. To fulfill his obligation to the analytic subject, the analyst must be informed by a concept of *transcendence*.

Analytic Technique: Romantic Style

The need for transcendence becomes palpable in the analysis when the patient becomes aware of the origins, pain, and steep cost of a lifelong pattern, but sees no escape. Or, if an alternative is contemplated it has the opposite form of the lifelong pattern (Summers, 2005a). For example, the passive patient tends to be drawn to megalomania, the sadist, to masochism. The seemingly opposite reaction is ready at hand for the patient because it is the other side of the object relationship coin. As Benjamin (1997) has emphasized, living in such a binary world encloses the patient in constricting patterns that suffocate her own freedom while objectifying the other. Whether or not such a binary manifests itself, the patient is lost, enclosed in a world of unpalatable options. The patient is then caught in an ambiguous space that can become a terrifying emptiness, a sense of falling apart, even to the edge of annihilation anxiety (Summers, 1999).

It is here, in this confrontation with the iatrogenic chaos of losing the guideposts by which the patient has led her life, the loss of moorings in the world, that the patient may feel most confused and lost. But, it is just because the space is ambiguous that creation becomes most possible. Eigen (1993b) refers to this moment as "breaking the frame, stopping the world," the point where structure has fallen away allowing new possibilities to arise. The patient, who might be wondering what she signed up for, is unlikely to see any virtue in this loss of a psychic compass; it is the analyst who must see the possibilities in the formlessness. If the analyst sees the dilemma as a threat to the analysis, she will attempt to fill the space, and the transcendental opportunity is likely to be lost. The key is for the analyst to see potential presence in absence (Green, 1975), or as Keats (1817/2005) called it "negative capability" and sustain it, as the poet said, "without any irritable reaching after fact and reason." The analyst's vision of the space as possessing the potential for the creation of new ways of being transforms emptiness into potential space (Loewald, 1960; Summers, 2006). This is the transcendental moment.

It is in this dilemma, this quandary of unpalatable positions, when the historical patterns do not work and cannot be continued, but no viable alternative emerges, that we can make especially productive use of our Romantic heritage. As we have seen, desire, interest, passion, and values all contain an imaginative component, albeit not always visibly. Pointed toward the future, desire includes a trajectory for what can and might be. Because each historical pattern that dominates the patient's life is a derailment of a disposition to grow in a particular direction, each avenue has within it a disguised expression of who the patient is striving to be. For example, the masochistic patient has a desire to connect expressed in subjugated form, and the sadistic other side is an effort to assert control gone awry. Embedded in each side of the object relationship is the potential for a new form of being. This way of viewing object relationships is a concrete embodiment of the Romantic notion that all experience, no matter how dark, has the potential for building the self. It may well be that a key to the difference between static and mutative insight is the appearance of the imaginative factor in the latter. By deploying the imagination, the patient can become, as Adam Phillips (1998) has said, "the artist of her own life," a virtual paraphrase of Novalis's concept of writing the novel of one's life.

For example, a young adult female patient, Martha, after exploring the roots of her history of compliance and seeing the abuse she suffered because of it, at the moment of her resolve to become more assertive, burst out, "I don't want to be obnoxious and demand that everything go my way!" This woman was expressing both a desire to affirm some degree of control over her life and a strongly held value of not subjugating others, without having any sense of how to accomplish these two tasks. The need for effectance had been infused with an omnipotent illusion; and the ethic was buried under a compliance rooted in abandonment anxiety. At this point in the analysis to interpret the patient's statement as only a wish to become sadistic is to miss the crucial fact that both the sadistic expression and the compliance were rooted in an inability to deploy her aggression. Such a strategy not only misses the patient's struggle, but also overlooks the possibility of transcending the compliance-dominance binary.

To be sure, the patient has a desire to dominate, but this wish is the presented form of the need to become effective, the obverse of her compliance. Hidden within her compliance/dominance binary were psychic dispositions for effectance and sensitivity to others, both of which were masked by their symptomatic expression. Such thwarted developmental needs are the "forward edge" of development that some self psychologists believe lie at the center of therapeutic action (e.g., Tolpin, 2002).

By bringing out both the desire and the value with which it conflicts, the analyst makes manifest the dialectical tension between two self states that impels the search for a third way. The often befuddled analysand then has to struggle with how to realize the desire in keeping with the value. In Martha's analysis, my strategy was to recognize both the need for effectance and her value of respecting other's wishes. This conflict emerged as her effort to gain control of her life by pursuing her interests without intruding on others. She would push her opinions, affects, and desires, rather than bury them to accommodate others, but she also believed in according others the right to be heard that she demanded for herself.

Initially, it was difficult for Martha to hold off on her opinions and desires because she associated such behavioral withdrawal with her former compliant pattern. But, when I asked about her motives, she saw that her intent now in holding her tongue was to respect others, an important value to her, while historically the purpose had been to allay abandonment anxiety. I pointed out the implication that it was not the activity of speaking, acting, or keeping silent that mattered, but whether the behavior was motivated by her convictions. Martha was creating her own interpersonal compass that told her when she should press her desires and opinions in conflict with opposing ideas and when she should accommodate to others. While her capacities for self assertion and empathy were both evolving from nascent dispositions, Martha's most fundamental new way of being was the exercise of her freedom to determine when and how to deploy her aggression and exercise her empathy. It was in this freedom to choose that she transcended the dominance/compliance binary.

This confluence of discovery and creation can be seen in the analysis of another patient, Zelda, whose case has been discussed in detail previously (Summers, 1999). This young, very attractive woman had an impressive social presentation, but was plagued by an inchoate, nagging dissatisfaction in her life. The feeling was articulated for the first time when the analysis evoked her humiliation and anger at being imprisoned in a narrow, stifling identity as an empty-headed beauty. At that point she surprised herself by unleashing a vitriolic explosion at her family for regarding her as academically incapable, intellectually shallow, and unable to fill adult roles. Implicit in the anger was a desire for achievement and self respect which gave birth to a vision beyond the directionless life she had always lived. The eruption of aggression with imaginative potential from the frustration of a previously unknown desire constituted the first step of a journey from the inchoate to form. Ultimately, she successfully pursued professional goals, but it would be inaccurate to say that her ambition was there waiting to be discovered before the aggressive explosion, nor can we say it was wholly created after it. Zelda's incipient motivation to transform her life had been in a dissociated state existing in *status nascendu*. The rage unleashed in the analysis led

56

to creating the form not only of her anger, but also of the ambitions that became central to her identity.

As the imaginative potential of desire emerges, patients begin to see not only the fulfillment of a particular longing, but also a future life trajectory built on affects. A classical approach to analysis, in the sense I am using it here, confines desire to its immanent appearance, thereby excluding its transcendent possibilities. This stifling of the imagination concretizes desire in a manner analogous to the physician described by Freud in "Wild Analysis" who misinterpreted the psychoanalytic concept of sexuality as orgasm rather than psychosexuality. From the viewpoint of immanence, Zelda was angry at figures from the past; from the viewpoint of transcendence, she was angry at the future denied her.

Clinical Illustration

Sarah came to analysis for help with anxiety and difficulty controlling her moods, as well as to see if she could understand why relationships were as difficult for her as they were important. She had never had an enduring romantic relationship and wanted to be married, have children, and have a group of friends, or, in her words, she wanted to "have a normal life." Raised on a family farm miles from any neighbors, Sarah grew up with her brother as her sole social contact. School was almost an hour bus ride from home. Her mother, a teacher and a revered member of their small rural community, was so busy with her activities she had little time for her daughter, and her father worked the farm alone from sunrise to sunset. Sarah spent many hours by herself swinging in a tree swing, often telling her mother, "Mom, I feel so empty." She drank water from the well in an effort to "fill herself." Her father would typically spend hours or even days in complete silence and then ramble incoherently, often when no one was within hearing range. Her only contact with him was to be an object of one of his frequent rants, usually about wasting money. Trusting no banks, he hoarded cash, stacking tens of thousands of dollars in the house while insisting that the family could not afford plumbing. The toilet was an outhouse, and when Sarah had to defecate at night, she used a chamber pot in her room and smelled the feces all night. For punishment, she was held upside down in the outhouse. Clothing and all household items had to be used until they fell apart. Disposing of an item such as silver foil before it disintegrated was cause for a tirade.

When Sarah tried engaging her mother, the older woman either gave her daughter something to occupy herself while she embarked on a project, or made a pretense of doing an activity "together," which involved her mother taking over the work while claiming the project had been a joint endeavor. Sarah's mother often did her daughter's extracurricular, or even curricular activities, and Sarah was at times humiliated by winning prizes for work her mother did. Sarah never celebrated a birthday and did not attend a party until she left home. Her first exposure to city dwellers and modern amenities was college where she felt like a "country mouse" in the city. Although intrigued and dazzled by modern electronics and the apparent affluence of other students, Sarah never felt she fit in, and although as an adult she lived and worked in a large city, she continued to feel she was not sophisticated enough to belong.

She had formed few friendships, and the only potential romantic relationships quickly fell to ruin around disillusionment with the would-be boyfriend. Once she became emotionally attached, she could not tolerate anything less than complete devotion and adaptation. The inevitable disappointments in the man's responses to her needs led to rage attacks, demands for immediate gratification, or hopeless despair, which at times became suicidal ideation.

Sarah made similar demands on me. Meeting four times per week, she strictly monitored the time, and often accused me of cheating her out of minutes, although in fact her sessions tended to run longer than the allotted time because she was often resistant to leaving. She called persistently, typically leaving dramatic, lengthy messages, and sometimes asking for a return call. She attempted to extend phone conversations as long as possible, and when I told her I needed to get off the phone, she would often demand more time and at times slammed down the receiver in anger. Frequently, she felt the same intense outrage at the ending of sessions, and weekends were inevitably periods of rage, depression, and multiple phone messages. When Sarah attacked, screamed, even ranted in response to a separation or my refusal to comply with a demand, I told her that I knew she feared losing our relationship and needed me to know how much fear and pain she felt.

Sarah was so overwhelmed with dread of abandonment that she seemed to lay claim to me with little recognition of a boundary between my personal and professional life. I felt suffocated, as though she was out to extract my very soul. I recoiled to preserve myself, but in so doing, I had unwittingly become her father, unwilling or unable to respond to her. But, whenever I accommodated to her, I feared that I was submitting to my own annihilation. In terms of Ghent's (2002) distinction between surrender and submission, I surrendered to the experience with Sarah, but rather than submit, I held on tightly to my own threatened sense of self. I was determined to maintain the tension between being one with her and holding onto myself, what Benjamin (2004) calls the "one in the third." Doing battle with the pressure from Sarah to yield my personal identity, I felt her desperation to see Sarah as a child desperately attempting to maintain a sense of self in the face of annihilation threats by a mother who refused to recognize her separate existence and a father who did not know she was there. Fearing imprisonment by this victimized, helpless young woman, I feared I would never be freed.

However, Sarah felt victimized by any assertion of freedom on my part such as ending sessions and phone calls, sticking to a schedule, and speaking when I thought best, not when she desired. We explored the parallel here to fledgling efforts by Sarah the child to establish separateness from her mother's overwhelming obliteration of her experience. Indeed, both parents had permitted neither collaboration nor cooperation, because there was no recognition of Sarah as having a mind of her own. When I complied with Sarah's requests I was an "all good" object with almost magical powers to meet her needs, but my subjectivity was erased; when I inserted my self by saying "no," I became an "all bad" depriving object inflicting only pain on her. In this oppressive binary splitting, one of us was imprisoning the other, jailer and jailed, no one was free.

The fact that the demands of such patients cannot be met in the way the patient seeks might seem to justify a classical approach of enforcing a reality to which the patient must adapt. However, to respond only to the symptomatic expression colludes with the patient's either/or reductionism, and the potential for finding other avenues of making affective contact is compromised. In contrast, the analyst with a Romantic sensibility responds to the patient's experience and rides the waves of the patient's demands, rage, hate, love, and the chaos of devouring greed and entitlement. While Sarah's insistence that I accommodate to her omnipotent illusion is unattainable, this very press contains possibilities that have not yet been, possibilities that can only be imagined. The analysand's experience is not exhausted by its present expression, nor even by the past meaning in its present expression; the experience includes nascent potential, what has never been, that is to say, transcendent possibilities.

This recognition of both immanent and transcendent experience motivates a clinical strategy that demands recognition of both levels of the patient's experience. When I told Sarah that she wanted to eliminate my separateness, I also emphasized that she was conveying a long buried need hidden among the weeds of hostility, demands, accusations, and self denigration, a need to which she had not yet given words. As we lived through her emotional oscillations, I kept the analytic lens focused on each of these affects, but I also continually emphasized the craving for human contact embedded in them. Not only her anxiety, but also her rage and vituperative attacks on me, were understood as her longing for the human connection she feared would never be hers.

The fact that I responded to her pain and demands without judgment, that I understood the loneliness and abandonment anxiety that fueled her rage without any effort to diminish them or take them away, was unique in Sarah's experience. She felt that we had a bond in which she felt understood and recognized for who she was. Feeling that her desires were recognized, whether they were met or not, she codified them for the first time. In response to her suffering and absolutist demands, I responded that she was so fearful that no one would ever stick with her that she was attempting to grab me and never let go. One day she spontaneously blurted out, "I just want to be loved! I want to be safe!" I replied that she felt she would only get it if she demanded it. Sarah cried.

When Sarah acknowledged her desires for love and safety, she was at that moment not making demands of an obdurate world, but engaging the desires embedded in the unfulfilled demands. Sarah's appreciation of this emotional bond allowed me to tell her that while she felt victimized by me, when she became rageful and threatening, I felt trapped by *her*, so that we seemed ensnared in a mutual jailhouse. She was shocked to hear that I was affected by her behavior, but she felt that pressing me was the way to get her needs met, and her only alternative was to give up on the interpersonal world and withdraw to an isolated, abject state of despair. I noted that the contemplation of the latter was not a change, but the other side of her conviction that meeting needs can take place only through an obliteration of boundaries, an annihilation of self that she suffered in her relationship with her mother, as when her mother did her projects under her name.

The awareness of holding me hostage opened her eyes to both sides of her relational pattern, but she could not alter either. This is where we can see both the value and limits of bringing to consciousness patterns enacted in the analytic dyad (Bromberg, 1998; Stern, 2010). Sarah was confronted with two unacceptable patterns, and the freedom to choose between them did not help extricate her from the dilemma. When I questioned her assumption that her only options were for me to meet her need for perfect attunement or accept isolation, she gave me a stunned look as though turning her metaphorical palms upward. I inquired about her objections to each role. The thought of persecuting anyone was abhorrent to her, recalling her own victimization by her father's hostile attacks, but she felt her only alternative was to submit to me, as she had to her mother, thus abdicating all desire and control over her own life.

My simple inquiry constituted the pivotal analytic move because it implied that she could create a way of relating not limited to the options she saw before her. I joined Sarah in the openness of the analytic space by noting that in her need to annihilate me she had a longing to be loved, and in her impulse to withdraw lay her need to respect herself. She said she wanted to feel connected to me without intruding on me, but did not see how that was possible. When I asked for her associations to that dilemma, Sarah exclaimed that she was offended by her own efforts to deny my reality, to make me an instrument of her control. She immediately followed with an expression of fear that I would not put up with her demands and emotional volatility. I said the implication was that if I am a real person with my own experience and was in any way disturbed by her demands, I would not stick with her. She hated the thought of violating others' boundaries, as her mother had, hers. I highlighted the other side: that she feared being abandoned and left alone. Sarah felt caught between intrusion and isolation. When she despaired of finding a solution, I asked her again to tell me what came to her mind.

She said that even though she found relief in my response to her states, she had until now seen me only as someone to cling to, a human life preserver. But, she went on, if she were to rely on me, depend on me without intruding, then she would have to see me as a real, flesh-and-blood person. It was at that point, in the open space between intrusion and isolation, that Sarah realized that to cease victimizing me was not just a matter of seeking more limited goals, but would include recognizing me as a person with my own experience. Confronted with my limitations, Sarah's experience of me was transformed from a cardboard figure to a real person with desires of my own. But, that meant she had the ability to make an impression not just "on" me, but "in" me, that I could keep her "inside" me. This realization evoked the fear that I might not keep her safe, but she did not want to cling to me, she wanted an emotional exchange, a connection with an other who is seen as separate but on whom she could rely. On the other hand, because my recognition of her experience came from me as a person with my own subjectivity, it made more meaningful and real the states I saw in her. Sarah realized that the relationship she sought could be achieved, and only achieved, if I am a person in my own right. Sarah found herself in the midst of a unique life experience: an emotional connection with another person experienced as having a mind of his own. She was no longer bound to the binary of fusion/isolation. In experiencing this new way of relating, Sarah felt the freedom of a transcendent moment.

The change began to crystallize one day when she believed I was late to start the session and began to get enraged, realized she was about to launch into a tirade about my mistreatment of her, and then stopped herself, and said with strong resolve, "I don't want to be crazy today." Moments of dissatisfaction in that and subsequent sessions were cause for a resolution of this type. The determined way she repeated this commitment to herself indicated a decision, a conscious choice to form her anger into a state decisively different from her usual outbursts. Each such instance was a transcendental moment, a decision not just to act differently, but to *be* different. She was deciding not just to give up her angry outbursts, but to create herself as someone who can tolerate failings in a relationship from which she derived a great deal. And, in so doing, she exercised her newly emerging capacity to form a relationship with a real person, limited in what it could provide for her. She was creating herself not as Sarah who demands unfailing accommodation, but as Sarah who found ways to sustain relationships of various types with varying degrees of value and satisfaction.

At this phase, transcendental experience began to dominate. The confrontation in the analytic space with the binaries of victim-perpetrator, jailer-jailed, and fusion/isolation provided the opening in which she saw ways she could pursue new possibilities for desire, longing for connection with others, and maintenance of her self. In affording me freedom, she made space for herself as someone who possessed desire, rather than being driven by need. She created this third way after she felt the analytic relationship had given her sufficient understanding and succor that she could tolerate its limitations. Once that happened, Sarah took advantage of the ever widening open spaces that appeared when the binary traps were recognized. Sarah used what happened between us to create a self who sought connection with others experienced as independent sources of subjectivity. The strength of the analytic relationship as well as the understanding that we both worked so hard to achieve served as a propaedeutic to creating herself as someone who could engage the intersubjective world.

Sarah learned not just a new way of forming our relationship, but how to transcend binaries with which she was continually confronted. This result was apparent in the development of lasting friendships, and, perhaps most tellingly, by the establishment of a stable, romantic relationship. She met a man with whom she enjoyed a strong synchrony, a spark of mutual connection that endured the inevitable pitfalls of disappointment and conflict. They disagreed on many lifestyle choices, and Sarah neither demanded her preferred route nor submitted to his preferences. In this relationship of mutual respect, Sarah was creating a way of relating that had never been a part of her experience. A new possibility had not only emerged, but also became a way of life. Last I heard from Sarah she was very happily married with two children and a satisfying job.

Conclusion

Sarah's analysis represents the application of the Romantic sensibility that has begun to define psychoanalysis. The shift of loyalty from theory to experience has brought analysis in line with one of the great traditions of the humanities, the Romantic concept of the highest good, *Bildung*, the realization of self potential. This redefinition makes the analytic process a means for transcending the limits within which we live, thus expanding the human experience into unknown territory, a transcendence that is possible not only for each individual but also for humanity. Indeed, the unimpeachable obeisance to the patient's experience has allowed us to see that any view of analysis as a normative model of the psyche or way of living is "wild analysis," an unjustifiable imposition on the patient's life experience. Analysis has become a means for self transcendence, a way to overcome constricted ways of being and relating.

Once the patient transcends previously reified patterns in analysis she finds that the self is not a fixed product in which one is encased, but a living relationship that can be continually renewed, created as it is affirmed. Certainly, this is one of Kierkegaard's (1849/1985) legacies to our age: The self is not a thing that can be put into a mold, analytic or otherwise; what we call the self is always in relation to itself and to others, and is either continually created and reborn or risks the death of reification. As Heidegger (1927/1961) famously observed, the human condition is not static, it is ek-static, always moving beyond itself.

In this age of reductionism, psychoanalysis is one of the few bastions of human subjectivity still standing. As such, it cannot afford to fall prey to the temptation to reify the psyche. The Sarahs, Marthas, and Zeldas of the world need analysts who are not deterred by the naysayers of limit setting and normative theorizing. Like all patients, they need someone who believes in them, someone who detects in them possibilities to which they themselves might be blind, but are nonetheless there to be seen by those willing to apprehend the latent potential of the human subject. Sarah's most enduring and growth-promoting change was not any particular ability, not even the capacity to form relationships with real people, but the ability to create herself, to use her own experience to create ways of being and relating. In those precious acts of self creation, Sarah realized that she was achieving what she had been searching for. And once people see that they can be more, they see what the Romantics saw, that all experience can be more than its immediate appearance, that the growth of human potential never ends, that there is imagination in all psychic states, that the self never is, it is always becoming, creating as it affirms itself. So, as William Butler Yeats once said, "Happiness is not wealth, not property, not even virtue. Happiness is no particular thing. We are happy when we are growing."

5

UNCONSCIOUS PSYCHIC ACTS AND THE CREATION OF MEANING

We have seen that contemporary psychoanalysis views the human being as an experiencing subject to whom the analyst must stay closely attuned without the imposition of a theoretical structure. That is to say, if we remain close to the foundation of analytic thought in Husserl's and Heidegger's phenomenology of experience, we sustain our immersion in the patient's world in its manifold variations and possibilities and avoid any conceptual reification of psychic process. This view of analysis raises the question of how "the unconscious" fits into a concept of analytic therapy that maintains a resolute view of the psychical as experiential process. Indeed, analytic theories that have emphasized empathy, such as self psychology, and relatedness, as in relational theory, have been accused of neglecting the unconscious level of experiencing, the hallmark of the analytic paradigm (e.g., Curtis, 1985; Rangell, 1982). The psychoanalytic vision of openness to the patient's experience and the facilitation of its transcendental possibilities would seem to suggest a different way of viewing unconscious mental acts. In this chapter, we will examine the concept of "the unconscious" in the light of the psychoanalytic vision of the experiencing subject.

The Unconscious

Freud (1895b) created psychoanalysis by uncovering sedimented layers of meaning that made sense of what otherwise seemed like incomprehensible symptoms. The procedure outlined originally in *Studies on Hysteria* consisted of following the patient's associations from the most conscious level to increasingly unconscious thoughts and events that led eventually to what he called the "pathogenic nucleus." In that work, focused on the psychoanalytic process with hysterical patients, Freud delineated a psychoanalytic method that followed a concatenation of associations. When the flow stopped, the analyst was to help the patient overcome the resistance to open a new series of associations until finally the process arrived at the "pathogenic nucleus."

An "association" was a thought or feeling linked to another mental event by a meaning connection. For example, Elizabeth von R.'s symptom was a hysterical inability to walk, which was connected to a walk she was on with her brother-in-law when she found out her sister died, and she reacted by thinking, "Now he is free!"

This reaction was so abhorrent to the young woman that she could not allow it into consciousness and developed the hysterical inability to walk.

The connection between the symptom and forbidden thought occurred by mental concatenations linked by meaning. Walking meant "I am relieved my sister died" and that thought was so guilt-ridden it was repressed and could be expressed only in the symptom. Elizabeth was quite conscious of her inability to move her legs, but not conscious of her wish to marry her brother-in-law and her positive reaction to her sister's death. Walking was associated with the guilty wish, so the symptom was the inability to use her legs. For the present purpose, the significant fact is that Elizabeth's hysterical paralysis was connected to the guilty thoughts by meaning, not by level of consciousness. In fact, as is typically the case, the meaning connections cut across the distinction between consciousness and unconsciousness.

Freud demonstrated in abundance the associative connections the mind makes. Elizabeth von R. associated walking with her wish to marry her brother-in-law and relief that her sister was dead; the Rat Man, his "bad thoughts" with his father dying; Lucy R., the smell of burnt pudding with her wish to marry her boss; the Wolf Man, a woman scrubbing the floor with sexual intercourse from behind. Freud's cases are replete with such connections in which separate psychical acts are brought together by their similarity of meaning. In each of the associations mentioned, seemingly disparate wishes, scenes, and memories are linked by meaning.

Any psychoanalytic clinician observes such connections in her patients and herself on a routine basis. Recently one patient was speaking about her husband's failure to listen to her when an image of her father appeared. She immediately realized that she felt her father had regularly been too preoccupied to listen to her and that she had historically felt inadequate to capture a man's attention. Conscious of feeling her husband did not listen to her, this patient was not aware that she had felt the same way about her father, nor of the fact that that relationship was connected in her mind with all potential relationships with men. Another patient was getting increasingly angry at trying to please his apparently chronically unhappy wife when he remembered his father looking at his report card and criticizing him for two Bs, the only grades that were not As. He then recalled his father's constant criticism of the way he handled his business, even when he completed a successful deal. Such memorial and image linkages are the stuff of ordinary psychoanalytic therapy, and what they all show is that the patient associates to memories, images, and thoughts that are linked by meaning to the current event, not by their topographic level. In any given case, the association may be to either an unconscious or conscious psychic event, but the link is via meaning, not level of consciousness.

Neither Freud's patients nor today's analytic patients connect two unconscious psychic events to each other by virtue of their sharing a topographic level. In all the examples cited, the patient connected a conscious event to an unconscious psychic act with similar meaning, indicating that topographic state does not determine psychic organization. Consider that the same patient who grew up in fear of his father's criticism had an unconscious belief that all women were engulfing, but until his analysis was unaware that this conviction was an outgrowth of his mother's exploitation of him as a "sounding board." This unconscious belief was not linked to his unconscious fear of his father's criticism even though both beliefs were unconscious. Simply put, the mind makes connections according to meaning, not levels of consciousness, and in fact will cut across levels of consciousness to connect psychic events with similarity of meaning.

How Did Unconscious Become a Noun?

In *Studies of Hysteria* "unconscious" and "conscious" described the topographic level of a mental event. They were not nouns, but adjectives modifying a psychic act by level of awareness. That changed when Freud (1900) began to develop his metapsychology in Chapter 7 of *The Interpretation of Dreams*. In formulating his view that dreams were disguised pictorial representations of repressed unconscious wishes, Freud needed a "psychical locality" for the dreaming experience (p.535). He argued that the instrument that "carries out our mental functions" is analogous to a compound microscope, and psychical locality is then a point inside the apparatus in which an image begins to appear. And here he makes his critical shift. The "compounds" of the microscope he calls "systems," which stand in spatial relation to each other much as lenses in a telescope are arranged. He coined the phrase *system ucs.* as distinguished from the *system pcs.* and *cs.*

Freud conceptualized a fixed order in which in any given psychical process the excitation passes through the systems in temporal fashion. The relevance here is not Freud's theory of dreams, which will be discussed in detail in the next chapter, but the conceptualization of "unconscious" as a system in itself. Freud provides no argument that "unconscious" is a "system" other than drawing the analogy to a compound microscope. Based on Fechner's idea that the scene of the dream is different from that of waking life, Freud contended that there must be a psychic location for dreams, and then analogized the mental systems to the compound microscope, the components of which are "agencies" or "systems" (p.536). Once he made "unconscious" into a system, it became *"the* unconscious," an entity with its own psychic organization. Note that now "unconscious" has been transformed from an adjective to a noun. So, "unconscious" is now the *system ucs.*, an organization of psychic processes presumably structured around their shared unconscious status.

This concept of "unconscious" as a system of psychic organization was codified in Freud's (1915) definitive statement on the issue. His classic metapsychological statement in his paper "The Unconscious" conveys clearly that Freud regarded "unconscious" not as a descriptor, but as the thing described. At this point there can be no doubt that "unconscious" and the other levels of consciousness have been hypostasized. Nonetheless, Freud's arguments for "the unconscious" apply to the existence of unconscious psychic acts, but do not constitute a justification for his *ontological shift*. He pointed to the gaps in consciousness of everyday life: memory slips, parapraxes, dreams, and associative connections that seem to appear as though from nowhere. Freud's contention was that these seemingly random events make sense only if one posits unconscious mental acts. And, indeed, it is difficult to imagine another hypothesis that would account for the evidence he lays out so well. However, none of the data warrant the codification of the phenomena in question into a "system." Even the most convincing proof of unconscious mental phenomena cannot be used as evidence for the existence of a noun called "*the* unconscious." The evidence Freud elucidates shows that the mind operates unconsciously, but that does not justify the ontological leap to a *system ucs*.

Freud argued from the fact that most of what is psychical, such as latent memories, is not conscious, to the conclusion that there must be "an unconscious," or, a *system ucs*. However, the fact that the latent nature of psychical events such as memories are not available to consciousness at any given moment does not mean that such acts form an unconscious mental organization. The postulation of a *system ucs*. goes much further than inferring unconscious psychic acts; it implies *a component of the mind* that is characterized by its lack of consciousness. But, as we have seen, mental events connect not by level of consciousness, but by similarity of meaning.

The sudden emergence of a memory does not mean that it came from a *system ucs*. It means that the memory was evoked in relationship to an event in the present moment. In fact, the analytic inquiry assumes that the unconscious psychic event bears a relationship to the symptom, and a "thing" could not be in such a relationship. The dynamic assumed in all analytic work militates against any notion of an entity that could be called "the unconscious."

If the psychic event were part of a "thing," namely "the unconscious," it could not be in a dynamic relationship to other psychic acts, conscious or unconscious. It makes sense to pursue dynamic meaning only if psychical events are processes. As the analyst wonders what unconscious affects and thoughts might make sense of the presumably unintelligible, she is treating psychical acts as motivational processes related by meaning to consciousness. The assumption that unconscious thoughts and feelings can motivate changes in consciousness contradicts the metapsychological postulate of an entity "the unconscious." It is difficult to conceptualize a "system" or entity as motivating a psychical event or pattern. The very fact that unconscious mental acts can motivate psychical behavior, such as slips, forgetting, and dreams, conflicts with the idea that what is not conscious is bundled together with other unconscious material in a "system." If it were, how would it motivate anything in consciousness?

The gap in intelligibility here is precisely what Freud described as the indication of unconscious interference in conscious thought process, the very foundation of psychoanalytic inquiry. The analytic attitude (Schafer, 1983) consists of the effort to find the intelligibility in this seemingly "automatic pilot" operation. It is this gap of which Lacan (1977b) made so much in his discussion of the nature of "the unconscious." Following Freud, Lacan avers that the gap in conscious thought is the intrusion of "the unconscious." Lacan, like Freud, believed the purpose of the analytic process is to read "the unconscious" in order to bring it into the realm of consciousness. But, Lacan also thought that the result of that process is to help the individual disentangle the demands and expectations of others from her desire. To assume ownership of desire is to become a subject, the ultimate goal of a Lacanian analysis. What I wish to emphasize here is that the goal of becoming a subject works precisely because the unconscious memory is able to become part of the patient's conscious understanding. If the memory were part of an unconscious "system" one wonders how it can be dislodged and enter into the patient's conscious experience. The memory, in becoming conscious, does not act like it is part of a system, but does act like a disavowed experience that is related to the patient's conscious life.

There is another line of argument Freud uses to bolster his claim for the *system ucs*. Perhaps the best case Freud makes for the existence of a separate *system ucs.* is his observation that unconscious material defies the laws of logic and reason obeyed by conscious life. It is this difference that is the fulcrum of his distinction between the merely latently unconscious and repressed unconscious psychic wishes and thoughts. He argues that because the former consists of material that differs from consciousness only by level of awareness, while the latter is different in psychic quality, it makes sense to distinguish *systems cs.* and *pcs.* from a separate *system ucs.* Dynamically unconscious psychical acts not only defy the laws of logic, space, and time, but also possess no degree of uncertainty, doubt, or negation. They consist only of contents with highly mobile cathexes, or primary process, utilizing condensation and displacement. Time and reality do not apply to mental events that replace external by psychic reality, and that is what distinguishes the *system ucs.* From the fact that unconscious mental acts follow their own rules, Freud concluded that anything unconscious must be part of a separate mental system.

At first blush this argument appears to be convincing, but again, there is a subtle but decisive and unwarranted inference in this reasoning. Freud successfully shows that some mental phenomena operate in violation of logic and reality under certain conditions. Typically, when a desire is overwhelming or the defenses overpowering, the patient may have beliefs, desires, and even delusions fueled by emotional need that overrun logic and reality. The result can be irrational beliefs, fantasies, illusions, or in extreme cases, delusions that are held despite their irrational or unrealistic nature. It is routine to hear from patients, "Rationally, I know this is not true, but . . ." and examples that fill in that sentence can be "I think everyone is noticing that I chipped my tooth," or "people are all thinking that I am a cheat," or "a group of people left the party because they did not want to be there with me," "I feel responsible for anything that goes wrong," or "everyone is talking about me." One patient believes that by repeating a thought continually, she will prevent injury to a loved one, another believes his wishes can cause harm to his wife. A new father begs forgiveness from his infant for injuring the child with his thoughts. Every analyst can recount dozens of examples of such illogical and unrealistic thinking from daily practice.

The fact that under certain conditions some psychical phenomena follow their own illogic neither presupposes nor provides evidence for an organized *system ucs.* that operates by defying logic and reality. It only means that the psyche is capable of producing its own rules, following its own procedures in defiance of logic and reality when the emotional need to do so is sufficiently intense. The Rat Man's guilt over his aggressive wishes from childhood was so great that he believed his thoughts could kill an already dead father. Logic and time succumbed to the power of the patient's guilt. But, that does not mean that a separately organized system was in operation. It means that an affectively dominating experience, such as guilt, can overpower logic and reality. As humans, we possess the capability for illogical thought processes that can be evoked when needed to cope with overwhelming affect. Such a capacity is no more an argument for an entity with those characteristics than the ability of the mind to do mathematics is an argument for a mathematical system of mind.

To conclude that because the mind has the capability to operate illogically there is a separate system characterized by illogic is equivalent to drawing the conclusion that because the mind uses metaphor there is a separate "metaphor system" of the mind. The various illogical mechanisms that Freud enumerated like collapsing time and space or conflating thought with deed are capacities the mind possesses that can be called upon when needed. The same is true of mathematics, metaphor, aesthetic experience, and many other capacities. To equate the existence of such capabilities with a "system" of mind is to reify mental acts. The mind can call upon a variety of capabilities, some of which are illogical and unrealistic, but those qualities render them no less psychical than any other psychic capacities and do not warrant a separate ontological status.

Furthermore, it is not the case that primary process and illogical, unrealistic thinking are always unconscious. As we have seen, it is common for patients to be aware of the unrealistic nature of their thoughts, but still have them. The Rat Man was aware of his thought that his wish could kill his dead father. It was only the motive for the thought that was not conscious. So, his conscious thoughts were using the illogic that Freud regarded as characteristic of "the unconscious." It is routine for patients to believe in full consciousness that random events are directed at them even as they know such thinking is not realistic. The illogical and unrealistic thinking patterns Freud identified as proof of the *system ucs.* can be either conscious or unconscious. Consciousness is no guarantee against irrationality.

An unconscious psychological process has a much stronger connection to a conscious psychical act with similar meaning than to an unconscious mental event with a different meaning. So, it is clear that topographic levels do not organize the mind. "Unconscious" is not a noun, but a description of the level of consciousness of a psychic act. To speak of "the unconscious," which is still common in the most psychoanalytic circles, is to reify psychical acts.

So, If It Is Not Reified, What Is Unconsciousness Anyway?

In the analytic process, we have seen that the psychical material that emerges from the associative train is related to the conscious thoughts and feelings by shared meaning, not topographic level. Thus, the psychoanalytic data show that the psyche is organized by categories of meaning, any one of which can have various levels of consciousness. The alternative to reification is the recognition that psychic events are grouped into meaning categories that contain a spectrum of conscious levels. One patient becomes anxious because he associates the analyst's mistake with his mother's neglect; another sees his father's criticism in the analyst's interpretations. These connections are typically analogies, connections between events or things made by the patient out of shared characteristics that may not be consciously identifiable.

The associative train need not be a product of psychic conflict. People associate to events with similarity of meaning in conflict free areas. A scene evokes a childhood memory with similar characteristics, a person reminds one of another with similar physical or psychological features. The tendency is to view people as members of categories, so that in meeting a new person some aspect of their appearance or behavior may evoke the image of another person with a similar attribute. Such associations are simply the way the mind operates. In fact, it is the halt in the associative train, the "gap," in Lacanian terms, that suggests conflict, not the association itself. Some of these connections are highly creative, others much less so, but they all are creative in the most general sense of creating connections by putting together disparate events. The fertility and uniqueness of the human mind may well lie in this analogical capacity. Additionally, Freud's (1895a, 1895b) concept of *Nachtraglichkeit* is another piece of evidence for the creativity endemic in the way the mind works. Looking back at an event to discern meaning unseen at the time is an act of creating and weakens the reified notion that what is unconscious is a fixed "system."

Data from outside the psychoanalytic process support the view that the mind is organized by categories of meaning. The linguists Lakoff and Johnson (2003) have argued convincingly that metaphor is not just a figure of speech used primarily by poets and fiction writers, but a way of thinking built into our conceptual system. Metaphor is "understanding and experiencing one kind of thing in terms of another" (p.5). While we do not notice it, metaphor saturates our language in everyday discourse. Consider ordinary phrases, like "time is money," "language is a conduit," "I am up today," "I am feeling down," "she is overflowing with joy," "I am drained," "she is a knockout," "he had a look of extreme gravity." One could go on endlessly to show that metaphor is built into our thought process, and language follows.

To think metaphorically as we do is to create and elaborate meaning. To use Lakoff and Johnson's most discussed illustration: "Argument is war" shows that we think of argument the way we think of war: trying to gain ground, defending our position, seeing the other's position as indefensible, attacking weak points, honing in on a target, and many others. So, for our purpose, the significant finding of these authors is that we do not simply register experience, but routinely think of our immediate experience in terms of other events and experiences that share a similarity of meaning. Metaphorical concepts are the ordinary way of experiencing and talking about much that we do although we are not aware of using metaphor in most cases. So, in demonstrating the ubiquity of metaphor Lakoff and Johnson also showed the creativity built into everyday speech and thought.

Chomsky's (1975) linguistic theory buttresses this conceptualization by demonstrating the creativity inherent in language learning and usage. Chomsky showed that language is not learned by memorization, but by rules from which sentences are generated, a process he calls "generative grammar." Children and adults are able to utter meaningful sentences they have never heard before because language is learned in rules from which the speaker can generate her own sentences. This is most easily observed in children's mistakes when learning to speak. In saying "goed," for went or "doed" for did, they are not modeling anything they have heard, but generating speech from rules no one explicitly taught them.

Solid evidence for the mind as organized by creating meaning categories comes from Edelman's (1987) theory that memory is not a registration of events as they happen, but rather a filing system in which we place events into mnemonic categories. Each act of memory, according to Edelman, includes an act of creation because we have to find the right category in which to place the event or create a new category, rather than recording a veridical occurrence. We interpret the experience according to our predilection and then place it into a category from which it can typically be accessed under conditions that evoke it.

Tomkins's (1978) theory of affective spreading provides evidence from developmental research for the inherent creativity of mind. His work shows that infants connect very different scenes with similar affects. Affect spreads to events that share similar characteristics, but are not completely the same. A degree of similarity along with a clear difference appears to be what is required for the child to connect events and spread affective experience. Affective meaning connections constitute the links tying different experiences and events to each other. He calls this process "psychic magnification" because meaning is magnified by connection with other scenes. Eventually, connected scenes enhance magnification into "scripts," rules by which one lives (Tomkins, 1978, 1987). As can be seen from this brief synopsis of Tomkins's work, it is affective similarity that determines categories of experience. Most important for the present purpose, the infant connects experience by analogy, a creative linking of seemingly unconnected experiences often separated in space and time.

So, Tomkins's developmental research, Edelman's theory of memory, and Lakoff and Johnson's and Chomsky's linguistic theory all provide demonstrable support for the findings of the psychoanalytic process that the mind is organized via creative meaning connections. In all these areas of psychological investigation, the findings are that the mind puts together disparate experiences in accordance with meaning categories that are often not apparent until the connections are made. Meaning and creativity are inextricably linked in normal psychic functioning because new memories and experiences are understood in terms of and must be categorized with old experiences. Whether the existing rubric is changed or new categories have to be created, connections with the world and other psychic events are expanded by a creative process.

And for those who might suppose scientific thinking is decisively different, it is worth noting that this analogical capacity is very much a part of the scientific world. Briefly, the concept of mind as creative is supported by the well-established principle in the philosophy of science that many scientific discoveries are essentially creative analogies in which one well-known or even mundane event is related to another perhaps equally ordinary happening (e.g., Bronowski, 1965). When Newton saw the apple fall from the tree, he did not "discover" gravity, he made the analogy between that event and the moon's orbiting the Earth. He guessed that the same force that brought the apple down holds the moon in its orbit around the Earth. Calling this force "gravity" was not a discovery, but the naming of a force he conceived by analogizing disparate events. The contribution was in creating the connection. For Bronowski, this type of creative linking of apparently unrelated events is the essence of science. Newton's scientific contribution lay in drawing an analogy that understood the world in a new way, but the process of analogizing itself is everyday mental activity. What makes an analogy scientific is its use for understanding the world.

Reification of Mind and the Psychoanalytic Process

Why is all this important? Clearly I am not arguing for a simple change in "the unconscious" from noun to adjective. But, I do believe that such a shift in language reflects a critical difference in the way unconscious motives and meaning are conceptualized, and that difference matters clinically. To repeat: The conceptual and clinical problems created by making "unconscious" a noun is an argument not against the existence of unconscious mental phenomena, but against the way they are conceptualized in psychoanalytic theory. Furthermore, this hypostasizing of unconscious mental acts has not been affected by the many changes in psychoanalytic theory and technique that have taken place since Freud. Even in the most contemporary psychoanalytic literature, one finds "the unconscious" used routinely (e.g., Bollas, 2005; Altman, 2006; Davoine, 2007; Elise, 2007; Grossmark, 2007; Ringstrom, 2007). Every psychoanalytic theory uses "unconscious" as a noun. The question before us is what effect such hypostasizing has on the analytic process.

When Freud's way of conceptualizing unconscious psychical acts is carried through to its conclusion, the unconscious psychic act is removed from the realm of the human subject. Analytic discourse frequently refers to "the "unconscious" as a separate actor in the patient's psychic drama. "The unconscious" "does" strange things, "plays tricks" on us, or "operates" on its own rules, and even "knows." That is, the unconscious motive is anthropomorphically categorized separately from the motives of the subject. In analytic writing, psychic states such as desire, love, hate, or belief are attributed to the patient, but "the unconscious" may have its own conflicting motives, as though the second group did not belong to the experiencing person. Such language disowns one part of the psyche as though it were a separate motivational system. And Freud did seem to regard it that way, but from a contemporary point of view, as we saw in Chapter One, such a desubjectified motive is antithetical to the very subject of psychoanalysis, the experiencing subject. If the unconscious acts, then who is the actor? The *system ucs.* is an "it" rather than an "I." So, how can an "it" act like a subject? By abandoning the reified concept of "the unconscious," the language of psychoanalysis befits all experience, conscious and unconscious, as belonging to the experiencing subject, and that discourse is consonant with the purpose of the analytic encounter. The therapist's conceptual tools then are fitted to her mode of inquiry.

Schafer (1983) has put forward an extensive argument opposing the use of language that implies "the unconscious" is somehow acting on its own. He proposed that every psychic event is an activity and therefore psychic acts should be depicted

71

only by active verbs, a view he calls "action language." In proposing this type of language for psychoanalysis, Schafer is opposing the "desubjectification" of both experience and analytic concepts that dominates classical metapsychology and replacing it with a language of the experiencing subject.

From a philosophical viewpoint, we have learned from both phenomenological and ordinary language philosophy that all experience makes sense only in the context of an experiencing subject (e.g., Husserl, 1913; Strawson, 1959). There can be no desire without a person desiring, no hate without a person hating. So, to attribute such a state to an entity separate from the subject is not defensible from either a philosophical or psychoanalytic viewpoint. It is this type of ontological error that led Sartre (1943) to attack Freud for proposing a "lie without a liar."

As we have seen, a major analytic task is to discover connections in order to show that what appears to be unintelligible is, in fact, a sensible outgrowth of unseen experience. For example, one patient became anxious and depressed in response to coming down with the flu, a connection that mystified both of us until a childhood memory suddenly erupted into consciousness. He recalled being home alone with a broken leg and being left by himself for hours on his own, feeling abandoned and depressed. Other similar memories of being alone for extended periods during his many childhood injuries and illnesses were evoked by the first memory. The depressive episode appeared when the adult illness stimulated the helplessness and loneliness of the childhood events.

Psychoanalytic inquiry of this type shows that apparently unintelligible psychical expressions emerge from meaning connections with unconscious psychic motivations. The irony is that the presumptive unintelligibility of such eruptions is used to justify hypostasizing unconscious psychic acts while psychoanalysis shows that such eruptions are, in fact, an outgrowth of an unseen level of meaning. Once the connections between the visible and invisible, conscious and unconscious, have become evident, the basis for hypostasizing "unconscious" has disappeared.

The standard analytic rejoinder is to say that the purpose of the analytic process is to bring the unconscious motive into consciousness so that it can be brought under the control of the ego (e.g., Arlow & Brenner, 1964). As is well known, Freud (1923) made the purpose of analysis the shift from the "it" nature of unconscious thoughts and wishes to "I," or from id to ego. Whether this shift is conceived in classical language or as the move from dissociation to agency, in a successful analytic process what was a nonsubjectified experience becomes part of the patient's subjectivity. The problem with this response is that it does not allow the analyst to speak to the patient as a subject when talking to her of unconscious motives and meaning. It is virtually impossible to imagine that speaking of psychic acts as removed from the patient's subjective experience would result in their becoming part of that subjectivity. If unconscious meaning and motivation is to become psychically owned, it must be addressed as the patient's experience, however deeply unconscious it may be, not as existing in some impersonal location.

We have seen that the core of the analytic project is the engagement, illumination, and ultimately transformation of the experiencing subject. Given that goal, for the analyst to regard the patient's unconscious psychic motivation and meaning as beyond the purview of her subjectivity fosters dissociation and colludes with any dissociative tendencies the patient may have. Any discourse that desubjectifies experience promotes self objectification and is therefore countertherapeutic. Maximum engagement of the patient's experience implores recognizing all her psychic acts, including those disavowed, as expressions of the experiencing subject. In fact, one of Fairbairn's (1958) objections to what he called "impulse psychology" was that it promotes a discourse distant from the patient's experience.

To be sure, many analytic therapists do not speak to patients about their unconscious motives in the depersonified third person, but instead direct themselves to the patient as subject, in a manner similar to the way motives are spoken of at the conscious level. But, that very fact demonstrates that analytic therapists do not find it clinically useful to conceptualize unconscious psychic phenomena as "the unconscious." If the analyst regards the language of "the unconscious" as countertherapeutic, that is good reason to abandon the concept. Why hold onto a concept that has to be discarded to capture the patient's experience and the clinical process?

Consistent attention to the analytic task requires that "unconscious" be used to modify psychic acts, not replace consciousness with a different arena of mind. Insofar as the analyst remains directed to the analytic goal of bringing all aspects of the psyche under the ownership of the subject, "unconscious" will be deployed as a quality of thought or feeling so that the focus on the experiencing subject can be consistently sustained.

As the analyst attempts to bring unconscious motives to consciousness her struggle is to get the patient to see that psychic acts are in fact psychological experiences. Patients tend to assume that the way they see others and the world is veridical. The clinician routinely hears statements such as: "You do not care about me," "People are hostile by nature," "No one really likes others," "My mother preferred my sister," "You prefer other patients," and similar assertions stated as though they are observed facts of the world. Their authors do not see these perceptions as psychological experiences, but as observations of the way the world is. Fonagy et al. (2002) has conceptualized this phenomenon as *psychic equivalence*. Analytic struggles are often fought around the analyst's attempts to get the patient to move from psychic equivalence to what Fonagy calls *mentalization*, the recognition that one's experience is a psychological process. When that change occurs, transformation becomes possible.

So, the reification of "unconscious" into a separate system of the mind is an ontological error with tangible clinical consequences. Reifications have a tendency to become rigid entities into which experience is fit, so they attract psychic material almost magnetically even if the experience does not fit the reified area of "the unconscious." The danger of reductionism is great because the assumed psychic entity is fixed and easily becomes a path of little resistance for fitting new psychic acts into the reified conceptual system. Such reified notions by their nature impede new experience by drawing potentially new ways of feeling and thinking into existing conceptual categories. If the resulting analytic process is not a crudely preprogrammed journey, it is at minimum likely to be influenced by presuppositions, as in the examples we have seen. Thus, the potential consequences of reifying unconscious psychic acts go beyond interference in attending to the patient's experience to stifling the creation of new ways of being.

If, on the other hand, the analyst views "unconscious" as a quality of meaning categories, filling in the gaps in the patient's associative connections is not intended as a definitive statement of a discovered truth, but as a "pointing to," a recognition of something missing that requires attention. And here we come to the pivotal clinical significance in seeing "unconscious" as a quality of meaning making. The implication of this view of unconscious mental phenomena is that analytic understanding is conveyed not as a reduction to a different state, such as a childhood stage, but as an *evocative* response to the patient's associational flow. The evocative remark illuminates the unseen connections that make sense of the gaps in the patient's intelligibility. Simultaneously, it suggests that the patient's interpretation of his situation has been limited by the previously unseen connection, and other ways of experiencing are possible. This does not mean that the analyst cannot interpret the relationship between childhood patterns and adult behavior, but it does mean that such a connection is used as a way of highlighting the patient's constricted ways of being by continuing the pattern. *Evocative* remarks emphasize that the patient is unconsciously limiting her possibilities by the repetition of childhood patterns. Such a remark is intended to stimulate the patient to consider moving beyond the narrow confines of her historical patterns. By way of contrast, the reductive interpretation seeks only to provide understanding in terms of a defined motive, such as a childhood dynamic. The distinction between *reductive* and *evocative* interpretation is the decisive technical difference between clinical theories embedded in the two ways of viewing unconsciousness.

Comments that evoke new possibilities are consonant with the analytic goal, as we have defined it, of creating new ways of being and relating. When the analyst evokes questions without prejudging answers the patient may be disrupted, but that very disturbance motivates the exploration of new possibilities. We have seen that the aim of the process is not only to understand *what is* but also to create what *has never been*, and the evocative remark, unlike the reductionist interpretation, points toward new possibilities and therefore fits the need to create new ways of being.

Winnicott (1971) consistently emphasized that if he had a word that he believed captured the patient's unconscious meaning, he preferred that the patient come to it herself because its emotional impact would be greater and more enduring if the patient is the agent of the insight. I would add that the most efficacious way to facilitate the expansion of the patient's experience is to respond to the patient's affect with an inquiry or comment that does not admit of truth or falsity, but stimulates the patient to experience something new.

The evocative response designed to disturb unquestioned assumptions recalls Socrates's role as the gadfly who questioned purported knowledge of which his interlocutor was confident. Lear's (2011) concept of irony brings out the similarity between the evocative analytic interpretation and Socratic irony. Lear notes that Socratic irony does not make known something that has previously been unknown, but disrupts what is "known" so that previously assumed knowledge now appears to be problematic. Socratic questioning disrupts the interlocutor's certainty. Socratic irony makes the "known" unknown. Does the Christian know what it is to be a Christian? The politician, a politician? The doctor, a doctor? Lear illuminates the fact that ironic inquiry shows that such identities fall short of their aspirations and therefore disturbs the certainty of what is thought to be solid knowledge. Questioning purported knowledge, to move from what is thought to be known to a state of uncertainty, which may be disorienting, is Socratic irony, according to Lear. It is also what we have called the evocative analytic interpretation. The purpose of the Socratic questioning was to stimulate reflection on assumed knowledge, whereas the analytic comment is intended to evoke questioning of living patterns to open the patient to new possibilities.

As we saw in Chapter Four, in what we have called the expressivist turn in psychoanalytic theory, the aim of the process is the realization of arrested aspects of the self, that is, the creation of new ways of being and relating. Creating new psychic configurations requires the analyst to accept not knowing and hold a space of "negative capability" within which the patient can create new form from the analytic interaction. This attitude of receptivity and willingness to hold ambiguity is in the spirit of Bion's (1995/1970) insistence that not knowing is a more productive analytic attitude than knowing. This clinical strategy implores the analytic therapist to utilize evocative interpretation, eschewing the attitude of possessing knowledge in favor of becoming an agent of new creation.

This analytic stance does not mean that the analyst cannot suggest connections between symptoms and the patient's previous life experiences, childhood events, and other formative experiences that may help understand the current picture. It does mean that such conceptualizations are most effective when they are not statements for the patient to endorse or refuse as though they are the end result of the process. To the contrary, such remarks are offered a resource from which it is hoped the patient may be able to fashion something useful. Although complete acceptance or rejection is possible, the interpretation works best if the patient utilizes it to create new meaning. In that case, something new has been created that can become the basis for new psychic configurations. The most successful analytic interpretations disrupt the patient's established patterns and open the space for potentially new ways of being and relating in a manner remarkably similar to Lear's depiction of Socratic irony.

As we have seen, the patient who is stuck in historical patterns is often unable to move despite possessing good understanding of his dynamics. An evocative intervention is designed to go beyond understanding to transcend historical patterns. If something new is to be created, the analyst must be willing to adopt two roles throughout the analytic process: interpreting *what is* and facilitating the creation of what *has never been*. The purpose of the evocative interpretation is to make conscious a connection so that a new possibility might be seen. For patients who seem unable to dislodge themselves from lifelong patterns what is most needed are new ways of being, and the evocative interpretation is designed to stimulate imagination, to see and eventually create new form.

This way of viewing psychic change suggests a shift in the metaphor for exploring unconscious mental phenomena from archeology to astronomy. In the *Phaedo* Plato uses the metaphor of the universe to depict the psyche. He analogizes our consciousness to a point on a planet within a solar system which itself is but one system in a much larger series of such systems. Our consciousness, then, is a point of reference within a grand psychological expanse, a virtually infinitesimal point in a universe of psychic potential. We can only be aware of what in this vast array of possibilities is available to us in a given moment. But that is due not only to underlying motive and meaning, but also to the fact that our psychic capabilities are far greater than our awareness. Matte-Blanco's (1998) infinity of unconsciousness is a concept that fit what Plato saw as the human psyche. If in normal consciousness we are limited to a small number of ways of being and relating, our potential experience is always far greater.

Analysands are limited to a constricted range of psychic forms, often to a very few ways of being and relating, and it is this limitation that keeps them repeating the same patterns long after they understand why they are there. The more traumatic one's early life, the less one is able to conceive of ways of living that depart from the childhood patterns. The agonizing struggle patients go through to conceive of a different way even if their pattern brings pain and dysfunction motivated Stephen Mitchell (1993) to conclude that all psychopathology can be thought of as a failure of the imagination. Evocative interpretations are aimed to stimulate the patient's imagination, to consider the possibility of bringing to fruition what has never been.

Some contemporary analytic thought is moving in this direction as the field achieves a growing recognition that creating new ways of being is the culmination of a full flowering analytic process. Ogden (2001), for example, uses Borges's poetry to illustrate the movement from the borderline of consciousness to the development of new psychic form. Borges directs our attention to what is just below the surface, and as we resonate with his illumination of experience, we are moved to see something new in the world, something always there, but not seen, akin to Bollas's (1987) "unthought known." As previously unseen feelings and thoughts begin to emerge, they show us something dimly sensed, but never before articulated. In the context of this new awareness, the potential of the underlying experience, if recognized by the analyst, can emerge as a new psychic property. For such a change to occur, the patient needs the recognition by the analyst that an aspect of the patient's psyche contains the potential for a new way of being (Winnicott, 1971).

So, while the hypostatization of "unconscious" may seem like a theoretically abstruse concern, in fact it reflects the way the psyche is approached, conceptualized, and responded to. If the analytic therapist views the psychical as an entity to be uncovered, it is difficult to see how the goal of realizing self potential is achievable because such a concept is foreign to the hypostasized unconscious. On the other hand, if the psyche is seen as the uniquely human way of being in the world, the patient's associations, memories, dreams, fantasies, and beliefs can be seen for their potential to create alternatives to the historically established patterns. Seeing the pregnancy of psychic possibility is ultimately the concrete clinical value of sustaining a

view of the psychical as a self sufficient domain that includes viewing unconsciousness as a topographic descriptor, not a separate realm of psychic existence.

Who Am I? How Did I Get Here?

The clinical impact of this way of viewing unconscious motivation can be seen in the
analytic work with Herb, an intellectually well-endowed, single, late 20s man who was
referred by co-workers who were very concerned about his mental condition after
he suffered what they regarded as a "breakdown." Herb was a very thin, tall, good-
looking man with wire-rimmed glasses and casual clothes, who gave the impression
of being an intellectual. He told me his story in a straightforward, well-organized
way, although he expressed shock and bewilderment about what had happened to
him. He had planned on an academic career, but when the advisor/mentor whom
he had gone to graduate school to study with died he felt no other faculty member
had the requisite expertise to help him pursue his intellectual interests, and he left
the academic world. After a period of floundering with no direction, he eventually
obtained an advanced degree in computer science. He then secured employment with
a fast-growing, quick-paced, highly entrepreneurial software company. He enjoyed a
meteoric rise through the hierarchy, and within a few years was offered the opportunity to run the company's recently opened office in a foreign country.

He built the operation quickly, many new employees were hired, contracts signed,
the work piled up, and Herb became overwhelmed. He found himself working
increasingly long hours, first into the evening, then into the night, and frequently he
slept at the office so he would not have to spend time commuting. Herb delegated
very little responsibility to others, preferring to take the leadership role in every contract he signed until his life became so consumed with ensuring the success of every
project that he slept and ate little, became overwhelmed with anxiety, and his frustration tolerance almost disappeared. When employees made mistakes or did not fulfill
job requirements, rather than give direction or ask for work to be redone, he did it
himself.

Eventually, he could not keep up the pace. Anxious and severely sleep-deprived,
Herb became increasingly fearful the office would not be able to meet its goals, and
he became disorganized, losing track of much of the work, a behavior that was so
uncharacteristic of him that his employees became worried about him. He began to
display visible anxiety symptoms and had difficulty concentrating and staying with a
project. Some co-workers tried to talk to him, felt they made no progress, and eventually contacted the CEO who flew across the ocean to find Herb in a disheveled,
disorganized state. Shocked at the condition of one of his prize employees, the CEO
concluded that Herb was "bipolar" and insisted he return to the States to receive
proper care. He entered a day hospital program near his hometown and lived with
his parents for several months. Upon discharge, his boss who clearly cared a great
deal about him, transferred him to an office in the States and referred him to me, but
he did not insist that Herb return to work immediately, allowing that decision to be
made by Herb in a therapeutic context.

Herb told me all this with a mixture of coherence and confusion over what had happened. Now at some remove from the situation, he understood he was "over-worked," and had no desire to repeat the overseas nightmare, but he did not have any insight into what he could have done differently. He agreed to come to three-times-per-week psychotherapy and took to the process with considerable investment and interest. This lengthy and intense analytic therapy had many facets, but for our purpose we will focus on the role of unconscious motivation and meaning and the clinical strategy to elicit them.

Early on, I inquired into some of Herb's behavior, such as his insistence on doing so much of the work himself. He said that he feared the projects would not be done properly, and when mistakes were made, he knew he had to take over. It was evident to him that attempting to do everything himself had led to an untenable form of existence, but he did not know how else to operate. He could not tolerate allowing work to fail while standing on the sidelines. When I commented that he seemed to become job focused from fear of failure, he resonated with that idea, but felt that was a natural and universal motivation. Early in the process, Herb recognized he had been motivated by a deep fear that the office would collapse and he would return to the United States a failure. Never having allowed himself to be aware of this thought before, it was so horrifying to him that he became highly anxious discussing it in session. I commented that he seemed to assume that either work became an all-consuming activity or he would fail. He immediately acknowledged that he could not trust others because they might make mistakes that would result in the failure of the enterprise. He also thought that explained his lack of a social life when running the office: He was so fearful of failure and that others would let him down that he organized his life around his job to the point that he had no time for anything else. Herb regarded this understanding as a well-thought-out conclusion at which his therapy had successfully arrived and saw no need for further inquiry.

But, I had other questions. I saw unexplained mysteries in his narrative that apparently he did not see or was not bothered by, such as why he was so fearful of failure. When I asked him to associate to his fear of failure, his father came immediately to mind. In response to my request for further thoughts, he spoke extensively of his father's various business ventures, poor business judgment, and with outspoken contempt for his father, expressed certainty that his parents would eventually declare bankruptcy. He said that his mother went to medical school in midlife in an effort to achieve the financial stability his father could not provide. His father purchased a large, expensive plot of land that he could not afford, tried to sell, but could find no buyers. As a result, despite his mother's solid income, the parents were living on the brink of financial collapse. In fact, when his mother later became sick and could not work, his parents did, in fact, declare bankruptcy. In his lengthy disquisition of disdain for his father's business irresponsibility and irrationality, Herb saw that he feared becoming a humiliating failure like his father. Once again, he believed our inquiry had reached an end. I noted that he seemed to believe that becoming consumed with his work life was his sole protection against suffering the humiliation his father had endured. He concurred and saw no other way.

I asked if he ever thought of the impact of his work preoccupation on the rest of his life. Herb said that thought had not occurred to him, but the question made him wonder. That mode of inquiry led to his questioning why he had never had a relationship of more than a few months. He attributed his lack of romantic involvement for several years to the demands of his job. I emphasized to him that his role as the one who did almost everything and certainly had to correct all errors was his interpretation of his job. Herb was quite surprised at this statement and readily acknowledged that he did, in fact, see no other way and had never thought about any other possibility. I noted his unquestioned assumption that his role was all-consuming despite the steep price he paid for his overwork. I emphasized that he had a particular way of interpreting his role, seemed to assume there was no other way, and that his way precluded a social life. He readily agreed, asked me what other way there was, and I said what mattered was that he had not given any consideration to other ways of conducting his life.

My statement about his all-consuming approach to the job led Herb to see that the way he construed his position had made any life outside of it virtually impossible, even though he could not even imagine alternative ways of interpreting his role. While I acknowledged his fear of becoming his father was a major problem, I noted to him that the fear led to organizing his life without any room for other areas of living. He went on to say that he had never had many friends and had few and inconsequential relationships. He had always attributed that to the amount of work he had to do, whether in school or on the job. But when I noted that he had a tendency to construe his life so that it excluded a social network, he began to wonder if his life was work focused in order to avoid social contact. So, at that point the understanding of his fear of failure led to his anxiety about forming relationships, and that added a new dimension to his obsession with work. I asked him, "What would life be like if work was not so all-consuming?" This was an evocative question he had never before considered, but he was able to recognize that even asking that question made him anxious so that he could no longer avoid confronting his anxiety in forming relationships. His affective response gave him the answer: He avoided his social anxiety by interpreting all his work situations as total preoccupations.

At his point, one can see the use of evocative analytic technique. Herb thought we had arrived at a definitive formulation of his unconscious motivation at several points, and although we never discarded any of that understanding, I used it to see what further meaning could be evoked. In asking how he organized his life, I was stimulating a line of inquiry that caused him to rethink his preoccupation with work. He realized that in fearing failure and becoming consumed with work success, he avoided social connections, especially romantic relationships, which made him far more fearful than failing on the job. So, while he did fear failure and replicating his father's humiliating business experience, he also used that anxiety as a defense against awareness of his fear of being seen by others. He had reversed his arrow of causation from work preoccupation as a cause of isolation to avoidance of relating to others as the cause of his work-focused life. Both were true. Herb kept looking for psychological rock bottom, a reified "final cause," but we did not hit any, not with his social avoidance nor with his fear of failure. We arrived at meanings that were connected to other meanings worthy of their own exploration.

In this lengthy analytic exploration, I made no definitive statements of what I thought to be true of his motivations. I saw my role as evoking further questions and stimulating Herb to think of other ways of construing his life situation. While I made connections, such as his fear of interpersonal contact and his work life, I did so by noting that he made unquestioned assumptions without considering other possibilities.

We eventually went down the road of exploring his social anxiety, delving into his anxiety of rejection and intimacy that he feared would mean "being found out" for the inadequate soul he believed he was. In the discussion of his social avoidance, Herb saw that he was trying to distance himself from others as much as possible. I noted that he seemed to keep a similar distance from me by engaging me at an intellectual level. Stunned at that comment, he asked if he were doing something wrong in therapy. He then added that he felt throughout the course of our work that I would "find him out" and not like what I saw. He acknowledged a feeling of certainty that I must not feel accepting of him given what I now know, but I would not say that. This exchange led to the second level: I emphasized that, as with work, he made assumptions with me he did not question, such as the belief that the purpose of our sessions was to reach an intellectual understanding that could be a final product, like fear of failure. He said that he had never thought about that and felt a bit hurt, as though I was criticizing his use of the therapeutic process. I responded that he made assumptions often for self-protective reasons and then felt locked into one way, whether in work or therapy. I went on to say that he is made anxious by the recognition that he is choosing to construe the world as he does. He prefers to think that he is resting on some bedrock of "givens." Here I was interpreting Herb's reification of his own psyche, an attempt to deny his own psychology in favor of what Fonagy et al. (2002) call "psychic equivalence."

As we were in the throes of going over these conflicting emotions, as he was struggling with finding a way to work that would not overwhelm his sense of responsibility, a way to form meaningful connections with others, and to stretch the boundaries of his life, he returned to work and asked for a role in which he could use his creative talents without being responsible for a team. His responsive, caring boss readily concurred that his best role was as a consultant on new ventures, a type of consultant who could define a new project, but not implement it. If problems arose, he was available, but he did not have responsibility for directing or supervising work to see it through to completion. Herb thrived in this new setup. But, most important, it gave him time to work on other areas of life, to develop friendships and seek a romantic relationship.

With work, social life, and his relationship with me, Herb made assumptions that he had never questioned, and each such assumption contained an unconscious meaning: anxiety over failure, being known, and emotional contact with others. This confluence of fears combined to organize his life around frenetic work activity and an obsession with success. When Herb saw the meaning of this behavior in assumptions designed to avoid various anxieties, he began to consider whether he could find alternative ways to perform and relate.

As we talked about the fears, I concentrated on his avoidance of emotional contact with me, at which point he became more direct with me about feeling grateful that I listened to him and took his feelings seriously. He was timorous and halting as he said that he had never felt that way with anyone, and he felt scared telling me that. That expression of positive affect overcame a hurdle that led to a sense of accomplishment and pride. He then began to experiment with affective contact, an exploration that ended in meeting a young woman with whom he formed an immediate connection. She was taken with his intelligence, energy, and good looks. The couple shared similar interests, and the two formed a strong bond that ended in marriage. He had at this point made some social contacts, and his wife enriched his life in that way also, as her circle of friends became an important source of social support.

Eventually, Herb thrived in a new life of marriage and a work balanced with a social life. Enriched by his wife and friends, he made them a priority and was determined to never let his work become the priority of his life. The aspect of the analysis that is most poignant for the theme of this chapter is that his growth into new ways of being and relating was initiated by the very process of questioning his unconscious assumptions of how his life was to be and the motivation for forming what seemed to be rock-hard convictions. Before he achieved an understanding of what propelled him into a one-sided myopic rush to frenetic activity and instant decision making, he had slowed the process simply by questioning whether his assumptions were necessary.

The pivotal point was his decision to question even if he did not have a solution for himself. *Asking* in itself implied a recognition that his ways of viewing the world were interpretations, psychological processes that could at least be subject to scrutiny and modification, even radical change. Seeing the contingent nature of his *modus operandi* was a huge relief and allowed him to ask for a different way of being employed, the first concrete change in his lifelong patterns. In this way, he began to realize long dormant capabilities, such as the capacity to form relationships with others. Moreover, the ability to shift that central arena of his life emboldened him to try new forms of relating, such as expressing his emotions to me directly and later pursuing a romantic relationship. When he found experiments that worked, he had created something that had never before been part of his life. Each such new way of being was a product of a process of meaning making, rather than a definitive analytic conclusion.

Conclusion

Because no understanding Herb and I reached was regarded as final, the insights we did gain, as in seeing that his frantic obsession with work was driven by fear of failure, rather than becoming a resting place, tended to evoke new meanings. It is too easy to assume one has hit psychological rock bottom, and Herb longed for such a resting point. However, as we can see from the process with Herb, openness to what an understanding will evoke is critical to the evolution of analytic progress. In this continual mode of inquiry and discovery, Herb felt that he was developing psychological muscle, working out to strengthen some weak functioning. In this psychological exercise, he experimented with ways of being intimate, angry, confrontational, and emotional, among others. All of these were emotions he had never before utilized in his engagement with others.

The analytic process was successful by virtue of a fealty to Herb's experience and evocative understanding. It is not that we did not find unconscious meaning and motivation; it is that as we found them the analytic process remained open to the polysemous nature of meaning and in most cases new angles of meaning enriched the exchange. Awareness of the potential for ever new possibilities cautions away from a reified system of "the unconscious" and toward evoking rather than reducing new meanings. Herb then deployed those new understandings of meaning to create new ways of being and relating that stretched the boundaries within which his life had been so narrowly confined.

So, we have seen in this chapter that viewing the psychoanalytic process as evocative expands the patient's experience beyond historical patterns to stimulate new ways of experiencing and creating new meaning. This emphasis on evocative, rather than reductive, engagement leads the process toward creating new ways of being. Engaging the patient this way is founded on a new view of unconsciousness, a nonreified concept that "unconscious" is a descriptor, not a "system" or entity of any sort. With this view of unconsciousness, we were able to develop a clinical technique of the evocative, rather than the reductive. This way of conceptualizing unconscious psychic acts and the consequent shift in clinical strategy raises the question: What does this do to psychical phenomena that we regard as the *sine qua non* of "the unconscious," such as dreams? We saw that Freud built his theory of "the unconscious" largely around dreams. If dreams are supposed to be the royal road to "the unconscious," and we no longer have a concept of "the unconscious," what are we to make of dreams? And it is that topic on which we focus next.

6

LIVING IN A DREAM

The guiding idea of this book is that psychoanalytic thought has evolved to the point that it has become a unique form of exploration of human subjectivity. The analyst's fealty is to the patient's experience wherever that may lead. We have seen that for contemporary psychoanalysis to fulfill this mission, concepts and theories that reify the psychical process have to be questioned and reformulated to fit the nature of human experiencing. Returning to the fundamental understanding of human being as Being-in-the-world, we have seen that "the unconscious" is a reification that we have reconceptualized as a topographic descriptor of psychic process. Because dreams were the primary basis for Freud's view of "the unconscious," reconceptualizing unconscious psychic acts has inevitable implications for the theory of dreams. Furthermore, because Freud regarded his discovery of dream interpretation as his greatest contribution, any shift in the theory of dreams has important implications for the analytic process as a whole. In this chapter we will apply the psychoanalytic vision of fealty to the experiencing subject to the interpretation of dreams.

Although it is well known that Freud (1900) regarded his understanding of dreams as his greatest discovery, *The Interpretation of Dreams* is actually divided into two separate parts that could easily be two books. The first six chapters are, in essence, a hermeneutic on how to understand the meaning of dreams. His contention was that dreams are disguised fulfillments of forbidden wishes, and by following the thread of the patient's associations, the analyst could discover the latent dream thoughts hidden beneath the manifest content of the dream.

In Chapter 7 Freud shifts to a metapsychological explanation for how the psychic apparatus constructs dreams. In this chapter Freud did not limit himself to the construction of dreams, but saw in the dreaming process an example of how the psychic apparatus functions. In this chapter, then, Freud delineated his first model of the mind (Gedo & Goldberg, 1976). He argued that psychic activity begins with stimuli and ends in innervations. At the sensory end perceptions are received and at the motor end is the outlet for motor activity. In normal waking life, psychical processes advance from the sensory to the motoric systems, but in dreams, due to the repression barrier, the excitation moves backward from the motoric to the perceptual system, and that is why Freud regarded dreams as regressive. Regression may occur in waking life, also, but it stops at mnemic images, whereas in dreams, Freud believed, the reverse excitation reaches all the way back to a "hallucinatory revival of the perceptual images" (p.543) which we call a dream. The dream images are, for Freud, epiphenomena that disguise the dream thoughts, or latent content, hidden beneath the manifest content of the dream. Because each dream image represents a repressed wish, the dream can be broken down into constituent dream thoughts, and the dream interpreted by uncovering the meaning of the individual dream elements.

For approximately 60 years after Freud first published his dream theory, analytic contributions in this area were predominantly derivative of this core theory, such as Lewin's (1946) work on the dream screen. Even applications of alternative theoretical schools, such as Kleinian theory, assumed the wish fulfillment model. With regard to dreams, Klein and her followers departed from Freud in the content of what dreams mean, but not in their structure and motivation. More recently, suggested changes challenge one or more of Freud's central ideas. For example, several theorists have argued that the manifest dream is not merely an arbitrarily assigned symbol but a valuable source of information in itself (e.g., Pulver & Renik, 1984; Bonime, 1989; Mendelsohn, 1990; Greenberg & Pearlman, 1999). French and Fromm (1964) showed that the manifest dream, in fact, expresses both a focal conflict and an attempt to resolve it. Bonime (1989) has presented a compelling case that the manifest dream and its affect can provide a useful understanding of the patient.

Even more fundamentally, self psychologists have questioned the cornerstone of Freud's ideas: the wish fulfillment theory. While Kohut (1984) accepted Freud's theory for most dreams, he believed that a minority of dreams are "self state" dreams that express not wishes or their fulfillment, but the state of the self. Subsequent self psychologists have proposed that dreams are not a composite of constituent wishes, but statements of how the self is functioning (e.g., Fosshage, 1988; Greenberg, 1989). According to this view, rather than repressed wishes, dream symbolism suggests the issues with which the dreamer is struggling *and* how s/he is attempting to cope with them (Greenberg & Pearlman, 1978). Thus, the self psychological approach tends to coincide with the tendency to emphasize the value of the manifest dream.

Contemporary self psychologists see dreaming as serving a broader and psychically more significant role than is encompassed by the wish fulfillment theory. They regard dreams as providing regulatory, restorative, and conflict-resolving functions (e.g., Fosshage, 1988). Perhaps the most comprehensive of the self psychological views of dream interpretation is provided by Stolorow and Atwood (1982) who see the dream as a reflection of the "salient concerns of the dreamers' life." The dream concretizes in visual symbolization the self and other configurations of the dreamer's life in order to reinforce the dreamer's convictions about these psychic patterns. So, the motivating force of the dream for these theorists is not so much that it provides potentially new information about the dreamer's unconscious life as that it dramatizes self and other configurations more vividly than they are experienced in waking life.

The self psychological formulation of dreams breaks decisively from the classical view by changing the function of the dream from finding a way to circumvent the repression barrier to a means for conveying the depth and intensity of meanings of which the dreamer may well be aware. Like some current thinking about dreams, this view gives pride of place to the manifest dream, but unlike much other theorizing, it blurs the distinction between waking and dream life.

While the self psychological view abandons Freud's metapsychology, Robbins (2004) sees in it the unique language of dreaming that he believes is missed in the traditional view. Robbins contends that the dream cannot be broken down into "thoughts" because thinking is a secondary process activity and the dream is dreamt in primary process language. The mental activity of dreams is a sensory-perceptual occurrence based on a "complete hallucinatory cathexis of the perceptual systems" in which the dreamer plays an active part. According to Robbins, the use of condensation and displacement which substitute the concrete *is* for the symbolic *as* are not necessarily means of symbol formation because they may simply be the language of the dream, the way the dream conveys its message. The manifest dream, then, is a complete expression in its own language that cannot and need not be reduced to the thoughts of waking life. The traditional dream theory, in Robbins's views, confuses the dream with its translation into ordinary language.

Pontalis (1974) also believes the uniqueness of dreaming is missed in the classical approach. He distinguishes between the dream as dreamt and its translation into words in the analytic process. For Pontalis, the dream is important as an object of the analysis, the way it is experienced by the patient as dreaming and in the patient-analyst interaction. Khan (1989) also believed the classical view ignores the dreaming experience and agreed with Pontalis that dreaming is a different psychic event from the remembered dream text. The lived experience of dreaming, according to Khan, brings the self to actualization, but it cannot be interpreted. Using components of the dream, a narrative is constructed that can be communicated and interpreted. In agreement with self psychologists, Khan believed that the dream is a unique experience that portrays psychic life in the most condensed, vivid manner possible. In a similar vein, Bollas (1987) views the dream as a unique opportunity to see how the dreamer locates herself in the object world. Where the dreamer as a subject in the dream places herself reflects how she understands herself to fit into her interpersonal environment.

These views break down Freud's clear distinctions between waking and dream life and between the latent and manifest dreams. In so doing, these theorists transform the purpose of the dream from wish fulfillment to a statement about the current psychic situation. They do not see the dream as a disguised wish, but, based on their clinical experience, these analytic authors, in various ways, see the dream *as dreamed* as a telling and meaningful representation of major dynamics in the patient's life. All agree that dreams are meaningful and a rich source of clinical data, but the kind of meaning expressed in the dream from this contemporary viewpoint is more directly expressed in the act of dreaming than is true of the classical theory.

Systematic studies of what people dream and the effects of dreaming support this concept of dream life. Both animals and humans, if deprived of dreaming, suffer major losses in complex and creative cognitive and emotional functioning, but not in the completion of simple tasks (Pearlman, 1982; Greenberg & Pearlman, 1999). Subjects deteriorated significantly in the ability to organize new or emotionally significant information (Greenberg et al., 1983). It seems that dreaming aids the ability to manage complex and affectively powerful material, and, therefore, facilitates conflict resolution capacity. Greenberg and Pearlman (1999) conclude: "The manifest dream is not a disguise for a drive. Instead, it is a different language that portrays the dreamer's problems and illustrates the efforts to find solutions" (p.758–9).

Whether one agrees with the conclusion of these particular researchers or not, the clinical and research data both indicate strongly that dreams serve a variety of functions. In dreaming, problems of daily life are confronted and sometimes solved. In fact, traumatic and anxiety dreams are disturbing because they do not contain a solution. At times dreams represent an interpersonal situation, at other times a work conflict, in some instances, they are wish fulfillments. But, the question then presents itself: According to Freud's metapsychology of dreams, repressed wishes form dreams to circumvent the repression barrier. If this is so, the manifest dream is a disguise. If Freud's metapsychology of dream formation is valid, how is it possible that the manifest dream, the experience of the dream, is relevant and the dream itself reflects the patient's psychic life rather than a disguised wish? It seems that the more recent clinical and research data indicate that Freud's metapsychology of dreaming must be reexamined.

The Phenomenological Critique

While there is much to commend Freud's elegant theory of dream formation, his metapsychology suffers from a fundamental flaw due to his belief that a dream is a hallucination composed of blocked visual excitations. Freud's metapsychology of dreams is built on the assumption that a dream is a distorted perception, but a hallucination is a misperception of an object in extended space. In hallucinations, objects are seen as existing in waking life that are not there, as in Anna O.'s belief that she saw snakes (Breuer & Freud, 1895). Subjects in sensory deprivation experiments hallucinate objects they believe they see, such bugs or space people (e.g., Hebb, 1955). As can be seen in these cases, visual hallucinations are constructions of nonexistent objects in space. A dream is not a misperception in extended space; it exists in its own space and therefore is not a hallucination, nor even a poor perception. When objects are incorrectly perceived, they are misrecognized, as when a highway on a hot day looks like a lake. Such a misrepresentation does not fit the dream because a dream does not take place in extended space. A dream cannot be reduced to a visual misperception in extended space nor duplicated in any other experience. The fact that the dream has believability to the dreamer while dreaming does not make it a hallucination. The hallucination is a visual concoction of extended space, while the dream takes place in a theatre of its own making.

Furthermore, dreams are typically dramaturgical, that is, they possess all the attributes of drama: writer, director, protagonist, and an audience. Unlike the theatre, in the dream the dreamer performs all the dramaturgical roles. Freud's metapsychology of dreams, based on the assumption that a dream is a poor perception, did not grasp the uniqueness of dreaming and therefore neglected the dreaming experience, including the experience of being in the drama of the dream. Indeed, his theory constitutes a reductionism in two ways: it regards the "manifest content," the drama played out in the dreaming experience, as an epiphenomenon of dream thoughts, and it reduces dreaming to a type of perception, distorted though it is. Freud's theory overlooks the lived experience of dreaming, a critical lacuna noted by some self psychologists as well as Bollas, Khan, and Pontalis.

Because a dream is not a poor perception, it is not the case that a dream is composed of dammed up visual excitations. Dreams are pictorial, but not visual. There is no reason, then, to assume that every dream is a wish fulfillment. While some dreams include the satisfaction of repressed wishes, the fact that a dream is not a visual outlet for blocked motoric discharge indicates that the motive for constructing dreams is not the provision of an outlet for repressed desires, although a particular dream may serve that function in an individual case. In short, the fact that dreams are not distorted uses of the "perceptual apparatus" collapses the foundation of Freud's metapsychology of dreams.

While the meaning of the dream may be arguably unconscious, the dreamer is living in a dreaming consciousness while dreaming, just as a perceiver is living in her perceiving consciousness, the mathematician in a mathematizing consciousness, the fantasizer in the consciousness of fantasizing. That is to say, if one eliminates the prejudice of privileging perception, the dreaming experience is as much a form of Being-in-the-world as perception, judgment, thinking, doing mathematics, aesthetic experience, or any other.

This view of dreaming has an affinity with Boss's (1977) pure phenomenological account, which is constructed on the edifice of Heidegger's philosophy of Being-in-the-world. Boss highlights the fact that the dreaming experience cannot be reduced to any other way of thinking or being; it is a unique way of Being-in-the-world possessing its own characteristics and cannot be reduced to misperception any more than perception is a misperceived dream. However, Boss's theory adheres so closely to the dreaming experience that he confines the value of the dream to its revelations regarding the relationship between the dreamer and the objects dreamt. Boss does not believe associations or any other technical procedure can be deployed to understand a dream because any such maneuver distances the dreamer from the dreaming experience. In one of his examples, the dream is of a "primitive jungle," and for Boss this dream tells us how the dreamer experiences jungles (p.38–42). To regard the jungle as a symbol is, for Boss, an unwarranted theoretical prejudice that removes the dreamer from the dreaming experience.

Boss's emphasis on the experience of the dream is an invaluable clinical move because it focuses the analysis on the patient's experience, but to refuse the possibility of meaning beyond that is to deny that meaning can be sedimented in experience, a realization that is, in fact, recognized not only in psychoanalysis, but also in phenomenological philosophy (Husserl, 1913). Boss's putatively pure phenomenological perspective has difficulty explaining why a dreamer would dream of any particular object, such as a primitive jungle. Moreover, adhering to a purely phenomenological approach makes any comment about the dream beyond its retelling vulnerable to the charge of distancing from the immediacy of the dream. Consequently, Boss gives himself the Herculean task of expanding the phenomena dreamt without going beyond the immediacy of the dream. Tellingly, Boss's depiction of the objects in patients' dreams comes from Boss's ideas about those objects. To continue with our example, Boss declares that a primitive jungle is "inherently a dark, untouched region of nature, teeming with plant and animal life, and barely permitting access" (p.39), but we do not know if the patient would describe a jungle in this way or if the attributes Boss selects would be salient to the patient. Such an imposition of the analyst's way of experiencing the object is precisely the error Boss claims to be avoiding.

Indeed, the best testimony to the lack of utility of Boss's purely phenomenological approach is the fact that he abandons it himself. For example, one subject dreamed of attempting to decline a Latin noun whose masculine ending hides its feminine gender, and Boss claimed that a symbolic interpretation would have overlooked the fact that the patient was hiding her femininity behind a masculine appearance. Somehow Boss did not see that he interpreted the dream as a symbol of the patient's attempt to hide her femininity beneath a masculine façade. While one can empathize with Boss's insistence that the dreaming experience must be allowed to "shine forth" as itself, his theoretical refusal to acknowledge that dreams have interpretable meanings is not clinically viable. Boss cannot demonstrate the value of dreams without interpreting in a way his theory says he should not. The fact that the dreaming experience is significant in itself and typically has an impact on the patient's life does not imply it is devoid of deeper meaning; to the contrary, giving priority to the dreaming experience is the most reliable way to make the associations meaningful and discern the meaning of the dream as a whole.

The Experience of Dreaming

The untenable phenomenological basis of Freud's metapsychology of dreaming debunks the wish fulfillment hypothesis, but not the thesis that dreams are meaningful. If we rush to interpret the dream without understanding its nature, we risk robbing the patient of an enriching, perhaps creative, experience. On the other hand, if we stay with a purely descriptive approach, we risk missing the depth of meaning contained in that experience. The challenge for psychoanalysis is to formulate a theory of understanding dreams without reducing them to an epiphenomenon. That is, to recognize and appreciate the experience of dreaming while understanding the sedimented meaning that inheres in it. To do that requires beginning with the nature of the dream world.

As the protagonist in the drama of the dream, the dreamer is participant as well as audience. The dreamer's perspective is from inside the dream. During the experience of dreaming, the dreamer lives in the dream. That is why there is not only believability to the dream, but also a unique quality not replicable in waking life. The dream is, as Boss contended, a lived experience. Looking at the experience of dreaming, a dream is not something we "have" or "make" as much as an experience we live (Wilkerson, 1997).

The dreamer sees herself not as an actress, but as a participant in the story while playing out the drama and watching it simultaneously. The dreamer is carried away by the experience, immersed in the drama that unfolds in dreaming consciousness. The dream is a pictorial production filled with emotion and a sense of having been in a realm of experience hermetically sealed from all other forms of consciousness. Robbins is correct, then, to argue for a decisive difference between the modes of communication in dreaming and waking consciousness, but it is prejudicial to define this difference as the distinction between primary and secondary process. Living inside a drama in a space set off from the perceptual world makes the dream a fundamentally different way of being from waking life.

Because so many bizarre occurrences take place in dreams that violate the laws of space, time, and logic of waking life, it is difficult to grasp the fact that the dream is a way of experiencing the world with the same status as any other psychic activity. Furthermore, the immediate move past the dream to its associations and search for hidden thoughts dilutes, or even ignores completely, the experience of being in the dream. If we remove this prejudgment in favor of allowing ourselves to engage, and help the patient to engage, the dreaming experience as it is experienced in the dream, seemingly "bizarre" occurrences in the dream can be fully lived and their depth experienced as a reality of the patient's psychic life. The novelty of the vivid portrayal in the dream will then be revealed. The dreamer finds the power and meaning of the dream in the affective environment in which she is immersed as protagonist in the dream.

It follows then that if the analyst looks at the dream as a series of symbols hiding meanings, the emphasis on the associations to decode the symbols either trivializes the dreaming experience or overlooks it completely. Meanings may well be uncovered, but they will replace the experience of the dream rather than add to it and therefore the richness of the dream may be missed. If, however, the dream is regarded as a textured way of experiencing the world, the analyst will encourage the patient to recount the experience of being in the dream as much as possible, or it might be more accurate to say, to live in the dream as remembered in the analytic session. The analyst's question will not immediately be "What does it bring up?" but, "What was it like to be in the dream?" The experience of *being* in the dream, if it can be relived to some degree in the analysis, offers the new experience that can shed light on psychic life and often add to it by revealing new potentialities.

Clinical Illustrations

Barry came to analysis for help with overwhelming job anxiety and a history of sabotaging his successes. In conventional terms, he was an Oedipal victor, the clear favorite of his mother who was openly devaluing and contemptuous of her husband. She would share alcoholic drinks with the patient as a young boy while the pair enjoyed belittling the father's failures and weakness. After struggling mightily against a powerful guilt that drove him to sabotage his successes, the talented patient enjoyed exceptional success working for a company that was about to be sold during the recent economic crisis, a transaction that could put his job in jeopardy. He dreamed he was fired and was dreading that he might "end up back with" his mother.

I asked him, "What was it like to be in that dream?" He said simply, "Horrified." In the dream he was filled with dread, expecting a catastrophe to happen. The meaning did not require complex deciphering once he expressed how he felt in the dream: He feared the engulfment with his mother that would be his punishment for achieving success. In previous jobs he had undermined himself after receiving raises and promotions, and in his current position he had worked hard for years to achieve a senior level position with a substantial income and consistent praises from his bosses. In the dream he was threatened with a return to his childhood hell. From within the dread he felt both in the dream and in retelling it, he experienced an uncanny horror he had never felt in waking life. In the dream he felt the depth of his fear of regressing to maternal domination, a fate that his two adult brothers lived out. Neither had formed a long-term relationship, one lived with his mother, and the other, near her. Unconsciously, Barry had lived with the ghost of returning to his mother's control. Beneath the fear was his belief that he should be punished with the destruction of his current life for the crime of colluding with his mother against his father and then daring to succeed where his father failed.

The impact of the dream lay not in deciphering symbolic meanings, but in the experience of living the dread, the depth of fear that he now knew resided within him, and reliving it in the analysis. The effect of the dream did not appear from thoughts he had uncovered, but from the strength of the dread and guilt he lived while in the dream. It was the experience of living through the dread in the dream that showed him that his fear and guilt were powerful enough to sabotage his successes and resist all positive life events. At this point Barry was able to see the extent to which his life had been arrested by the specter of returning to the maternal orbit, a fate he feared, felt he deserved, and believed awaited him.

When Barry relived the experience of dread and guilt in the dream of returning to his mother, he felt the continuous pull his mother still had on him. To presume that his fear in the dream "really" represented a "wish" would be an unfounded imposition that did not fit his experience in any way. The dread and guilt were the meaningful experiences, and they both dominated his state in the dream. In seeing this, Barry felt a new affective dimension to his maternal relationship. He saw that his mother's shadow was with him and that he had been deluding himself to think her influence was in the past. He now had a deeper understanding of his anxiety than he had ever before achieved.

In my clinical work I have found that by asking about the patient's experience in dreaming, the exploration of the dream tends to be affectively intense. Sometimes the patient feels a depth of affect when recalling the dream, as in the example above, but at other times, the patient reports the dream with little emotion. In the latter cases, if the patient and I follow a train of associations, the affect usually changes little and the discourse tends to remain at an intellectual level, but if I inquire about the experience of being in the dream, the patient typically responds with emotional intensity.

A good example of this type of emotional revelation was dreamt by George, a 50-year-old, highly successful businessman, who originally came to analysis for help with an acute depressive episode. The evolution of the analytic material became concentrated on the extreme unhappiness he felt in his highly lucrative work life. He received no gratification from his business ventures except the derivative benefits of wealth and power. Although he originally insisted the considerable admiration and remuneration he received from his professional success had no meaning to him, in the analysis he became aware that the narcissistic satisfaction of wealth and power were, in fact, so irresistible he could not risk losing them by giving up the misery of his daily work life. Despite a painful process of arduous analytic work, he could not disentangle himself from his business. He feared he would feel lost and forgotten without the status of and income from running a successful operation.

At this point he dreamed about a friend who surprisingly appeared at a dinner revealing himself as a transsexual dressed in outlandish garb with clown-like face accessories, such as fake lips and oversized glasses. A theoretical prejudice might tempt the conclusion that the dream is an unconscious expression of a desire to be a woman or homosexual. However, when I asked George what it was like to be in the dream, he immediately replied, "I was envious of this guy. What impressed me was how comfortable he was in being a transvestite. He was saying, 'This is me. I am who I am.' He didn't care what people thought. I was so envious! I want to be like that." George quickly added that if he were "like" his hero in the dream, he would sell his business and seek a different way of earning a living. The strength of his envy enveloped him both in the dream and in retelling it in analysis. In the analytic discussion of the dream, George felt his needs for both self expression and adulation with a new intensity.

The depth of George's fear of leaving the business was now clear. He feared the loss of others' approbation would leave him with little sense of self, but acknowledging the importance of the gaze of the other made him feel "weak." The envy was a new experience for George, but he did not feel the importance of the dream lay in the awareness of envy, as much as the experience of feeling his very sense of self was dependent upon the adulation of others. The envy in the dream was a way of showing himself how much he longed to be free of others' views of him and how unable he was to free himself from the need for admiration. In the dream, for the first time he experienced envy of those he regarded as free, the longing for liberation, and his self-imposed trap. As with Barry, the intensity with which he felt this stubborn and fundamental motive was the contribution of the dream to his life.

A different sort of trap was revealed to another patient, Charles, in a dream from which he awoke startled. Charles had been enmeshed with his mother for most of his life. His role was to provide support and advice on her many life problems, including her conflictual relationship with her husband. Performing this function since childhood made him feel important to his mother, and he derived great satisfaction from knowing she preferred him to his father. It was not until the analysis that anger at his mother's exploitation of him surfaced, although he acknowledged feeling gratified by being the mother's specially chosen confidant. In the analysis, he realized that despite the self-enhancement he felt in the maternal relationship, he was paying a huge price for it by assuming the burden of sustaining her emotional well-being and living with the fear of how he would fare without her. He sought her approval for all he did and rushed to console her out of fear that if she were distressed in any way, he would lose his major source of emotional sustenance. He was constantly anxious that if he did not receive her endorsement for any anticipated decision or life activity, he could not go through with it.

As these realizations came to the fore, Charles began to take steps to distance from his mother, reducing their contact appreciably. His mother was disturbed by this change, and he felt guilty as well as caught in a conflict between his desire to disentangle himself from the enmeshed bond and the guilt of separating from his mother. In one session he was agonizing over his guilt at attempting to put more distance between himself and his mother when he recalled a recent dream that his parents and three brothers were going somewhere without him and did not tell him, an event that would have been inconceivable in waking life. When he asked them where they were going, one brother replied that they were going to Europe on vacation. He was shocked and awoke startled.

Charles said the dream evoked little affect or thought. But, when I asked him what it was like to be in the dream, he immediately blurted out "lonely." At that moment Charles felt a sense of alienation from his entire family, and as he talked about his grief at needing to separate, he felt enveloped in isolation and abandonment. He began to weep. Prior to this session, he had been only aware of a vague sense of loneliness. As he continued talking about the dream, the feeling intensified until he felt "all alone in the world." He feared the conflict between isolation and responsibility for his mother was unresolveable.

At that point Charles associated to brief periods in his life when he had attempted to become relatively more autonomous from his mother's influence. In each case, he fell into such deep despair that he resumed the old relationship with her. At those moments of attempted separation, Charles lacked any sense of orientation to the world and felt lost without her continual presence. As a result, he felt desperate to resume the historical relationship in order to feel reconnected to the world, and his anxiety was allayed when it was. In this session he felt similarly bereft, without any sense of orientation or direction. It became clear to him that his use of his mother was as exploitive as hers of him: He needed her to avoid the panic of loneliness.

The dread of abandonment and isolation appeared in his next reported dream, which, again, he recalled while expressing guilt at separation. He was in a cave with no one around, suddenly someone appeared, and he tried to find out who it was, but he could not. Again, Charles reported the dream without emotion, but once asked what it was like to be in the dream, he did not hesitate: "All by myself; with no one and nothing, I could make no contact." Again the despair of existing without human connection consumed him in the session, and he felt helpless in the face of it.

These dreams brought home to Charles the terror of losing all contact with the human world if he disentangled himself from his mother. It should be noted that Charles's associations helped in grasping the power of the dream, but the associations were of benefit in response to the experience of isolation in the dream. After Charles felt the power of this emotion, the associations became affectively meaningful. It may also be noted that both dreams were remembered when the issue of separating from his mother was being discussed. As Charles became aware of his feelings about separation, the dream was evoked, and the recalled dreaming experience was a dramatic, vivid, pictorial expression of what he had touched on in the session. The material that evokes the dream is a clue to its meaning because the dream is a dramaturgical representation of the dynamics under discussion.

As can be seen from the method employed in interpreting the dreams of George and Charles, the phenomenological basis for dream interpretation does not dispute that associations are important for understanding the meaning of dreams. The phenomenological approach, however, differs from the classical psychoanalytic way of looking at dreams in its insistence that associations are of most help after the patient has recalled not just the dream, but the experience of being in the dream, what it was like to be the protagonist of the dream drama. Once that experience is felt in as much depth as can be captured in an analytic session, the associations are more likely to be affectively alive. So, when Charles associated to previous periods of loneliness, he did so from inside the despair of his isolation.

Conclusion

In all the dreams discussed, the dreaming experience shed light on the dreamer's life, but typically by the vividness, the texture of the experience, more than in new insights. All three patients felt something deeper and more real in feelings they knew they had in the pre-dream state. Barry was aware of his fear of success and the punishment of returning to his mother's control, but in the dream of being fired, he knew the horror of failure and guilt for success in a way he had never able to experience them in waking life. George knew he felt enslaved to the adulation that came with the success of his business, but in dreaming his envy of the friend dressed in a clown costume, he felt a longing for a new life that he had not been able to experience while awake. Similarly, Charles knew he was anxious about separating from his mother, but in dreaming of the family going to Europe without telling him, he knew the depth of his dread of loneliness. In brief, dreams are dramas precisely because their dramaturgical nature provides a setting in which the patient can experience a way of being that is unavailable in waking life. Patients rarely find something wholly new in the dream, but they do live new experiences by dreaming. In so doing, they are realizing new modes of being in the world. By living in the drama of the dream, the themes and struggles of the patient's life are lived in a different way, a way that realizes potential dormant in waking life.

The prejudice that the dream is "unreal," or even a hallucination, that must be reduced to thoughts of waking life fosters an analytic discussion that attenuates rather than intensifies affect and depth of experience. The principle of focusing on affect and avoiding intellectual distancing is strictly adhered to in virtually any other analytic arena. If the patient reports an incident at the workplace, or with a friend or spouse, the analyst will want to know what the experience was like for the patient. If the patient reports an intellectualized version of the event in question, the analyst will see this response as a defense and seek to uncover the protected affect. While analysts would claim to adopt a similar approach to dreams, the standard technique emphasizes connections to the dream over the experience of being in the dream. Although no analyst searches for an intellectualized report of a dream, the technique of immediately seeking associations is likely to move the patient toward connections that lack affective intensity and away from the vividness of the dreaming experience.

Ultimately, life in the dream shows the dreamer a potential that he did not know was in him. A dream, as we have seen, is a way of being in the world that allows for a different form of living, a different way of existing, than is possible in any other mode of consciousness. Dramas of the waking imagination do not have the power of the dream to evoke believability, a sense of participation, of living there, as the dream does. That is why ultimately Freud was right to say that the dream is a royal road. However, we might now modify Freud's statement to say that the dream is a royal road to a way of being that cannot be lived in the waking world.

The analytic exploration of the dreaming experience, then, leads the patient to bring to waking life a new way of being, and in reliving the dreaming experience in the analytic session, the patient is exercising a new psychic capacity. And in this creation of a new way of being we find the therapeutic action of the analytic process. We have seen that the analytic engagement of the patient aims for the realization of self potential, and in dreaming we find a unique road for bringing to fruition new modes of experiencing. But, now we may ask: If the analytic process is about creating new ways of being and relating, if it is focused not just on understanding what is, but on bringing to realization what has never been, then the patient is understood not just in terms of her current patterns, but also for her possibilities of new ways of being. The other is not limited to who she now is because her identity includes who she *might become*, And, so, now we turn to this new way of experiencing the other embedded in the psychoanalytic vision.

7

THE OTHER AS TRANSCENDENTAL EXPERIENCE

We have seen that defining psychoanalytic therapy as a unique mode of inquiry into human experiencing goes beyond the engagement of who the patient *is* to the stimulation and facilitation of who the patient *may be*. With the breakdown of the conflict/arrest distinction, unrealized self potential becomes a central component of who the patient is, and, consequently, of the analytic process. While the analytic aim of bringing to fruition unrealized self potential is a logical outcome of the developmental arrest model, it implies a profoundly different view of the other than is found in conventional analytic thought. Theories as far removed from each other as ego psychology, the Kleinian school, and relational theory tend to see the other in terms of who she is now and how she became that person. There are some significant exceptions, such as Loewald's (1962b) suggestion that the future is an essential part of the analytic stance. However, Loewald's view was limited to the superego; he did not recognize the embeddedness of the forward trajectory in all psychic events. The more significant theoretical advance is Stern's (1997) concept that analysis is about the articulation of the unformulated. Stern sees the analysand/other as suffering from states that have not been brought to fruition. For Stern, the analysand has unformulated states that may become articulated in the analytic process, and in this way Stern has provided a major step forward in the analytic conception of the other.

Loewald and Stern have illuminated the importance of seeing the potential for new experience in the other as a component of the therapeutic process. But, these advances have not resulted in a theory of how such recognition fits into the analytic process, and, as a result, psychoanalysis has not had a theory consonant with the promise of self realization. The purpose of this chapter is twofold: (1) to build on the thinking of Loewald and Stern to elucidate a theory of the other that includes unrealized possibilities; and (2) to show the clinical implications of this way of viewing the other. Or, to put this another way: This chapter will demonstrate how viewing the other as potential for who she may *become* results in an analytic strategy that enriches the analytic concept of therapeutic action.

In contemporary psychoanalysis, one thinks of empathy as the primary tool by which the analyst knows the other. The most common meaning of empathy is captured by Sullivan's concept of "contagion." As phenomenological philosophers have demonstrated, no inference is made to know the other's affective states (e.g.,

Merleau-Ponty, 1985). One feels the other's sadness, anger, pain, or joy immediately as though affects are contagious. We might call this *immanent empathy*. This common usage of empathy captures the immediate communication of psychic states, but is insufficient to account for analytic understanding that aims to reach beyond immediate experience to grasp the reasons for the patient's states and configurational patterns. For the analyst to perform his task, he must understand not only the present moment of affective communication, but also the unconscious motives and meanings that gave rise to the current states and patterns. Analytic empathy goes beyond the phenomenological concept by seeking to understand states known immanently. Kohut's (1959) definition of empathy as "vicarious introspection" captures this analytic method. This type of empathy, unique to psychoanalytic inquiry, can be termed *analytic empathy* as opposed to the immanent empathy of everyday life. In the empathy of the analytic encounter, the analyst immerses herself in the patient's experience to understand the reasons for the current psychic configurations (e.g., Basch, 1983, 1990; Bolognini, 2004, 2009). What is essential for the current purpose is that both types of empathy are limited to the recognition of who the patient currently is and how she became that way and therefore excludes any consideration of the other as potentiality.

Transcendent Empathy

Any current state derives it meaning from its intentionality. At the micro level of everyday interaction, meaning that takes place in the future perfect tense, so the current relational patterns are not understandable outside of the goals toward which they strive (Schutz, 1932/1974). For example, to know that two people are talking is not tantamount to knowing what they are doing. What defines their activity is the purpose of the discussion. Whether the two met to negotiate a business deal, wager on a football game, socialize, discuss the problem of a mutual friend, gossip, or argue about politics defines their activity.

At the macro level, the life narrative is not exhausted by present and past; life is organized by goals. The desire to achieve something beyond the present situation dominates who the patient is now and who she has been. To know the patient's historical roots and current affective and relational patterns no more encompasses the whole of the patient's psychological state than the altitude, latitude, and longitude of an airplane in flight defines the location of the plane. To know where the plane is at any moment, of course, one needs to know its direction and the speed at which it is traveling. The analogy applies to the human process because life is lived in the perfect tense (Schutz, 1932/1974; Summers, 2003). The meaning of the present is to be found in how it fits anticipated goals; the perfect tense defines the present moment. Every state consists of a moment in becoming, so who the person may *become* is as important to understanding the person as who he has been. And who the person is to become is a function of unrealized potential.

One of the contributions of psychoanalytic thought is its emphasis on development over the entire life cycle (e.g., Greenspan & Pollock, 1991; Erikson, 1968/1994). The movement of the individual from one state to another, from one developmental level to the next, is the very essence of not only child development, but also the entire span of life. At the macro level there is always a new phase of development to undertake so the movement forward, the push toward ever new goals and experience, is a necessary component of understanding who the other is.

Here again Heidegger's (1962/1927) concept of human being as *Da-sein*, or "Being-in-the-world," clarifies the nature of human experiencing. What must now be emphasized is that in this relating to the world is a movement forward, what Heidegger called "ek-static," because there is no stasis in the human way of being; one is always comporting oneself toward the world in the mode of "having been done." The life cycle perspective of psychoanalysis is a concrete embodiment of Heidegger's view of temporality as movement forward. It follows that the other is experienced as having a trajectory, an anticipatory striving toward the future. Who the person is cannot be exhausted by present modes and past roots because the individual is attempting to achieve goals, fulfill projects, and the desire for what-is-not-yet is endemic to who the person is. It is an organic implication of Heidegger's thought that the other cannot be grasped within only present and past; to understand the other is to see her goals, aspirations for the future, the aims toward which her present is striving.

For these reasons, understanding the patient's current patterns only, no matter how comprehensively they may be grasped, misses an essential component of her life-world. In fact, the present life patterns gain their meaning from the projects in which they are embedded. Ignoring the patient's potential and future strivings omits: (1) the context within which the present and past make sense; (2) who the patient hopes to become; and, perhaps most tellingly (3) who she may be in the process of becoming.

Here again we see the importance of conceptualizing psychopathology as both conflict and arrest. While the evolution of an individual life is for all a process of becoming in which the "not yet" is omnipresent, those afflicted with pathological patterns and symptoms have significant components of the self that have never been realized. It follows that who the person is *not* is a critical component of who the patient *is*. The full recognition of the other embraces both what has developed and what is missing, the lack around which the patient leads her life. The other, the patient, includes in her very being unformed potential, and those unrealized parts of the self are the root of the patient's disturbance. Indeed, it is precisely this gap of nonbeing that typically motivates the treatment and impels the patient to seek something from the analyst. At the heart of the therapeutic process, then, lies the unrealized parts of the patient, both her longings and capacities. To be fully empathic with the patient requires immersion in and recognition of who the patient *is not and has not yet been*. This form of empathy is *transcendent empathy*, empathy that goes beyond *what is* to what *has never been*.

The Gap

It is this arrest, recognized by clinicians of a variety of theoretical persuasions, that leaves potential unfulfilled and ultimately issues in whatever conscious distress motivates the patient, at however many steps removed, to enter the consulting room.

Whether the ability to form relationships or sustain intimacy, the capacity to deploy aggression, the need for accomplishment, the capacity for separation, or any number of other human needs and desires, the patient lacks an ability relevant to the growth and development of the self. It is this gap that the patient seeks to fill, however unconsciously, to repair psychic wounds and complete a derailed developmental process.

The childhood prohibitions having issued in a developmental arrest that overrides strivings to complete unrealized potential, the individual continues his quest to complete the developmental project, albeit in disguised form. For example, if the child's aggression is met with stern prohibitions, the child may avoid aggressivity to maintain the bonds with the caretakers. The potential for the deployment of aggressivity being undeveloped, the patient does not allow aggression into any significant relationships. In this case, the avoidance of conflict may be not only a desperate attempt to sustain relationships, but also an inability to maintain a relationship in which aggression plays a role. As a result, aggression remains only as a potential way of being, a possibility if it can be exercised.

One patient emerges from childhood without the ability to be intimate, and the second without the ability to assert herself. The first case has not realized her potential for love or intimacy, the ability to be close to another person, and the second cannot sustain an aggressive form of relating. The unfulfilled potential in both cases dominates the patient's distress and is likely to sustain a haunting presence over her life. The gap between the patient's potential ways of being and her practiced interactional patterns results in a profound sense of disturbance that tends to motivate the pursuit of therapeutic aid. The potential to become something other than who the patient now is remains in a disavowed state, but the indomitable desire to achieve its realization evokes an unease that may emerge in a variety of pathological states, such as a gnawing lack of fulfillment, anxiety, panic attacks, depression, despair, or defensive constellations erected against those painful states, such as grandiosity or hypomania. Those symptoms reflect the derailed desire of the self to become who she can be.

These deliberations set into high relief the reality that the person is both who he *is* and who he *is not*. What we do not do, what we are not capable of doing, may be as present on our minds and influence our actions as much as what we do. Many patients are haunted by this absence in their lives. Common examples are those patients who cannot form a lasting romantic relationship. For many of them, the most dominant presence in their lives is this absence. To fail to take into account this "not" would be to miss a fundamental striving of profound importance in their lives. In general, the "not" may be a capability so far unrealized, or it may be something we are not and cannot become. In either case, the "not me" is an absence that is very present in the experience of the patient. The "not" defines who we are as much as the "is." What one cannot become tends to be disavowed, but its presence remains, much like Loewald's "ghosts," the haunting presence of the undefined and even unnamable, but very much present and often profound in its influence on the direction of life.

For Lacan (1977a), too, lack is the motivator, but for Lacan the gap is the human condition and the patient must confront the reality that it cannot be filled. There is no room in Lacan's work for the environmental impingements that lead to developmental arrests that, in turn, cripple individual aspects of self development leading to specific dysfunctions. The "lack" of which Lacan writes is a pure ontological negative, a crack in human existence. Such an ontological lack should never be confused with the psychological deficit suffered by the traumatized individual. It is unnecessary to argue Lacan's point about human nature to see that some children are subject to physically, sexually, and/or emotionally abusive early environments from which they attempt to protect themselves by erecting rigid defenses. Such children suffer from gaps that are contingent on the abuse to which they were subjected. Traumatic events of this type cannot in any useful or meaningful way be equated with the human condition. Indeed, it would be a harsh dismissal of the suffering of abused and traumatized individuals to equate the absence in their lives with the essence of being human. To respond to the traumatized patient as though she is suffering from the human condition would deprive her of needed engagement with the specifics of her traumatic experience out of theoretical prejudice. The essentialism of Lacan's "lack" leaves little room for the patient's unique history, the specific experiences of her childhood. As a result, his thinking ignores the unrealized capacities of the self that are the product of environmental intrusion or neglect. Even if he is correct about an ontological lack in the human condition, that gap should never be confused with the psychological deficit produced from contingent early experiences.

Transcendence in the Therapeutic Relationship

The purpose of analytic understanding is to analyze, or break down, the historical patterns, so that they can be replaced with new, more productive ways of being. As we have seen, a decisive break from the past in psychoanalytic thought is the realization that understanding, no matter how thorough, is rarely sufficient for analytic change (e.g., Stern et al., 1998). If the interpretive process goes well, the patient becomes aware of her historical patterns and seeks to change them, but typically patients can conceive of no alternative and feel at a loss. As discussed in Chapter Four, if new ways of being are to be created, the burden falls on the analyst to detect possibilities not visible to the patient (Summers, 1999, 2005a, 2005b). That is to say, the analyst must be able to recognize indications of unrealized psychic potential. Because unrealized psychic capacity is not a disavowed self, nor even a "part" of the self, but a potentiality, a not-yet-been, the analytic task at this point is not to discover what is, but to detect the potential for what may be.

It is at this point that the analyst's transcendent experience of the patient is most essential. So, while the analyst will not find suitable alternatives to the patient's historical ways of being ready-at-hand, neither is she in the dark. Unrealized potential is discernible to the analytic therapist who is willing to adopt a stance that includes two fundamental components: (1) a shift in perspective to the facilitation of new ways of being at key points in the process; and (2) a search for transcendent possibilities in the patient's strivings and efforts to cope. The discovery that symptoms possess veiled meaning virtually inaugurated the field, but the fact that the patient's search for a future is embedded in current patterns has been buried under the attention given to the roots of pathological behavior in the past. While it is not the analyst's job to create those new parts of the self, it is his role to detect possibilities that may become new ways of being and relating. This strategy shifts the way the analyst sees and engages the patient. The analytic role at this point is to see not only who the patient is, but also who he may become. That is to say, it is incumbent on the analytic therapist to recognize and stimulate the patient's transcendental possibilities. The analyst now looks to see what in the patient has potential for transcending current patterns.

The recognition of transcendental possibilities is a more subtle process than interpretation of formed affects and patterns because truncated affective states and patterns of interaction can only be indicated by efforts distorted by environmental assault or defensive occlusion rather than demonstrated through behavior or formed experiences. Such potentialities are not entities whose roots can be understood as much as dispositions that need to be brought to form. They cannot be understood in the usual analytic sense because they are not formed psychic entities, but they can be detected and stimulated; their growth, nurtured.

For an example of how this process works, consider patients who possess seemingly intractable defenses against experiencing negative affect. The child learns to tolerate distress with the help of a caretaker who promotes positive affects and helps overcome painful states (Demos, 1992). The nature of the help depends on the developmental level of the child, so, for example, it can be nonverbal in the case of an infant or a verbal perspective for an older child. The mother brings a presence in the former case, and a different, more positive viewpoint in the second. In both cases, the caretaker is responsive to the child's state, and offers, in addition, an experience the child does not have on her own. The empathy of the caretaker gives the child a feeling of connection so he does not feel left alone with the pain. By introducing a presence or viewpoint something new is brought to the scene that reduces the dominance of the painful feeling. So, the child is not left alone, but the caretaker does not make the pain vanish. The mother, or caretaker, does not relieve the child's pain by herself; she helps provide relief by offering a presence and a perspective the child does not have.

The outcome depends on how the child uses the caretaker's help. In each instance in which the child's pain is relieved, she takes a step toward developing the ability to master negative affect. The interventions help the child learn that negative affects can be overcome and other perspectives brought to bear even in the midst of pain. As the child learns to provide new perspectives for herself to overcome distress, she gains the ability to manage psychic pain along with confidence in her ability to tolerate, relieve, and master negative affects, including injury and attack. The child does not simply internalize the mother's functions, but uses them to create ways to cope with disturbance (e.g., Demos, 1992). When the process works best, the child reacts to the mother by fashioning her own means of coping out of the mother's empathy, encouragement, and the new perspective she offers.

If, on the other hand, the caretaker does not provide this crucial psychological help, the child has little means for combating negative affects and tends to become overwhelmed by their appearance. The lack of caretaker response to pain and injury leaves the child alone to cope with painful mental states, and the child becomes easily overwhelmed in the face of disappointment and disturbance. Extreme measures are then required, such as withdrawal from contact with others, or, more commonly, the erection of a grandiose defense to drown the flood of painful affect in narcissistic gratification. Such vulnerability with only grandiosity as protection leaves minimal tolerance for withdrawal of attention and lack of responsiveness. Tolerance for negative affects and the capacity to cope with them does not develop.

Lacking the capability to cope with negative states, patients will erect powerful, sometimes intransigent, defenses in a desperate effort to avoid feeling them. And now we come to the crucial technical point. Because the patient is so well defended, if he is to gain the ability to master negative states, the analyst must see the potential for this development. Using grandiosity as an example, the analyst can see the patient's anxiety around vulnerability and the need to overcome psychic pain with a self-gratifying bath of grandiose beliefs about himself. The analyst's empathy for the patient's need to sustain his grandiosity brings the patient's struggles to cope with untoward experiences into the analytic space. But the therapist must do more than that. Once in the analytic space, the potential of the grandiosity can be utilized to therapeutic benefit. The positive affects embedded in the grandiose defense provide a potential counterbalance to the patient's negative states. It is incumbent on the analytic therapist to make use of this potential.

Grandiosity as an effort to cope with negative affects is not visible to the patient; it is a disavowed state in which a nascent psychic function is embedded. I make every effort to bring out this truncated and brittle psychic potentiality by helping the patient use positive affect for the purpose of counteracting painful affective states. I often say to a narcissistically vulnerable patient who is defending against a rejection, "You must feel that you cannot endure the pain of not being preferred, so you defend against that awareness and substitute all the good feelings you can muster as though to wash away the bad feelings before they get to you because you see no way to overcome them. At the moment of a bad feeling, you feel helpless against the pain, so you eject all negatives and let in only the most flattering feelings about yourself." The purpose of this type of interpretation is to highlight the patient's effort to use positive experiences to cope with vulnerability and to bring this intent into the analytic space. Grandiosity is an attempt to deny the existence of psychic pain, so by engaging the grandiose defense directly, I try to demonstrate its pitfalls while showing the patient I recognize his effort to use positive affect to overcome painful states. The goal is to recognize and appreciate the patient's ability to access positive experience and its potential to master negative affects. Enlisting positive feelings suggests that they can be effective in the effort to overcome psychic pain, and at the same time, I am conveying the belief that the way the patient is going about it will not achieve the desired result. That is to say, I am telling the patient that his distress can be counteracted with resources utilized in his current defensive structure but without defending against awareness of the negative states. The grandiosity has embedded within it positive self experience that can be deployed to counteract negative states which, therefore, need not be walled off. This view of the patient's grandiosity transcends its immediate function as a defense in order to grasp its potential for good feelings about the self to help regulate psychic pain.

In this situation I note to the patient that he has indeed attempted to obliterate painful feelings, but to no avail; they persist despite his grandiose defense. However, I make a point of emphasizing both the consequences of his method and the effort to bring in positive affect to counteract the fear negative feelings will inundate the psyche. The analytic strategy is to sustain the openness of the space so that the patient may come to grips with alternatives that embrace the variety of his life experiences. The way this is done is unique to each individual, but the commonality is the use of latent dispositions, in this case the deployment of positive affects, to articulate a new *modus operandi.* The same overarching strategy is applicable to a variety of clinical problems, such as narcissistic vulnerability, self-hatred, or fear of intimacy. In each case, the potential of occluded psychic capabilities is called upon to initiate the creation of new ways of being. And for this to happen, the analyst has to be able to detect possibilities that transcend the patient's lived patterns. This analytic attitude has the unique ability to embrace the transcendental possibilities of all the patient does.

Such a therapeutic posture establishes the analytic space in which it becomes possible for the patient to create a means for acknowledging injury without collapsing in despair. At this point the distinction can be made between the patient's desire to use positive experience to balance negative feeling and grandiosity as an effort to obliterate psychic distress. This welcoming of the patient's use of positive affect facilitates its potential to overcome painful states. It is in this analytic space that the patient may experiment with ways to bring forth positive events, memories, and affects in order to develop means for overcoming psychic pain. The purpose is to open a space in which psychic pain can be articulated and positive feelings brought out and efforts made to utilize them as ways of coping. The analyst's role is to stimulate the patient's positive feelings as a potential means for mastering pain so the patient can find ways to overcome her helplessness. In seeing and utilizing the potential of the positive affects embedded in grandiosity, the analytic therapist is seeing the transcendental possibilities of the grandiosity. The process is an experimental type of play with a myriad of possible outcomes, but once the patient has found ways to counteract and cope with negative feelings, he can begin to relinquish the grandiosity that has now outlived its usefulness.

So, for the vulnerable patient, the defenses used, such as grandiosity or hypomania, indicate the truncated efforts to overcome pain and trauma. By emphasizing the purpose of the defense, the potential of the positive affect and the means to bring it forth come into the analytic space. The analyst highlights the patient's efforts to extinguish the pain that threatens to become overwhelming. Such a patient needs the analyst to aid in the regulation of negative states by encouraging alternative viewpoints and contexts for the patient's distress, but to provide the content would rob the patient of the opportunity to develop his own way of managing negative experience and the skills needed to combat stressful situations. The purpose of analytic ministration is to facilitate the patient's creation of a new psychological ability.

The transcendental approach bears some similarity to, but must be differentiated from, the approach of self psychology which aims to strengthen the patient's self through analytic understanding to increase tolerance for the inevitable disappointments and failures of the interpersonal world (Kohut, 1971). According to this viewpoint, empathy for the patient's pain and understanding the injury provide a calming effect that allows the patient to struggle with distressing experience in a new, more benign context. The patient ultimately internalizes the analytic soothing to form new psychic structures that provide what had been missing (Kohut, 1984). While the emphasis on analytic empathy bears an important similarity to the approach advocated here, there are decisive differences. The self psychological strategy is not sufficiently consonant with developmental observations and research on the acquisition of the capacity to master negative affects (e.g., Tomkins, 1991; Demos, 1992). As we have seen, the child is helped most by a caretaker who facilitates mastery of painful experience by her availability, attentiveness to the child's distress, and aid to the development of the child's coping strategies. The child does not "internalize" the parent as much as utilize parental input for the creation of coping strategies.

The patient who is easily overwhelmed by negative affects needs succor from an analyst analogous to the assistance that should have been provided by the caretaker. In the clinical arena, the empathic connection, while necessary, is rarely sufficient for the creation of new ways of being. The analytic relationship opens the space so the patient can access experience other than the immediate distress. There is a decisive clinical difference between "internalizing" the analyst's function and using the analytic space to create one's own means of mastering psychic pain. The self psychological strategy, while seeing the power of empathy, emphasizes what the patient takes in from the analyst. The therapeutic action, from this perspective, comes from the therapist's empathic attunement to the patient which is internalized by the patient. By casting the patient in this passive position, self psychological theory is not oriented to helping the patient create something new from historical patterns, which is to say it does not have, as yet, a concept of transcendental empathy.

While a successful strategy for the patient will typically include accessing positive feelings and putting injury into a broader context, this process is not equivalent to the Kleinian concept of integrating good and bad part objects into the same object (e.g., Klein, 1957; Segal, 1982). For the Kleinians, the purpose is to bring the positive and negative together in one object. Such an integration is not tantamount to creating the ability to withstand and sustain the self in light of negative experiences, for which purpose access to positive experiences is required. In contrast to the Kleinian approach, the strategy advocated here is the provision of an analytic space in which the patient, with the aid of the analyst, develops his own coping skills for handling negative experiences. While gaining access to positive feelings is one aid to tolerating psychic pain, the ability to sustain narcissistic injury will be solidified if the patient finds a means for experiencing painful psychic states and gaining mastery over their influence. The patient is most likely able to create these new ways of being if the analyst sees the potential in the psychic wounds and the defenses used to keep them from awareness, that is, if the therapist sees the transcendental possibilities in what the patient is doing. The result is transferable to other situations because the patient can utilize the newly created skill to confront other difficult experiences and events. As the patient uses the analytic space in this way, she is bringing to fruition her previously arrested psychic capacity for deploying positive affect to master pain and negative affects. At that point it becomes possible for the grandiosity to be relinquished.

Clinical Illustration

Some patients with similar conflicts over negative experience sustain their relationships by compliance. In these cases, the anxiety is about losing the other in response to self assertion or any aggressive expression. They differ from the grandiose patient in that they are not made anxious by any negative affect or vulnerability, but are primarily threatened by aggression which they associate with loss of the other. For example, Sarah, a chronically compliant 26-year-old woman, had avoided anxiety over conflict and aggression all her life, but when we analyzed her anxiety, she saw that her self assertion was suppressed out of fear that any expression of aggressivity would threaten relational ties. She had unconsciously traded off the ability to control her life and influence its events for the safety of conflict avoidance and conflict-free relationships. Sarah came for help due to a fundamental lack of satisfaction in her life, although she saw no relationship between her unhappiness and her strongly ingrained pattern of "pathological accommodation" (Brandchaft, 2007). The dissatisfaction was experienced symptomatically as the frustration of trying to please all the figures in her life, the consequent anxiety that she could not do so, and the loss of control over the course of her life. In the analysis, it emerged that she had been a strong-willed young child asserting herself against her parents' strictures, but had lost access to the assertiveness of her early years after her willfulness evoked her mother's catastrophic fear her daughter would have no friends. In response, the little girl accommodated to the wishes of others and buried, she thought forever, her feistiness.

As Sarah saw the roots of her compliance, she became increasingly conscious of the fact that her lifelong accommodation to the desires of others gave her little control over her life and was the source of much of her dissatisfaction. Bringing her unarticulated dissatisfaction into the analytic space made possible the transformation of her inchoate distress. It would not be quite accurate to say that she had been defending against anger because she had not formulated her dissatisfied state into anger. Her vague feelings of dissatisfaction and frustration had not yet *become* a way of being angry in the world. Nonetheless, her dissatisfaction and nascent feeling of aggressivity motivated Sarah to attempt to pursue her own desires, but she found herself unable to overcome her need to please others. Her frustration was building at her own inability to, as she put it, "get off the dime." When I asked her about that expression, her frustration intensified both at me and herself for her paralysis. I noted that her disturbance seemed to be an unarticulated, vaguely negative mood, difficult to define. In this phase of the analysis, her inhibited life and the lack of ability to follow her interests appeared in her reaction to the slow pace and tortuous path of the analytic process as she languished in a formless, inchoate morass of indecision and conflict. I saw this state as the symptomatic expression of her long-buried efforts at self expression. That is to say, I viewed the very frustration which caused her so much pain as an indication of her unfulfilled longing to push ahead with her desires, a transcendental possibility buried within the dissatisfaction simmering beneath her compliance. I illuminated Sarah's frustration in an effort to stimulate the arrested potential for aggressive expression she once practiced as a child, but had never brought to fruition as an adult.

Sarah's compliance bore within it the value she placed on sensitivity to the needs and interests of others, and it was this ethic that she believed was in direct conflict with aggressive expression. Making conscious this conflict and seeing how little control she possessed over her own life fortified Sarah's growing desire to assert herself, even if it meant being aggressive, but she feared the effects on others. If insensitivity to, or even denigration of, others was the only alternative, she saw no better path than the one on which she had been traveling. Her mother's anxiety over her spirited independence of early childhood had left Sarah with a simplistic equation of assertiveness and loss, on the one hand, and compliance and connection, on the other. She saw either *subservience*, which became unacceptable after it became conscious and its origins manifest, or *selfishness* to which she was ethically opposed. For Sarah, it was a case of the concrete "do it my way" or "I do it yours." Frustrated in her futile efforts to overcome helplessness with selfishness, Sarah believed her only options were to comply with others' demands or demand that others bend to her will. Finding both avenues unacceptable and seeing no alternative, Sarah felt trapped.

It is at this critical juncture that the therapist's ability to perceive transcendental possibilities in the patient's binary becomes pivotal. In her refusal to express the hostility that had now become a part of her fantasy life, Sarah was holding steadfastly to a value of according others respect that would need to be a part of any therapeutic outcome. In her unwillingness to continue her lifelong pattern of accommodation, Sarah was asserting her growing conviction that she had a right to self expression. In this phase her affective expressions were construed as reflecting a desire to pursue her interests, affects, and beliefs as she saw fit, that is, to use her experience to guide her in the interpersonal world. Although excited by the idea that she was unconsciously expressing her desire for a life of self expression, Sarah no sooner felt buoyed by that thought than she feared becoming self-absorbed and insensitive to others. I noted that this concern reflected the deeply held ethic of according respect to others, and that the existence of this value was a transcendental possibility embedded in her excessive compliance.

The intensity of Sarah's anger and dissatisfaction, now that it was expressed, indicated that her new anticompliant position was the product of an arrested longing to lead a life based on her affects and interests. Nascent desires for self expression and the assertion of her will had been disavowed, set off into a dissociated state while still unformed. That is to say, Sarah possessed an aborted desire to live according to her experience that had been buried by her anxiety, but was now beginning to emerge in her anger and dissatisfaction. This truncated need for self expression, arrested in a fledgling state in childhood, remained a transcendental possibility for a different way of living. The dissatisfaction with which she had entered the analysis was a symptom of her newly emerging desire to live in accordance with her experience, rather than continuing to be "lost in the desire of the other" (Lacan, 1970). In highlighting Sarah's newly overt opposition to compliance, I interpreted her aggressive strivings as a movement forward, a step toward the ability to pursue her desires and interests. Her frustration with her life was not only the result of her mother-induced anxiety over object loss but also a product of the future she feared was being denied her.

By expressing her anger and frustration, Sarah was indicating a belief in her right to pursue her own desires, a transcendental possibility previously shrouded in her dissatisfaction with pathological accommodation. Analogously, her aversion to self-absorption indicated that she did not wish to assert herself by demanding all for herself, an attitude she found abhorrent. I saw this antipathy not as a defense against entitlement, which under another circumstance might be the case, but as a value of respect for others that she hoped would guide her future, that is to say, a transcendental possibility embedded in her pattern of compliance. Her lifelong accommodation was now found to be distasteful because it buried her pursuits under an avalanche of self-devaluation resulting in a loss of control over her life. I emphasized to Sarah that she did not know how to assert her wishes, desires, interests, and passions because she did not know how to transform them in a way that was consonant with her value of respecting the rights and interests of others. I went on to say that she was drawn to accommodation because it expressed a strong appreciation for others' interests and desires, and she was attracted to selfishness because it permitted the pursuit of her own. But, each by itself was an enactment of a devaluing attitude, the first toward the self, and the second, toward others.

I indicated to Sarah that by refusing to adopt a position of denigrating others, she was telling us both the great importance she placed on maintaining her ethic of respect for others. In this way, I was bringing to light the transcendent value embedded in her excessive compliance. I interpreted to her that the accommodation that caused her so much confusion and dissatisfaction contained a value central to her very identity: respect for others. That value, I went on to say, was enacted in her current life, but the other preeminent value, the desire to lead her life according to her experience, had been in little evidence. She longed to live according to the ethic of both attitudes, to respect others while pursuing her own desires, but felt the two attitudes were incompatible. The former was well practiced and honed, but she had little experience with the latter.

When I encouraged her to tell me about the emerging desire to live her own life, we embarked upon a discussion of her struggle to sustain aggressivity within a relationship and her anxiety about pursuing her desires in the face of opposition. This moment is an illustration of what we have previously described as the transformation of the analytic space into potential space, an open relational space between patient and therapist that provides an opportunity for the patient to find a way of being that transcends the binary in which her life has been ensnared. From the present perspective, we may add that this is a point of transcendent empathy, a pivotal analytic moment in which the patient's potential buried within her historical object relational patterns becomes visible in the analytic space. Rather than adopt Sarah's binary assumption that her life was impaled on two unworthy attitudes, I drew out the transcendent possibilities of each. I indicated that her otherwise pathological lifetime of accommodation reflected a deep respect for the needs and rights of others, and her fantasies of hostility and denigration of others, although abhorrent, showed a need for self expression and control over her own life. Each of these coveted ways of being was distorted and buried in a pathological attitude because she had internalized a strict binary rooted in the anxiety of childhood. In the analytic space, by bringing out both positions, we were able to see the possibilities in each side of the antinomy.

The momentum of the analytic process was diminishing Sarah's need to comply, but the dropping of this default position did not immediately translate into an easy replacement because Sarah's fantasies of aggressive expression were unacceptable explosions of rage and devaluation of others. For example, she thought of screaming at her mother with a string of insults for robbing her of the ability to assert herself, but the tone and invective were distasteful to her. Although she felt caught between her ethic and her rage, I encouraged Sarah to articulate in the analytic space both the affect and the principle with which she believed it conflicted. In her most hostile moments, she unleashed caustic attacks on the analysis and me as the practitioner of such a lengthy and uncertain treatment. But, this devaluation of which she was not proud invoked a struggle for how to express dissatisfaction and anger. The analytic structure then became the play space for Sarah to experiment with various ways of articulating her anger, each with a different level of intensity. Sarah expressed her frustration, dissatisfaction, and anger at me in a variety of ways, from spontaneous explosions of rage to mild annoyance and piquishness. I noted that the rage was not only about the analysis, but also a product of her mounting frustration with a lifetime of inhibition and embedded in it was her truncated desire to pursue her interests and passions without fear of doing injury to others. It was then that Sarah began to consider expressions of anger and dissatisfaction that were direct communications of her negative states without any of the judgment she found so disrespectful. She determined that she could convey her negative states, even her strong feelings of anger, without devaluing her mother, me, or any other figure. She expressed her frustration with the analytic pace without casting aspersion on my character. In this way, Sarah created a new way of being based on the transcendental possibilities of each side of what she had considered an entrapping binary.

While analytic authors have occasionally recognized inhibitions and related phenomena as inabilities rather than only anxiety-driven conflicts (e.g., Gedo, 1981), seeing such inhibitions and dysfunction as containing the potential for the creation of those very abilities has not been a recognized component of analytic strategy. Sarah's analytic process demonstrates the importance of seeing what in the patient's experience contains the potential for new, productive ways of being. It has been recognized for some time that understanding is rarely sufficient for analytic change, and therefore many have averred that a new relationship is the crux of therapeutic action, but one must define what that relationship *is*. The concepts of empathic immersion, enactment, intersubjective awareness, provision of psychic functions, and similar concepts all involve immanent and analytic empathy, but lack transcendent empathy. Without empathy for who the patient is *not* and *might become*, the analytic therapist has difficulty seeing a way out of the patient's binary and often becomes trapped within it. The new relationship of which many now speak is maximally effective when it contains transcendental possibilities. Analysts tend to shy away from remarking on the patient's potential and future possibilities out of fear of influencing the patient and becoming fortune tellers. But, that position, understandable though it is, misses the other side of the issue: Without a sense of the patient's potential, the therapist is greatly limited in his ability to facilitate the patient's creation of new ways of being (Loewald, 1960). A focus on the transcendental possibilities of the patient's binary encasement evokes a new relationship that points toward a different future.

Conclusion

We can observe from these clinical examples that the empathy for the other so emphasized in psychoanalytic clinical discourse is a more complex matter than is commonly recognized even taking into consideration the subtlety of unconscious affects and thoughts. At one level this complexity is due to the human condition, which in its essence is about continual becoming, a process we have called "ek-stasis" following Heidegger. That alone would make understanding the other a difficult, nuanced, and complicated matter. But, clinicians experience an even greater degree of intricacy because they are confronted with the reality of having to detect potential ways of being in unformed psychic dispositions. And this recognition of who the patient may be requires an inference beyond understanding who the patient now is, that is to say, a transcendental experience of the other. But, nothing less is required of the analyst because who the patient may become is an essential component of who the patient is and how the analysis may evolve. So, the analytic process, in its most fundamental sense, is about the transcendental experience of the other.

With this recognition, psychoanalysis has reached a new phase in its historical evolution from Freud's original positivist leanings to a view of analysis as a very human process of engaging the experiencing subject and recognizing the transcendental possibilities of human subjectivity. The transcendental consists of the pregnant possibilities of the psyche, what it may become. With this move, we have made the turn from a static concept of the person to a view of human being as continually becoming. And that pivotal turn places the future at the center of analytic theory and therapy. In this way, the third temporal modality has become an essential component of the analytic process. And it is to this critical dimension we now turn.

8

TEMPORALITY AND FUTURITY IN THE PSYCHOANALYTIC PROCESS

In the last chapter we saw that understanding the patient is not exhausted by a grasp of the patient's current ways of being and how she came to develop them. The patient's experience includes her potential, the goals she is striving to meet, and the possibilities for new ways of being and relating. This experience of the other as transcendental possibility means that an appreciation of the patient's relationship to the future is central to understanding who he is. Because the life trajectory and anticipation of goals define the meaning of past and present, the future is not an "add on," but a dimension central to the understanding of the patient's present life. This inclusion of the patient's experience of her future, or what might be called futurity, in the analytic understanding of the patient has profound implications for clinical strategy. In this chapter we will explore and draw out the implications of including futurity in understanding the analysand in order to delineate the way inclusion of all three temporal modalities informs and transforms the analytic interaction and ultimately its therapeutic action.

Temporality in Psychoanalytic History

Because psychoanalysis originated with Freud's discovery that symptoms can be traced back to repressed memories, and later fantasies, psychoanalytic inquiry in its early years was focused primarily on uncovering the past and its influences on the current symptom picture (e.g., Breuer and Freud, 1895; Freud, 1906, 1917, 1924). Although Freud's use of time was complex and varied, his focus throughout was on how past and present influence each other (Green, 2008). This emphasis on discovering the meaning of symptoms in childhood experiences has remained central to clinical strategy among analysts from theoretical schools as diverse as early drive theory, ego psychology, the Kleinian school, Winnicott's object relations theory, and self psychology (e.g., Ferenczi, 1931; Rapaport, 1960; Racker, 1960; Winnicott, 1960, 1962; Kohut, 1971; Basch, 1977, 1985; Kohut & Wolf, 1978). Historically, the trend in this thinking was to assume a linear concept of time in the relationship of early development to adulthood. Freud's case studies primarily treated the patient's narrative as a series of childhood events occurring in linear succession. In the Wolf Man, for example, Freud (1917) reconstructs the "Grushna scene" as taking place before the sexual molestation which is succeeded by witnessing the primal scene. From an ego psychological perspective, development is viewed almost exclusively as a series of successive stages (e.g., A. Freud, 1936; Rapaport, 1960; Busch, 2005; Blum, 2010). Despite her theoretical claim that the paranoid and depressive positions oscillate in development, Klein (1937, 1940, 1945, 1957) treated pathological events in linear fashion, as did many of her followers (e.g., Bion, 1957; Rosenfeld, 1987; Segal, 1983). Kohut's (1971) developmental theory, despite its radical difference from classical thinking, also assumed that formative childhood experiences, such as the relinquishment of grandiosity and idealization, took place in linear succession. This concept of time is spatialized, the measurable time of clock and watches.

As the transference became the focus of therapeutic action, the here-and-now relationship between patient and analyst became increasingly emphasized by a good number of analysts from the same range of theoretical paradigms (e.g., Busch, 1995; Gray, 1973, 1990; Sugarman, 1995; Bacal & Newman, 1990; Bacal, 1985; Kohut, 1984; Winnicott, 1971; Bollas, 1987; Joseph, 1985, 1992; Rosenfeld, 1987; Aron, 1996; Mitchell, 1988). The Boston Process Group has placed central importance on "now moments" in therapeutic action (Stern et al., 1998; Stern, 2004), and Gill's (1981, 1994) model of analysis as focused exclusively on the current transference interaction rendered the reconstruction of the past virtually irrelevant to the analytic process. This emphasis on working through the analytic relationship in the here-and-now transference–countertransference interaction shifted the analytic emphasis on temporality from the past to the present. At this moment in analytic history, for some, the present is as important as the past, and for others, it is the very heart of therapeutic action displacing the role once accorded the patient's childhood experiences.

Nonetheless, no matter how much emphasis is placed on the here-and-now, it is highly problematic to disregard the patient's history given that an essential component of being human is our historical nature. Because human lives are organized temporally, unpacking the meaning of the current patient-analyst relational patterns includes finding the traces, and in some cases even the imprints, of the patient's past in the current transference perceptions. Even for Sullivan (1953) who viewed psychopathology as problems in interpersonal relationships and analysis as the offering of a new way of relating, the patient's problematic patterns were to be found in the residue of childhood relationships. Tellingly, Thompson (1964), who extended Sullivanian thought by replacing the past with character, believed the patient's irrational beliefs must be traced to his childhood origins.

Heir to the Sullivanian tradition, the current relational movement views the analytic process as an exploration and expansion of the present relationship between patient and analyst, but it nonetheless uses the patient's history as a guide to understanding (e.g., Mitchell, 1997). Aron (1996) who sees analysis as a "meeting of minds" uses a developmental model to explain the evolution of the child's sense of self as both subject and object (p.72–4). These contemporary views eschew the developmental reductionism sometimes characteristic of older theories while according a significant role to the influence of the patient's past on her current patterns. The difference is that in contemporary relational thinking, as in other forms of today's analytic theory, the relationship between past and present is more fluid, contingent, and subtle than the reductionistic views that equate present patterns with past experience. We can unequivocally reject a veridical relationship between past and present, but we can never be disconnected from our past experiences and their legacy. As Ogden (1990) has noted, subjectivity begins with the birth of the historical subject.

Time and Temporality

From a philosophical viewpoint, Husserl (1905) emphasized long ago that the experience of duration is very different from the spatialized , measurable time of clocks. To clarify our nomenclature, let us call "time" the objectivized, measurable series of events, and "temporality," the experience of duration. Husserl showed that all experience is retentive, meaning that some elements of the past are included in the way experience manifests itself in the present. Unlike natural objects, we bear a relationship to our history; it is both unique and fundamental to the human experience to see oneself historically, and, beyond that, to relate to one's past as meaningful (e.g., Bergson, 1910/2010; Husserl, 1905; Heidegger, 1927/1961; Schutz, 1932/1974; Ricouer, 1984). It is not simply a case of the ability to recall past events, but of giving meaning to the past and experiencing that history as a significant component of one's identity. That is why virtually all psychoanalytic clinical theories, even those with strong theoretical allegiance to a here-and-now approach, find a place for the patient's history in the clinical process.

To these considerations we must add that to be a temporal being is to experience temporality in both directions. As Husserl (1905) brought to light in his phenomenological investigations, all acts of meaning include not only retention, but also protention, anticipatory possibilities. To know the meaning of any psychic act, whether it be a judgment, perception, dream, fantasy, or any other, is to see its possibilities, what it might be and may not be. Every psychic act, Husserl noted, points toward a future of possibilities and limitations. Heidegger (1962/1927) expanded on Husserl's phenomenological investigations by showing that because we are temporal beings, our psychic meanings are never static, but "ek-static," movements forward. The "ek-stases" of time are the temporal dimensions that constitute a "horizon" of possibilities for all experiences. For Heidegger, these "ek-stases" of time are fundamental to the human experience, that is to say, they inhere in every psychic moment.

Consequently, for Heidegger the temporal is not simply a fact of life, but the defining ontological structure of human being. That is, the "ek-states" constitute the way we relate to the world. The very nature of human being is our temporality, our "throwness" toward the future in which we encounter present and past. So, to neglect our futurity is to miss the very essence of human experience. In our temporality, we find the horizon of our possibilities, and our possibilities define who we are. Authenticity, for Heidegger, consists of our "ownmost possibilities," so authentic human existence comes to fruition within the horizon of possibilities that unfold in the futurity of our existence.

The upshot is that for Heidegger (1962/1927), building on Husserl, the temporal is first a trajectory toward the future, and it is in this anticipation, this movement forward, that one experiences the present and runs into the past. Without a concept of futurity, past and present cannot be understood. The present moment is grasped fully when its role in the anticipated future is seen. Any act gains its meaning from the protention into which it fits. The movement toward the future cannot be reduced to a repetition of the past because the life trajectory always contains something more than a replica of what has occurred. The future is not an epiphenomenon of the past, but an autonomous temporal modality that must be taken on its own terms, and, in fact, is conceptually prior to the past and present. These considerations implore an exploration of the psychoanalytic concept of temporality and the role of futurity within it.

The conceptual priority of futurity has been clarified and its relevance to the human sciences shown most clearly in the work of Alfred Schutz. Building on the philosophical work of Bergson (1910/2010) and Husserl, Schutz (1932/1974) demonstrated that life is lived in the future perfect tense, and consequently, the meaning of life events has the character of "will have been done." The meaning of any action lies in what is portended, conceived as completed in the future. No experience in the present can have any meaning without its intentionality, the aim toward which it is directed. The present moment derives its meaning from how it fits into the plan of action, however simplistic and implicit it may be. The past becomes relevant insofar as it is encountered in the trajectory toward the future. The future, then, is ontologically prior to both present and past.

Even the simplest activity cannot be grasped without reference to its project. For example, the meaning of a person walking depends on its purpose, what the projected outcome of the walk is anticipated to be. Walking for exercise, to buy groceries, to meet a friend, or to be on time for a business meeting have completely different meanings because their purposes differ. In each instance the activity is walking, but the meaning of the behavior is different in each case because meaning is a function of intention. One can see then even from this simple example that the meaning of the present is dependent on how it fits into the future perfect, not vice versa. Therefore, it is illusory to think that the present can be understood outside of its projected movement toward the future. To grasp the meaning of the present includes seeing the intention within which it fits, and, that purpose, in turn, can be understood only if one sees the history within which it is embedded. To return to the example, for any individual to know the meaning and motivation for walking one needs to know the goal the walking is expected to achieve and the past experiences that led to the belief that the end result is worthwhile. It is clear then that any effort to dislodge the present from past and future is tantamount to robbing the experience of its meaning.

But, as Ricouer (1984) has shown, meaning does not consist of a series of disconnected acts and sentences. Building on Husserl's phenomenological explications, Ricouer (1984) has shown that the meaning of individual acts is a function of how they fit into the life narrative. Meaning and narrative, Ricouer convincingly argues, are inextricably intertwined. Ricouer (1984) adds to Husserl's phenomenological findings the insight that meaning takes place in a life narrative, and narrative consists of temporal organization. To look at a life without narrative construction is to extinguish its meaning. The conclusion we may draw from this philosophical analysis of temporal experience is that a life narrative consists of the future perfect within which the present gains its meaning, and the past is viewed. Seeing the patient from the perspective of temporality, rather than time, makes the future perfect, the present moment, and past experience all interrelated in analytic understanding.

In the psychoanalytic world Schafer (1992) among others has underscored the fact that lives are lived as narratives, and the meaning we give to an individual act involves its narrative context. However, narrative as used in psychoanalytic theory, irrespective of epistemological position, has historically been focused on past and present. Schafer's work is a representative example of viewing narrative as past and present only. But, as we have seen, to know the other includes a sense of the other's relationship to the future, what possibilities and goals are envisioned and even abandoned. Essential to the sense of one's life narrative is the trajectory of what is expected and not expected, wished for and relinquished, in short, the sense of futurity.

There is a second, more current, and fast-growing trend in the psychoanalytic theory of temporality, perhaps less recognized but potentially powerful, that does greater justice to the experience of temporality. This concept of the temporal views temporal modalities as interpenetrating and cycling among themselves, rather than organized in a linear fashion. In his earliest formulation of psychoneurosis, Freud made clear that early sexual assaults were not in themselves traumatic (Breuer & Freud, 1895). What acts traumatically, for Freud, are not the disturbing events themselves but "their revival as a *memory* after their subject has entered on sexual maturity" (p.164). Freud (1896) stated explicitly that childhood sexual experiences have their major pathological effect not at the time of their occurrence, but at a later phase of development after sexual maturity has been achieved. As Modell (1990) has emphasized, Freud's concept of *Nachtraglecheit* was a recognition that temporal experience is an interplay between past and present, rather than a linear arrow from past to present to future. Any event may gain its meaning at a time other than the moment of its occurrence, and Freud (1896) believed traumatic events inevitably do so.

Laplanche (1985/1970) has added to Freud's concept, commonly translated as "deferred action," by noting that the original event, prior to the traumatization, is neither repressed nor conscious, but remains in what Freud called a "separate psychical grouping." In this limbo state, it is not linked to the rest of the psyche. It is only after sexual maturity that the sexual molestation becomes a trauma and is repressed. For our purpose, the important point Laplanche makes is that the meaning of the trauma does not take place in linear time; the future gives meaning to the past event.

Modell (1990) notes that Freud recognized that the past is recategorized in the context of present circumstances and the current developmental phase, just as the present is influenced by the past. Further, one memory is insufficient so the traumatic event must be continually reworked in a cyclical manner. Modell's understanding of Freud betokens the fact that despite Freud's tendency to write his case studies in linear fashion, the founder of psychoanalysis conceptualized temporal modalities as mutually influencing each other so that events and their meaning do not necessarily exist at the same point in linear time.

Modell has made an important contribution to the psychoanalytic view of temporality by showing that temporal experience is a cyclical process of interpenetration between present and past. However, the third temporal modality, the future, is strikingly absent from Modell's characterization of lived duration. While he quotes Augustine and Elliot on the mutual influences of all three temporal modalities, Modell sees the transference as an interplay between present and past only. As we have seen, the present achieves meaning only within the context of the future perfect, so this omission leaves a critical lacuna in the psychoanalytic concept of temporality and the way transference is conceived. The same may be said for the conception of the temporal advanced by Freud and Laplanche. The willingness to see temporal modalities as interacting puts this psychoanalytic view of temporality closer to the philosophers' interpretation of lived temporal experience.

Loewald (1962b) not only introduced the future as an important theoretical concept, but also recognized the centrality of the patient's experience of the future in the analytic process. In his first contribution to the problem, Loewald (1962) identified each temporal modality with a psychic structure: The id is the realm of the past, the ego, the present, and the superego brings the concept of the future into analytic thinking. In a subsequent paper, Loewald (1972) goes further by distinguishing between objective time as a linear succession of events and the experience of temporality characterized by a relationship of reciprocity between three active modes of psychic life. The three temporal modalities, for Loewald, are not successive, but interactive, determining and shaping each other. In the transference, the present is influenced not only by the past, but also by "the wished for or feared future" (p.144). More precisely, we may say that Loewald recognized that the present is affected by the future perfect. And this sense of futurity both "wished for and feared" is typically not conscious. So, Loewald's work leads to a concept of the *unconscious future*. The present is influenced by the unconscious future, and "the present relationship and the expectation it engenders activate the past and influence how it is now experienced and remembered" (p.144). In this way, Loewald's work, although chronologically earlier, went beyond Modell to include the future perfect in the unconscious and conscious interplay of temporal experience.

Freud's concept of *Nachtraglicheit*, its elaboration by Laplanche, and Modell's cyclical notion of durational modalities, make this second psychoanalytic understanding of temporality consonant with the philosophical analysis of temporal experience. Freud, Laplanche, and Modell develop a fluid, cyclical view of the temporal that fits the human temporal experience, but they are limited to past and present. Loewald adds futurity, but does not draw out the clinical implications of this expanded view of temporality. The purpose here is to fill this lacuna by including the patient's experience of the future in both the analytic process and the concept of therapeutic action. By according futurity the role it plays in the patient's experience, the implications for therapeutic action of Loewald's concept of the temporal as mutual influence of past, present, and future can be brought to fruition.

Linda, Woman Interrupted

To illustrate the use of temporality, we may consider the analysis of Linda, a case chosen for its very typicality. Linda came for analysis because she was depressed and had the feeling that something was wrong with her life, although she could not see what it was. Married with two teenage children, her husband had supported the family in an affluent lifestyle. In recent years Linda had returned to school to receive an MBA and was now becoming successful in the business world. Nonetheless, she found herself in an increasingly dysphoric state for reasons that were mysterious to her because she had not suffered any recent traumata or losses. She did know that she had been sexually molested continually between the ages of 9 and 12 by her grandfather, but that was not a recent realization. Her mother had died two years before Linda entered analysis, and she guessed that the death must have deeply affected her because immediately after the burial she had a brief, two-week affair. Her relationship with her husband, she felt, was missing both sexual and emotional intimacy, but it provided her with companionship, and she felt their life together was "good enough" despite its drawbacks.

Her father being a successful businessman, Linda described her childhood as a materially comfortable, suburban, upper-middle-class upbringing. She did note that her parents chose to give the burden of child care to servants, and when they were not available, to Linda herself as the oldest child. Her affluent parents, busy with their professions and many hobbies, were distant and paid little attention to Linda or her three younger sisters. Linda showed little indication of any affective reaction to the parental neglect, although she did characterize her childhood as frequently lonely. With regard to the sexual abuse, Linda was surprised and embarrassed by the gratification she received from it. Ashamed of her willingness to respond to her grandfather's advances, she felt she was to blame for their sexual relationship. Under the sway of unbearable guilt as a child, she had mustered the courage to tell her mother who responded, "Now, now, dear, we mustn't tell tales." The abuse continued for years thereafter.

Linda's parents put such stringent requirements on her activities that a social life was virtually impossible. From an early age, she was expected to be responsible for her younger siblings when household help was not available. On one family vacation in Europe, the parents decided to travel to another country and left Linda, at age 9, in charge of her sisters. A neighbor became aware of the situation and took in the children. When the parents returned, they were enraged that Linda had put herself and her sisters in the care of other people. In her recounting of being left in charge of her siblings in a foreign country at age 9, Linda showed little emotion and no animosity toward her parents. She seemed only vaguely aware that there was something fundamentally wrong with her parents' behavior.

Despite being largely isolated from her peers, as an adolescent Linda became sexually active early, and when her father discovered her sexual behavior, he flew into a rage, slapped her, accusing her of being a slut. Nonetheless, she regarded sex as the most satisfying part of her pre-adult life and continued to be sexually intimate. Although she never overtly protested, Linda continued to sneak out to meet boys, and her parents not infrequently discovered her stealth. Conflict with her parents over her romantic life continued throughout her adolescence.

Although Linda was an outstanding student, her parents had no intention of sending her to college, but, for the first time in her life, she opposed them openly and insisted on being given the opportunity. They finally relented, but only on condition that she go overseas. They sent her to a foreign country by herself with no arrangements for what she would do when she got there. She knew no one and arriving with only a suitcase in hand, she had to find her own living quarters and learn the customs of an alien culture. Linda related all these events with no discernible affect. When asked, she acknowledged being puzzled by their behavior and the pain it caused her, but expressed little animosity toward them. There was no outrage at her parents for sending her to another country without any preparation or the means to care for herself.

Most alarming of all, Linda expressed no anger at her mother's failure to take her confession of sexual abuse seriously and allowing it to go on. Linda certainly knew all of this parental malfeasance was wrong, but this knowledge seemed to have little emotional impact on her.

Despite Linda's history of abuse and neglect, the early issues that surfaced in the analysis were not the revisiting of her childhood as much as her deepening frustration with the emptiness of her marital relationship. While Linda had always been aware of the lack of emotional gratification in her marriage, she said that she now found her frustration with George mounting, although she showed no such affect in her voice or tone. After recounting her years of attempting to foster an emotional interchange between them, she said that she thought she had accepted the limited nature of the relationship, but she was now finding it increasingly difficult to tolerate. Nonetheless, as with other neglectful and abusive events in her life, Linda did not express any overt distress about the situation even as she described her frustration. She seemed to not even consider doing anything about the stalemated marriage.

When we addressed the question of why she had chosen George to be her marital partner, Linda drew a picture of a pseudo-dependent bond. She felt helpless with most practical life tasks. If she wanted directions, needed gas, had to file an insurance claim, or perform any similar action, she counted on George to do it for her. Linda had never used an ATM machine or been inside a bank as a customer. George took all her paychecks and put them in various accounts, some of which she had no access to, and controlled the finances. Despite her increasingly frequent sexual contacts with other men, Linda had never given any thought to leaving her husband and assumed she needed him. As with her parents, she was aware of the emptiness of the relationship, but appeared to have little affective reaction to it despite its clearly dissatisfying nature and seemed to be resigned to a relationship characterized by distance and little gratification.

But, Linda now expressed a deeper feeling and raised a further question. She felt depressed and wanted to know why at this point in her life the emptiness of the relationship resulted in a deflated mood. She had lived with her husband for more than 20 years with a mixture of satisfaction and frustration, but she had never been this depressed. Furthermore, she had recently made great improvements in her life by obtaining an MBA and becoming successful in the business world. From the perspective of functioning, her life had never been better. It took only a quick look back to her first symptoms to see they dated to the time her first child left home. Now that her younger daughter was within one year of going to college, she was beginning to envision herself living without her children, and she was simultaneously becoming increasingly depressed. As she began to talk about her future living with only George, Linda burst into tears. The feelings she possessed about her relationship with her husband had been shrouded under the cloth of children and their activities. Contemplating a life centered on her marital relationship without the buffer of her children, Linda felt a sense of despair and loneliness growing within her. With the emotional shield provided by her children, Linda's life with George had been tolerable; without it, she sensed an intolerably empty, lonely existence on the horizon. Her mood had collapsed markedly as she had begun to contemplate living in the house with only George, a man she found unstimulating and with whom she found it virtually impossible to form an emotional bond.

It was only now that Linda gained a full appreciation of her fear of the repetition of her childhood feeling of abandonment. When she revisited her state of mind at the time of her wedding, it became clear that she felt driven into the marriage as an escape, as though it was the only refuge she could find from a world she feared contained the prospect of isolation and abandonment. George was a port in a terrifying storm, and she had not ever felt the freedom to consider the price she might pay for the life-saving maneuver of "docking" there. Linda had adroitly managed to avoid paying the full price by putting her main emotional investment in her children, the cottage in the country, taking care of the house, and eventually higher education and the business world. It took the prospect of living without the children for the full cost of this adaptation to become evident. An emptiness now emerged that she could no longer deny nor hide behind the curtain of her family life. Nonetheless, her overwhelming fear of loneliness made the thought of living without him seem as terrifying as the prospect of an empty life with him. With her youngest child on the verge of moving away from home, the depth of her dissatisfaction with her husband emerged in the analysis with utmost intensity, and she became even more depressed.

Linda's confrontation with the full force of her frustration with and anger at her husband evoked rage at her history of neglect as she meditated on the consequences of her parents' self-absorption. She realized that she had spent a lifetime trying to connect with both parents, but was especially distraught after her mother's death because it forced the realization that she would never have the relationship she sought. She now saw that she had lost not so much the real mother as the hope that she would someday have the maternal relationship she wanted. Linda's only comfort being sex, she used sexual relations as her means for soothing loneliness both in adolescence and in the aftermath of her mother's death. In this context, we drew parallels between the emptiness in her relationship with George and her parents, and her use of sex for comfort with her feeling that her grandfather's sexual abuse was the only expression of "caring" she received as a child.

During the course of the analysis, Linda and I were able to reconstruct her history of repressing her anger and then acting it out sexually. As an adolescent, her sexual activity constituted acting out her anger toward her parents, and in her adult life, extra-marital affairs were her means of expressing her anger at her husband for his lack of affection and sex. Nonetheless, in these sexual trysts, Linda felt a comfort and pleasure similar to her experience with her grandfather. He was the only figure whom she felt showed any interest in her in childhood, and she continued to experience sex as an expression of being desired and cared for. A major theme of the analysis was bringing to awareness repressed anger at her parents for the neglect and exploitation she had previously denied.

The importance to Linda of sexual intimacy raised anew the question of why she remained married to a man who offered so little in that regard. Linda quickly recognized that her attachment to her husband consisted primarily of the feeling that he would "take care of her" and never abandon her. She had married him knowing there was little closeness, but because he was 12 years older and owner of his own business, she felt he was an established person on whom she could rely. When she married him in her early 20s, she described him as "adult." At the moment of their agreement to marry, he told her she would "never want for anything." By marrying George, Linda felt that she had guaranteed a life without loneliness or danger of abandonment. Without having been aware of it, Linda had fostered a pseudo-dependent relationship with him in order to feel that someone cared and to justify to herself the intensity of her attachment to him.

In seeing the sadness of her childhood and the desperate need to avoid loneliness that lay at the basis of her attachment to her husband, Linda became aware of few new facts, but the old events took on a new meaning as she felt neglected by people who put their own pleasures above her needs. It was the sense of being left all alone that she dreaded in anticipation of having only George at home with her. Linda's present life was not as painful as the future she envisioned, which was based on her past of isolation and loneliness. As Winnicott (1974, p.104) once said, the patient fears what has already happened. This anticipated loneliness forced upon her the awareness of both her current and former isolation lying beneath the defenses of her adult adaptation. The memory of being sent to college in a foreign country elicited a deep sense of abandonment in addition to anger.

We might say that Linda was finding new meaning in the old narrative. She had always known that she had no connection with either parent, that she should not have been left so alone in general, that she should not have been in charge of three children for an extended period at age 9, that she should not have been sent off to college in a foreign country by herself with no living arrangements or contacts, and worst of all, that it was wrong of her mother to dismiss her revelation of the sexual abuse. Nonetheless, Linda had not been aware of the impact of these events on her life. She knew neither that she had been traumatized by these occurrences nor that she was spending her life both disavowing her anger about them and attempting to avoid repeating them.

In addition to the sexual molestation, Linda had suffered what Mhasud Khan (1963) called "cumulative trauma." Awareness that her life was organized around the fear of repeating the loneliness and abandonment of her childhood and her growing awareness of her anger about the childhood neglect gave these events a new and deeper meaning. The narrative of her past was becoming saturated with isolation, sadness, anger, and terror as well as her efforts to relieve these painful feelings. In this context, she was able to see that her marriage to George was a way to defend against any further abandonment and loneliness. Leaving George had never been an option, she now saw, because the purpose of the marriage was to ensure that her childhood pain would not be repeated.

I believe Linda's case illustrates the way the analytic process leads to insight into the present and past. When Linda entered psychoanalysis she had a narrative of her life we might call an "everyday narrative." In the course of the analysis, she replaced the original life story with a psychoanalytic narrative, that is, a narrative that unfolded from the uncovering of meaning. Her current state of depression led us to her marital relationship and the dread of her future, which, in turn, evoked childhood events which she now saw were filled with loneliness and abandonment. This affective awareness re-evoked the question of her motive for marrying George. Exploration of the experience with her husband in the present, in turn, sparked a greater appreciation for the depth and breadth of the impact of childhood events on her psyche. The awareness of how little parenting and guidance she received in childhood gave her a new understanding of the attachment to her husband and she became even more aware of a sense of abandonment in that relationship. The subsequent inquiry into the underlying motive for the bond to him moved the analysis back to the depth of anxiety and traumata of her childhood. In this oscillation among future, present, and past, some new events were uncovered, but more significantly, previously recognized events gained new and deeper meaning, and much of life in each temporal modality was seen in a new way.

The evolution of Linda's psychoanalytic narrative demonstrates the distinction between a timeline and narrative, and, in this way, shows the importance of all three temporal modalities in psychoanalytic exploration. It would not do justice to her depression to view the prospect of the second child leaving home as only the "precipitant" of her dysphoric state. Despite the dissatisfaction in her marriage, Linda was not depressed during the years of her children's upbringing. Dread and despair mounted as the future of living alone with George grew close to becoming a reality. The bleakness of the future was as much the source of her depression as the traumata of her childhood that left her with an overwhelming fear of abandonment. That is, the meaning of Linda's depression lay as much in her dread and hopelessness about the future as it did in the traumata of her past life. To ignore either would be to miss a crucial component of her dysphoric state. Moreover, the deepest meaning of the past and present could not be fully grasped until we explored Linda's anticipation of the future. The terror that appeared in the expectation of an empty life alone with George was a palpable display of both the void in that relationship and the loneliness of her childhood. Until that point, Linda had not felt the full force of her foreboding that the future might be a repetition of the past. Thus, awareness of her dread of the future evoked a full appreciation of the emptiness of the marital relationship in the present, which, in turn, led to awareness of the depth of her childhood loneliness. She was then able to see that her isolated childhood made her desperate to attach to an older figure whom she felt gave her a virtual guarantee of availability. In this way, exploration of all three temporal modalities worked together to construct her psychoanalytic narrative.

Temporality and Symptoms

The traumata of Linda's sexual abuse and the abandonment she felt, especially by her mother, overwhelmed her with anxiety. To master the horror of her isolation, she used sex, and, later, George. Both defensive strategies arrested her emotional development at the point of using immediate expedients for temporary anxiety avoidance. The blunting of her aggression, excitement, and capacity for intimacy robbed her of the ability to achieve emotional depth and utilize her feelings as guides for conduct. Her emotional life having been suspended in childhood by anxiety, her affects were little different from those she possessed at pubescence. Confined to emotional shallowness, Linda regarded most of her relationships much like junior high or high school peer groups. She befriended younger women and was concerned with peer group competition for friends. When conflict erupted, she preferred to withdraw from the friendship rather than communicate her anger.

The repetition of her attenuated affective responses into adulthood and avoidance of conflict constituted an arrest of the emotional trajectory of her life. The maturational process of structuralizing and articulating affects having been strangled by the events of her childhood, when she did begin to feel a spark of affective connection, she immediately sexualized the feeling. This pattern dominated the transference. Whenever she felt that I understood her or had been beneficial in any way, she became sexually excited. Often she responded to positive moments between us with a sexual dream about me. Not infrequently, at moments of affective contact, she would blurt out, "Why don't we just have sex?" She associated these points of affective connection with her grandfather, often repeating her belief that he was the only person in her family who valued her. This immediate sexualization of positive affect fortified the arrest of an emotional life that had not developed beyond its state during the abuse.

Because much of her affective life was split off from the motives and goals that fueled her behavior, the parts of her self that were available in the future perfect tense were emotionally diluted. But, as we have seen, life gains its meaning in the future perfect. Linda's denuded affective experience led to an impoverished future perfect the awareness of which was defended against by avoidance. Consequently, fear of a bleak future shadowed her existence with a vague, but disconcerting dread that she defended against by absorbing herself in her children's lives, occasional romantic trysts, and a general proclivity for immediacy of tension relief. While she made plans for the future, her affects remained in an endless series of present points. When the reality of her younger child's departure forced itself upon her, she was no longer able to fend off the emptiness of her anticipated life alone with George and fell into a depression that she had been holding at bay throughout her adult years.

By including futurity in the conceptualization of Linda's analysis, a new way of understanding symptoms presents itself. As we can see from the analytic process undergone by Linda, symptoms do not just appear at a given moment because precipitants evoke unresolved childhood conflicts. When defenses are erected to protect against threatening affects, not only is that aspect of development distorted, but also there is an inevitable fear that the adaptation will break down resulting in the reexperiencing of threatening childhood affects. In this way, anxiety about the future is central to symptom formation. In some cases, as was true of Linda, consciously held future perfect goals and ambitions are constructed to split off the dreaded future from conscious life. This adaptation can be effective by providing goals that yield some degree of gratification, but dissatisfaction is inevitable because these conscious life ambitions are affectively impoverished. Even more poignantly, there is inevitably anxiety that the superficial adaptation will break down and the feared experience will occur. When the anxiety-ridden future threatens consciousness, the full force of the negative affect is felt. In Linda's case, she feared abandonment and loneliness if her relationship with George was threatened. In other instances, defensive constructions are not as successful, and the patient is aware of the fear of the future. In such cases, the symptom is directly attributable to a feared fate. In either case, strangulated affect distorts the future perfect, a fact indicating that anxiety about the future is a major component of symptom formation.

To say this another way, the affects and self potential arrested remain in a limbo state removed from the temporal trajectory of the life narrative. Symptoms, then, may be seen as temporal abeyance, a failure to move along with the future perfect. In Linda's case, one can see that her affective life remained in an arrested state after failing to evolve with her chronological growth. The resulting psychopathology may be defined as the failure to move forward, to complete the temporal trajectory of the future perfect. Symptoms are a reflection of temporal limbo, a cutting off of the temporal flow. What does not move forward into the future perfect becomes the soil for pathological growth.

While it may be tempting to believe that this analysis of the temporal nature of symptom formation is an overgeneralization from one patient, psychoanalytic history tells a different story as can be seen by a quick perusal of Freud's early cases (e.g., Breuer & Freud, 1895). The first, Anna O., fell ill fearing the prospect of life without her father. Both Lucy and Elizabeth von R. became symptomatic due to repression of a hoped-for future with men they felt guilty for loving. Of course, these cases are complex with many features involved in the symptom picture, but the point for our purpose is that whatever conflicts these patients possessed from childhood, they also suffered from highly conflictual future visions of their lives, and they became ill when reality forced awareness of the illusionary nature of their hoped-for future. That is to say, the *unconscious future* played a critical role in the symptom outbreak along with the *unconscious past*.

Or, again consider the large number of cases that come for psychoanalysis or psychotherapy because of a recent crisis, such as the ending of a relationship, or a fear of a looming threat, such as the impending loss of a current relationship. If the relationship has recently ended, or some other crisis has occurred, the patient tends to feel that the future has been ripped away, and the trauma consists of the feeling that she now feels lost without the future on which she was counting. If they believe a catastrophe is in the offing, such as the ending of a marriage or long-term romantic relationship, such patients fear the future around which they have built their lives may disappear. In either case, the feeling is that because the world they counted on is no longer in their future, they feel bereft, without a world to belong to. Or, again, many patients come for fear they will never form a meaningful, lasting relationship. For such patients, the present would be tolerable if they knew the future would be different. Their distress consists in their fear that their lives will never change, that they may not have the future they seek. Unable to believe in a better future, the depression from which they suffer is not as much about the dysphoria of the present moment as about the dread that they will never fulfill an anticipated future life. All these patients fear the future, even if they are not always aware of what their vision of the future is. In brief, dread of the future is invariably a significant component of the problems for which people seek analytic help, and, often, it is the impetus for a sense of crisis.

Because symptoms impede the developmental trajectory, it is not only a dysfunction in itself, but also an occlusion of new possibilities for the life narrative. For example, Linda's inability to form a relationship or even sustain conflict and tension, as well as her need to discharge tension states via sexual activity, had remained from her adolescence until adulthood without change. This view of symptom formation suggests that the therapeutic action of psychoanalytic therapy includes helping the patient understand and resolve a problematic future perfect, a dread of what her life is becoming, as well as what it may be in the moment. The narrative reconstruction includes movement into the future, a narrative that directs her life toward a meaningful future, influenced by the past, but not imprisoned by it.

Therapeutic Action

Returning to the analysis of Linda, it may be recalled that the psychoanalytic narrative that replaced her everyday narrative consisted of all three temporal modalities. After making conscious the future perfect that she had so long avoided, we constructed a psychoanalytic narrative that included the anxiety-dominated anticipated future, the pain and isolation of her childhood, and the emptiness of her marital relationship in the present. Confrontation with the vacuity of her relationship with George evoked the anxiety of the anticipated future of living alone with him, and this dread was central to her depression. The exploration of the motive for marrying George led us to deepened understanding of her childhood traumata and the loneliness of that period of her life. Her fear of abandonment saturated the future perfect with anxiety and shed light on the isolation and trauma of her early years as well as the present attachment to her husband. Bringing together the anxieties and pain of each temporal modality resulted in a psychoanalytic narrative that replaced the everyday narrative with which she entered the analysis.

Making conscious the dread of her anticipated future shifted the analytic spotlight to her mounting frustration with her husband's inability to respond to her emotionally or even, to her surprise, intellectually. The more she tried to find a forum for interaction of any type, the more disappointed she was in his lack of reaction. Stifled by the tedium of the relationship, Linda was well aware that she was experiencing a repetition of her early family life. It became clear to her that she would never find any sustained emotional meaning as long as she felt imprisoned in the marriage. But, of course, having felt locked into a dependency on George, she feared living without him. The conflict between her feeling of imprisonment and her fear of being alone forced awareness of the impact of her childhood abandonment. That is, Linda only saw clearly the deep impact of the loneliness and emotional abandonment of her childhood after her fear of the future evoked the emptiness in her marital relationship and the prospect of living without distractions from it. The analytic lens was then focused on the future perfect she had disavowed until that point.

In our inquiry into the anxiety with which Linda foresaw her future life, Linda realized that her dependence on George was a pseudo-dependence in which she did not learn simple tasks so that she could feel a reliance on a protective figure, an experience her childhood lacked. When we broke down the components of the dependence, it was apparent to Linda that none of the tasks for which she felt she needed George were in fact difficult for her. She could easily use a cash station, figure out where to get gas, find directions, and perform for herself any of the myriad tasks for which she had relied on him. Despite this awareness, the anxiety of living without a figure representing childhood dependence felt insurmountable. Linda felt stuck.

This is where the transference relationship took center stage. In her expressions of pain, depression, and anxiety, Linda felt some relief in the persistent understanding provided by the analytic process. Typically, in her appreciation for the help she felt from me, Linda erotized the relationship. I persisted in interpreting that every positive feeling for me was immediately sexualized because only her grandfather paid attention to her as a child, and she was eventually able to see the immediate way in which she converted good feelings into sexual impulse. It was a major advance when Linda was able to accept that explanation and continue the analysis despite the frustration of her usual means for discharging excitement.

The understanding achieved seemed sufficiently gratifying that she became less persistent in her attempts to sexualize our contact. Longing for emotional and intellectual stimulation, Linda sustained the analytic bond despite its sexual frustration. Often she teared up as she expressed gratitude for analytic empathy, frequently asking through her tears, "What would I *do* without you? I *have* to come here and talk. It's the only relief I get!" I would typically respond by noting that she felt a strong and valued connection with me despite the absence of a sexual relationship. Linda's ability to sustain this deeply meaningful relationship without using sexual excitement to dilute the intimacy ultimately led to the feeling that she had the capacity to experience emotional depth in a variety of ways.

The evolution of our relationship from the transference of shallow affects and the desire to squash intimacy with sex to a deep emotional bond of closeness, love, gratitude, and aggression gave Linda some confidence that she could break out of her childhood repetition to learn new capacities and create other types of relationships. The discussion of her feelings of helplessness along with the recognition that she had greater capability for forming a variety of relationships and for functioning than she had previously thought issued in the conclusion that the future did not have to be confined to a repetition of the present. Now able to imagine a life without George, Linda was developing a sense of agency, that is, a belief that she could control her destiny.

As she constructed her new life narrative with the possibility of a different future, Linda gained an even deeper appreciation for what had been missing from her earlier life: the opportunity to exercise her emotional and intellectual capacities. The recognition of the depth of her loneliness and deprivation evoked a deeper, more meaningful understanding of why she had constructed her present life of imprisonment. Linda realized that she was paying a bigger price than she could afford for the purpose of assuaging abandonment anxiety.

Gradually, Linda started to perform routine tasks for which she would have formerly depended on George with a combination of excitement and trepidation. The dread was not because she felt the tasks would be difficult, but because she knew performing them meant she was separating from George and attempting to live without an object of dependence. In this way, the analytic relationship facilitated the construction of a future perfect very different from the one to which she had felt fated. The exercise of these new capacities eventually resulted in her finding a place to live on her own, signing a lease, and when her second child left for college, she informed George she was leaving.

The separation and eventual divorce had ramifications well beyond the marital relationship. Moving to a different part of town, Linda made new friends who stimulated her in a variety of ways. She began involvement in physical activities, something she had never done before. No longer feeling suffocated by the expectations and control of others, she created a life for herself that emanated from what she enjoyed. It was not the new activities and even friends per se she most cherished, but her capacity for making her own choices.

For our purpose, it must be highlighted that the therapeutic action in Linda's analysis was a product of analytic work in all three temporal dimensions. The understanding we won on her past traumata illuminated her depression, but the resolution of her dysphoria required breaking through the disavowal of the future perfect, that is to say, bringing to consciousness the unconscious future. In the affectively diluted life she had leading, Linda had disavowed her fear of the future, but the making conscious of that temporal dimension evoked her longing to use her affects and capabilities to direct her life. Understanding that her childhood trauma experiences were related to her dread of loneliness helped Linda see she did not have to be trapped in her present life, an insight that aided her growing contemplation of a different future. Within the context of the transference relationship, Linda developed new capacities that shifted her sense of possibility. As her fear of the future became more apparent, Linda saw that she needed to exercise her newly recognized, but dormant potential. In utilizing these capabilities, Linda created projects for her life and began to live in a new future perfect. The insights she had gained into her past and present came to fruition in the development of a new life built on the deployment of her emotional and intellectual resources. The construction of a new sense of futurity, in turn, was facilitated by deriving new meaning from her past experiences, but newly uncovered meaning, in turn, was fostered by the opening up of a new sense of the future.

Each of these shifts was closely connected to the vicissitudes of the transference. The evolution of the analytic relationship showed Linda new possibilities that eventuated in the reconstruction of the future perfect. Similarly, this new relationship highlighted for her how much she had missed in her formative years. With Linda, as with most analytic patients, a variety of interventions and processes contributed to the analytic result. Interpretation of the past, the use of the here-and-now analytic relationship, and the confrontation with the previously unconscious future perfect were all indispensable elements of her new sense of agency. However, it was her confrontation with the dreaded unconscious future and the realization she could create a new future perfect that was most closely connected to the development and exercise of new emotional and social abilities. The future perfect is the temporal modality in which potential becomes realized through a vision of who the person can be. In this exercise of new possibilities lies the unique contribution of this temporal modality to the therapeutic action of psychoanalysis.

Conclusion

To return to the dilemma we set out to resolve, we can now see that the construction of a psychoanalytic narrative as a temporal interchange of modalities rather than an objectivized timeline links such a narrative construction closely to therapeutic action. If we confine narrative to past and present, there is an unclear connection between the insights won and the ability to change one's life. Some patients will be able to find ways to deploy new awareness, but many will struggle to translate understanding into new ways of being and relating. Patients who see only a bleak future will have difficulty imagining how newly achieved understanding can have a significant impact on historical patterns. Therefore, the patient's relationship to the future, and especially the unconscious future, is an important part of the analytic work. As we saw with Linda, grasping new meanings of past and present will be enlightening but not sufficiently mutative unless the patient can use them to construct a new future. Once the analyst sees her role as facilitating new meaning in all temporal dimensions, she becomes an agent facilitating the construction of a new narrative, but even more importantly, the psychoanalytic narrative will achieve its full potential to help the patient create new ways of being and relating.

Part III

CULTURE AND THERAPY

9

THE EXPERIENCING SUBJECT IN A QUANTITATIVE CULTURE

Since Aristotle Western civilization has known that the self can appear and define itself only in a community of others, and the community is the natural state of human existence within which the self becomes articulated. When Aristotle (350 BCE/1985) said, "Man is a political animal" he meant that humankind is inherently community making. It is not just that people tend to congregate in groups, but that community inheres in the very nature of being human.

Psychoanalysis, which began as a strictly endogenous theory, took a step toward incorporating this ancient wisdom with the shift from ego to self and the experience of the other was recognized as inherent in the experience of the self. The recognition that the self needs the other and becomes itself only through the other seen as a subject distanced psychoanalysis from its endogenous origins (Benjamin, 1995). However, this appreciation for the intersubjective nature of the self did not explicitly include role of culture. The importance of cultural issues has finally become recognized in the burgeoning literature on race, ethnicity, gender, and sexual orientation in psychoanalysis, as we will see in Chapter Eleven. However, the dominant values of American culture have not yet been given an explicit place in the discourse of American psychoanalysis. At this moment in analytic history, a gap remains between the experiencing subject and the dominant values of the culture.

In Chapter Two we observed that the American value system of objectification, quantification, and materialism has motivated the positivist epistemology of American psychology. In addition, we saw that this powerful cultural influence is not limited to epistemology, but is emblematic of the culture-wide value system that seeks to delete the subjective from the societal picture. This aim creates conflict between the experiencing subject and the hegemonic ontological position that gives reality status only to the quantifiable. It is the task of this chapter to examine in detail the influence of mainstream American culture on the experiencing subject, the formation of the self, and the analytic process.

Happiness and the Evaluation of Life

Every culture and subculture brings to bear pressure on the shape of the self. As Lacan (1977a) has noted, every child is born into a preexisting culture, so culture and its history are the condition of the child's birth. Before the child is a historical subject, the history and culture of the society into which she is born provide the environment with which she will interact to form her self. So, while we have seen the importance of culture in epistemology, we now turn to an examination of how the hegemonic American culture dominated by materialist values influences the shape of the self and our efforts to understand and transform it.

Aristotle once said, "What is honored in a culture will be cultivated there" (as quoted in Torrance, 2003, p.277). We have seen that our culture honors the concrete, the quantifiable and the measureable, and so those are the values we have cultivated from the Industrial Revolution through the computer age to the current era of hand-held technology. The existence of these values might not be a cause for alarm if they were applied only to the natural world where these attitudes are most applicable. However, in American culture these values tend to be applied to every aspect of life, including human experience without regard to measurability, as though all phenomena are assumed to be subject to measurement.

We observed in Chapter Two that in the American value system quantification and measurability have become the standard for truth and reality. What a person experiences is "merely subjective," whereas quantification is given reality status as "objective." The value of a house is the dollar amount for which it can be sold, not its value to the owner nor its service as a dwelling. The natural beauty of coastlines and forests have no inherent measureable value, so they are valued in terms of the amount for which they might be sold. Consequently, they are often destroyed in favor of developments that can bring greater dollar value.

It is perhaps easy to attribute this spoiling of the Earth to greed and profit, and while these motives are very real, to end the discourse there is to end it too soon. One may ask the further question: Why is greed placed ahead of aesthetics on the American value hierarchy? Why is profit making so desperately sought even after hundreds of millions or even billions of dollars have already been made? Such value preferences are not built into the human condition. Greater care is paid to conservation than profit in many other countries.

The pursuit of wealth after a certain point brings not greater material comforts, but the satisfaction of gaining a higher score, a quantitative increase of a portfolio. It is this numerical increase that is sought in an endless pursuit for which natural beauty and resources are destroyed. While one can never discount narcissism in the effort to score higher than one's competitors, or the need to "win" as one of my patients described it, the question still presents itself: Why is winning defined as the dollar amount of the portfolio? Why is that figure called one's "net worth"? It could just as easily be a cultural value to define "success" by the good done for others and the preservation of natural resources and beauty. The satisfaction sought in heightened numerical values appears to be so great that many wealthy individuals who seek no greater material comforts are willing to eviscerate irreplaceable resources to attain it. If they buy art with the wealth, it is valued by its price.

I emphasize that the satisfaction *appears* to be great because the reality is that after a point well below extreme wealth, money ceases to buy happiness (Diener et al., 1993; Kahneman & Deaton, 2010). Up to $75,000 per year, the greater the income, the better are daily moods, and the more enjoyable is daily living. But after $75,000, increased income has little to do with the satisfaction of everyday life. However, by the measure of how Americans evaluate their lives, the greater the income, the more positive their life evaluation. These findings demonstrate what clinicians see in the consulting room: Americans assess their lives not according to their experience, not by what they feel, but by quantifiable, external standards that have little experiential referent. The American people continue to use quantifiable measures such as economic success as the criterion for a successful life even though income does not make their lives more satisfying, enriching, or enjoyable after a certain level is reached; ironically, that point is quantifiable.

Further research finds that the most sustainable form of happiness is fulfillment of self chosen pursuits (Lyubomirsky et al., 2005). Happiness is most stable when it is derived from the attainment of goals that fit who the person is, what researchers call "self concordant." Happiness researchers have discovered that after a certain level of income is reached, the more one's life is engaged in the pursuit of goals that fit one's sense of self, the happier the individual is likely to be. Ironically, the empirical research informed by the dominant empiricist epistemology finds that the key to happiness is to pursue self chosen goals. It is not the attainment of a certain quantity on a goal scale that matters, but whether one chooses one's own life pursuits. Nonetheless, Americans continue to judge their lives on the basis of the achievement of quantifiable goals.

These findings indicate that Americans' life assessment is based on a belief that increased quantitative accumulation, whether in concrete material goods or the numbers of a portfolio, increases their life satisfaction even though they experience no change in feeling states. The fact that with ever increasing income, people evaluate their lives more positively but are no happier indicates how removed from experience many Americans have become. This preference for an external, material standard irrespective of experience reflects a culture that valorizes the material and ignores the experience of the living, breathing human being. The myth of American culture is that life satisfaction is derived from the accumulation of quantitative scores, whether those numerical figures are on the pages of a portfolio, the rankings of a profession, or the compilation of professional victories.

Many patients expect economic and material gain to bring a transformation of their emotional states and are shocked and even depressed when it does not. The greater the portfolio numbers, the happier one expects to be, and the greater are the chances of disappointment and despair. Others who are unable to accumulate the wealth they seek feel their lives are a failure and become depressed. The use of an external criterion removes the person from her experience so that life pursuits are divorced from feeling, passion, and desire. The experiencing subject is left behind as quantitative increase in some area is pursued endlessly and futilely. When the desired state is not achieved, because no other road to happiness is imagined, efforts are redoubled to increase material goods or other quantitative accumulations in a desperate effort to dissipate the distress. The spiraling need for the material moves life in the direction of increasing unhappiness.

The Internalization of Numerical Value

What is not subject to measurement is relegated to the low status of the "merely subjective" if it is given any status at all. "Merely objective" is not a phrase one hears. The experience of the individual is "anecdotal," virtually without significance, as opposed to behavior that is assessed by measurement and therefore is given "truth" status. As a consequence of this dominant ideology, the American citizen is tested and evaluated on a multitude of variables from birth through all stages of the life cycle. While students of most countries are given standardized tests, the American child is inundated with local, state, and national scores on a bewildering array of competencies, well beyond the traditional academic measures. In addition to classroom tests, national and state tests are administered annually, some states have several different tests on different dates each year, and often local standardized tests are interspersed. Teachers not infrequently complain that they spend so much time testing they have little time to teach, and, when they do teach they are focused on "teaching to the test" rather than teaching what children need to know (Seeley, 2006). The testing does not stop with academic subjects. Physical fitness, mechanical ability, mental ingenuity, and creativity are also standard. Test results lead to a variety of numerical values inscribed in the minds of children and virtually emblazoned in the mind of the adolescent as she leaves home to make her way in the world. When children go off to college they are loaded down not only with their ACT, SAT scores and class rank, but also the rankings of the high school they attended and the college they are going to.

The purpose of mentioning all this is not to dispute the importance of evaluation, but to highlight the fact that its excessive nature in American society inscribes numerical rankings in the experience and identity of American children almost as soon as they enter school. It is a short step for the young people of America to assess themselves according to the numbers they have been ascribed from their tests and rankings.

Clinical experience reflects the results of this numerological self assessment. Whether their scores are high or low, high school students treat their standardized test results as incontrovertible facts about themselves, characteristics that inhere in who they are and confer a status upon them. Those whose scores are average or below are ashamed and convinced they have no intellectual value, and sometimes, no worth at all. Students whose scores are superior tend to feel inflated, but some fear that subjecting themselves to the give-and-take of competition could damage this self-image. Having been given the status of superior intelligence without having to demonstrate accomplishment, they can only lose by entering competition. Of course not all adolescents with outstanding test scores are subject to this syndrome, but the persistent testing and number ranking of children results in self definition by test scores, a fragile identity because it can be deflated by the next test score. Whether the student does well or not, the tendency of most children and adolescents is to reify the test results as a core component of their identity.

Numbers are internalized as self defining for both those with high and low test scores, making identity contingent and severely constricting, even for those who test well. While the use of test scores to define the self is understandable given the honor that American culture accords numbers, it leads to a reified, highly restricted, concrete self concept that excludes a wide range of experiences, ways of being, and possibilities that are potential components of identity. That is why so many patients, if asked about their conviction they are "stupid," will point to their standardized test scores, as though those numbers define their competence and ability to cope with life. Although standardized tests like the SAT have little predictive value (e.g., Baron & Norman, 1992; Esen, 2010), children and adolescents tend to emblazon them in their minds as permanent components of who they are.

One sees many patients whose sense of competence is defined by test scores, even if the tests were taken years before. Patients as well as the wider society imbue test results with the special power to detect definitive capabilities, and ultimately self worth. Therefore, many make the assumption that they can do very little if their tests scores are average or below. This assumption is faulty for several reasons. First, intelligence is far more than such standardized tests measure. Howard Gardner (1983) has found seven intelligences, only two of which are measured by academic standardized tests. Furthermore, in this complex world there are a wide array of abilities and competencies beyond even Gardner's seven intelligences that are useable for a productive and satisfying life. Persistence, creativity, practical judgment, communication skills, and the ability to see opportunities are just a few of the characteristics that have helped many become professionally successful and lead fulfilling lives. That test results vastly oversimplify the skills and competencies one needs in life is demonstrated by their low predictive value for life performance and success. For example, LSAT scores predict first-year law school grades, but not success in the legal profession (Shultz & Zedeck, 2008). The SAT does not purport to predict life success, and it is not even a good predictor of college grades, the one claim it does make (www. fairtest.org/satvalidity.html). But, in a culture that defines reality by quantification, numeric indicators become the means of self assessment, test scores are imbued with the illusionary ability to determine worth and skill, and those numeric results are internalized as core components of identity. The importance accorded standardized tests, such as the SAT and LSAT, by students, parents, and educators is important more for what it says about the culture of numbers than the capability of the student to be successful in life.

The Numerical World of Physical Appearance

The numerical system of value so permeates American life that it extends beyond abilities to physical appearance, the most measurable elements of which are endowed with extraordinary importance. Even in the contemporary age of feminism, girls typically measure their attractiveness, which for some is equated with value, by their body weight. Thinness is so valued that adolescent white girls hold rigid views of their attractiveness defined largely by low weight (Parker et al., 1995; Rodin et al., 1984). Conversely, negative body image tends to be closely associated with bodily heaviness, and overweight girls are routinely stigmatized (Neumark-Sztainer et al.,

1998). Chronically anxious about their weight, American girls with the most negative body images are likely to develop eating disorders (Rosen, 1990; Thompson & Stice, 2001). The preoccupation with thinness is endemic, and the incidence of eating disorders has grown commensurately with this measuring stick of attractiveness (e.g., Striegel-Moore et al., 1986). Preoccupation with weight is a major predictor of bulimia, and the media attention given to attractiveness as defined by thinness has also been found to be a major factor in its onset (e.g., Harrison & Cantor, 1997). As might be expected from these findings, body dissatisfaction is correlated with depression in adolescent girls (e.g., Stice & Bearman, 2001; Allgood-Merton et al., 1990; Ohring et al., 2002). All these findings fit with the obsessive preoccupation with weight one sees among females from adolescence to adulthood. Those who meet the technical criteria for eating disorders are but the most extreme form of the pervasive tendency to use weight as a critical indicator of self worth.

Furthermore, in today's America, these weight-related female anxieties cut across subcultures and ethnic differences. Caucasian, Asian, and Latin girls share similar levels of weight anxiety, and Afro-American women less so (Neumark-Sztainer et al., 2002). Although boys' body images are much less studied, there appears to be a correlative striving for musculature associated with male attractiveness, although less dominant than the female pursuit of thinness (McCreary & Sasse, 2000).

In the voluminous literature demonstrating the strong relationship between weight preoccupation, depression, and eating disorders among American adolescent girls, the American-European ideal of thinness is typically noted as a major factor pressuring young girls to reduce body fat (e.g., Garner & Garfinkel, 1980; McCarthy, 1990; Nolen-Hoeksema & Girgus, 1994; Davis & Katzman, 1999). While feminists have been quick to attack this value as an objectification of women who are appreciated only for their physical appearance, what tends to be overlooked is the more subtle cultural prejudice that body shape and weight are the concrete, quantitative measures of attractiveness. The two values join to assess girls on a measure much like any commodity. The use of the body as a physical indicator of value is itself a concretization of female worth, and the bodily yardstick of weight solidifies this concrete view of appeal. The woman becomes a body to be measured much like any piece of meat or commodity.

Body image being an important part of the experience of self, especially among adolescent girls, the dominance of physical measures of attractiveness contributes to a narrow and objectified sense of self. As a result, the tendency of the dominant society to value the quantifiable becomes central to the way the self is experienced. Self-image is reified in numerical assessments, and body weight and shape, especially for girls, are the ultimate concretizations of the self.

The Quantification of Self Concept

Human experience is unique in its ability to see and adopt a relationship to itself, what Bollas (1987) calls a fundamental "twoness" in the experience of self. Because children treat themselves as they were treated, the child whose self is objectified by the cultural value system will tend to view herself as a commodity much like any "thing." This self objectification is obvious in patients who overtly attack and even vilify themselves as "bad objects," but there are also subtle ways in which self commodification occurs. The adolescent girl who measures her worth by her body weight, the woman who judges herself by the productivity of her sales numbers, or the man whose self regard fluctuates with his billable hours are all concretizing and objectifying the experience of self. And, in this process, the hegemonic culture is colonizing the mind of each. The culture is internalized in the form of quantitatively measureable attributes and abilities, thus delimiting severely the range of experiences that can be appropriated as one's own and crippling belief in oneself.

The findings of the happiness studies confirm the common clinical experience with wealthy people who are deeply troubled and often suffer from debilitating depression. The accumulation of wealth, if they have amassed it themselves, will be the basis for a positive view of their life narrative, despite their deep dissatisfaction with daily living. Some patients regard their lives as far more successful than they ever dreamed they would be and are then surprised to find that happiness does not follow the money or other success. One especially wealthy young man told me he had never allowed himself to imagine that he would achieve the spectacular material success he enjoyed by his mid-30s, but he was troubled, dissatisfied, lonely, and unable to form a relationship. Calling his life "a great success" while acknowledging his despair, this deeply troubled young man could not make sense of his unhappiness. Mystified by the degree of his depression in the midst of his "success," when once he became aware of the emptiness he could no longer deny, he felt lost and disoriented, as though waking from a deep sleep.

Wealthy, unhappy people believe they are successful, but for that very reason their depression is confusing and disorienting. Although patients of this ilk are rarely able to overcome their unhappiness with worldly success, they cannot admit their lifelong pursuit of material wealth was ill advised and continue to accumulate material possessions while perplexed by their unhappiness. The pursuit of happiness becomes a mystery with no clues, and the regressive tendency to find solace in some type of quantitative measure is strong. Even when the patient becomes aware that measureable accumulations will never result in happiness, he pursues them as though they do. He knows no other way. Material goods for such people are transformational objects (Bollas, 1987), objects that are expected to transform the psychic state as the mother once did with her ministrations.

Other patients express the same distinction between life assessment and happiness in more commonplace terms. Therapists are accustomed to hearing "I should be happy, I have it all, financial success, good wife and family, kids doing well, live in a good neighborhood, but I am not happy." This type of life narrative is more compelling because the list of accomplishments is not confined to material assets. The inclusion of family appears to suggest a broadened view of values, but in the depth of clinical inquiry, one finds that a more subtle form of the concrete is often revealed.

For example, one patient insisted that his "great family" was more important than his considerable financial success, but when we explored his dissatisfaction with living, it appeared that he spent little time with his wife and made only perfunctory visits to his children's activities. His marital life had little passion or sex, and what was there felt robotic and unexciting. Preferring to ignore his children, this youthful father had little patience with them and rarely helped them with homework or any other part of their lives. He knew little about them, and when they needed his help, he seemed to feel intruded upon by any demands they placed upon him. Despite his belief that he had a "great family," he gained little daily gratification from his domestic life. When asked about his positive feeling toward the family, he said that the kids did well in a good school system, his wife was a good homemaker and cook, and they lived in a well-appointed house. For this man, these attributes constituted a model family. Unable to say one word about his children or wife as people, he appeared not to know them, but valued them highly according to external measures of success. His family actually brought him little daily gratification, but he assessed his family life as "great" on the basis of external standards.

For many patients who are successful in conventional terms but puzzled by their unhappiness, their accomplishments offer little beyond momentary satisfaction primarily because both family and professional success are sought to fulfill an image rather than for the enrichment of their lives. When the expected life transformation does not occur, they experience a deflation that can easily become a state of depression. The illusion that quantifiable success will produce a state of enduring satisfaction is so commonplace as to be a cultural phenomenon. Depression and other reactions to the failure of quantifiable achievements to bring lasting stability are not due wholly to family and other environmental pressures; they are products of the culture of numbers.

Clinical Application

We can see this devotion to numerical success and the disappointment in achieving it in Herb whom we discussed in Chapter Five. It may be recalled that Herb had become consumed with making his branch of a large company a success while neglecting his own life, including self-care. As we saw, Herb had transformed himself into a producer of company sales and profits to the point that he could not distinguish the success of the enterprise and who he was. This "producer self" was both fueled by and solidified his frenetic single-minded devotion to numerical success. Herb was so terrified of failing and repeating his father's life that he seemed to have lost all connection with the rest of the world. His only measure of success being sales numbers, when the business did well, he anticipated an end to his chronically dissatisfied state and even a sense of fulfillment, but when the expected transformation did not occur, Herb felt even more desperate to increase his sales figures to boost himself.

The despair in which such patients find themselves is not simply that they are "overinvested" in their careers, or that they conflate who they are with what they do. Their very sense of self has been reduced to a number or series of numbers on one or another numerical scale. Although such patients typically claim to value home and family, their behavior is marching to the tune of a different drummer. They are driven to achieve a measureable outcome because the very sense of self is fused with the score on the company sales sheet. They have a mental, and sometimes physical, quantitative model against which they assess their lives, and the fact that reaching these goals leads to no greater happiness rarely results in any questioning of the standard. In fact, as we saw with Herb, the very failure of the numerical criterion to work leads to a redoubling of the effort to increase the numbers in the hope of finally reaching the elusive goal they believe will be transformative.

Herb turned himself into a profit-and-loss statement, but for many patients the standard may be sports victories, real estate holdings, numerical rankings of their professional production, among others. Objectifying the self is not always about vocation. The particular measure used is less important than the fact that a measureable criterion constitutes the self concept, as it did with Herb. The equation of self with outcome, and outcome with quantitative factors combine to render experience of little importance in assessing one's life. It is not uncommon for children's athletic, music, or academic success to be the measure for many parents. When the self is conceived as a property with measureable, quantitative worth, it is reified, much like real estate. The key factor is the reduction of the sense of worth to a measureable scale of some sort, not the content of what is being measured.

As one of six children with parents suffering from their own characterological problems, Herb gained little recognition as a person of value in his own right. Possessing considerable intellectual talent, he sought a sense of value in academic success. Such satisfaction as he drew from life was derived from his grades, test scores, and Ivy League education. But, the most striking fact from the current perspective is that no one, including Herb, believed anything was wrong until he became so anxious and overwrought that he could not work. His intellectual success hid in plain sight the poverty of his existence. He had acquaintances, but very few friends, no meaningful relationships, and he derived little from his intellectual achievement. He had pursued academic success in the hope of finding some unarticulated and indefinable satisfaction, and he did the same when he threw his life into his job. But, no one, including Herb, could see the emptiness just below the surface of his manic work life, and, in fact, the unconscious anxiety of recognizing this poverty impelled an ever more frantic need to devote himself to quantifiable success.

Herb suffered from overwhelming anxiety and fear of failure, both of which emanated from an emptiness he was desperately trying to fill. When his compensatory, frenetic pursuit of professional success could not be sustained, he collapsed in a depressed state. The childhood roots of the depression can be traced to his overwhelmed and anxious mother of six boys and his alcoholic father. He reacted to his mother's anxiety and his father's erratic alcoholism by numbing himself, divorcing his behavior from all experience except intellectual activities, all sense of living as an existing human being.

Early in the analysis I tried to focus on his experience, but he responded only with descriptions of his behavior. His very sense of self seemed to be a series of behavioral patterns designed to form a product he called "success" that had no experiential referent. He described his state as overwrought, overwhelmed, and overtired to the point that his thinking was clouded. Nonetheless, in response to my inquiry about what led him to work so relentlessly, he stated simply that he was "doing his job" by trying to make the company successful. He could not articulate any feeling about his role in running his office. In lieu of feeling, he gave an evaluation of his job performance which he regarded as successful, but not good enough. Queried about what led to his psychic collapse, Herb said that he could not get the resources he needed, had few employees to rely on, and consequently had to do all the work himself. All of these factors were real, but Herb could never ask why it was necessary for him to fill the gaps in a warped system.

So, the family dynamics account for the vacuity of Herb's emotional existence, but his attempted solution, his belief that he could live a fulfilled life by hitting the right numbers for the company while ignoring his experiential state, is a product of contemporary American culture. To be sure, success motivation is not inherently problematic, but when quantitative measures of success substitute for self experience, as they did in his case, the person becomes transformed into a source of production, the experiencing subject gives way to external goals, and the activities of life are so removed from feeling that only an emptiness remains. Herb's obsessive preoccupation with professional success could not afford him any degree of life gratification because he was *doing* without feeling. His emptiness being just below the surface, it threatened to gain consciousness, motivating intensified activity to avoid awareness of the sense of meaningless that lay buried in a shallow grave, just below the surface of his consciousness. Of course, this objectification of self divorced from experiencing can take place in competitive nonvocational areas of life in which numbers or rankings are used for scorekeeping, such as sports competitions, computer games, gambling, or many others. It is not the content of the pursuit that squeezes life out of the experience, but the lack of meaning in the experience.

Patients such as Herb fit Joyce McDougall's (1996) depiction of alexithymia, inability to experience affect. While the inability to access an affective life is a cardinal characteristic of Herb and similar patients who live divorced from their own experience, McDougall's formulation defines the condition exclusively by what it is *not*. Absent from McDougall's formulation is the fact that the patient has an actively constructed self, formed and defined in concrete terms, albeit empty of meaning. When the therapist is able to identify this empty fortress, the process is directed toward analyzing the patient's constructed self, rather than focusing on the wholly negative concept of missing affect.

Attention to the self organization marks the difference between McDougall's concept of alexithymia as simply a lack of affect and the present formulation that an objectified self defined by productivity squeezes affective juices out of life and insulates itself against the world. McDougall's conceptualization does not capture the type of person-world relationship actively maintained by such a self. McDougall considered the psyche without regard for the person-world relationship and thus her formulation misses the essence of Herb's psychological makeup as a concrete, reified self reduced to quantitative measures. And, most poignantly, McDougall makes the common analytic mistake of ignoring the importance of culture in the construction of a "producer self."

In a desperate effort to achieve a sense of self, Herb had crystallized his experience into a schema designed for productivity and maximizing effectiveness. When, in the therapeutic process, I tried to engage his experience, he was unable to respond with anything except a description of his behavior. He was guarding his narrow, affectless self organization tightly and attempting to keep it enclosed, impervious to outside influences. Herb's reified self aimed to ward off any influences that would threaten to distract from his singular focus and open awareness to the foreboding dread he was desperately trying to avoid. His receptivity to new experiences being minimal, no process of *becoming* was possible. All was frozen into a repetitive effort to achieve a single goal, as though time was standing still. Here again, as in Chapter Eight, we see that symptoms constitute a freezing of the temporal flow and the disappearance of futurity.

My analytic efforts with Herb were directed to developing awareness that he had mental activity beyond thinking, that he possessed feelings, attitudes, beliefs, even convictions, if not in completely formulated states, at least in nascent form. I noted to him, as we saw in Chapter Five, that he was making assumptions lacking in any experiential basis. By emphasizing that he had reduced himself to a measureable commodity, I managed to gain his attention and stimulate curiosity about the way his life had gone. In taking notice, he began to wonder about his experience, and, as we have seen, ultimately transcended the narrow cage he had constructed to avoid all feeling. The analytic strategy, then, was directed to the reified self hardened into a commodity, not simply his lack of affect, and to undoing the numerical self assessment derived from the dominant culture by fostering a belief in experience, rather than external numerical standards.

Reification and Analytic Theory

The commoditization of self, as we saw in Herb, is such a powerful influence in American culture that it has infiltrated some of the most basic analytic concepts. A good example is the way analytic theory has conceptualized self-esteem. Freud (1914) believed self-esteem is derived from the residual of primary narcissism, the fulfillment of the ego ideal, and love returned. The first is infantile, and the latter two are contingent on meeting a value standard, the first, one's own, the second, that of others. The most commonly employed analytic view is that self-esteem is a function of the relationship between the ego ideal or superego and the ego (Freud, 1923, 1938), so that low self-esteem results from a major gap between the two structures. This concept *could* be psychologically cogent depending on what values are embedded in the ego ideal. However, if the ego ideal is an image of talent or professional or economic success, self-esteem will be contingent on the fulfillment of goals that depend on talent and life circumstances. The ideals may not be achievable and even if they are, that can change as skills and talent inevitably erode. The weakness of any concept of self-esteem based on the congruence of ego and ego ideal is that it depends on contingencies that are not controllable.

The same critique applies to Kohut's (1984) concept of healthy narcissism as a function of ambitions and ideals held together by the tension arc of talents. Kohut included the "tension arc of talents" so that self-esteem depended on the modification of ideals to fit capabilities. However, this view suffers from the same problem as the classical view: It makes self-esteem dependent on the achievement of goals that may not be achievable. For both conceptualizations, those with little productive capacity are consigned to a negative self-image.

Kernberg's (1976) conceptualization of healthy self-esteem as the "realistic appreciation of one's talents and limitations" suffers from an even deeper problem. While many people do in fact measure their self worth this way, the assessment of talents and limitations makes the esteem for oneself contingent on talents that many people may not have. Those with little talent, according to this formulation, should have low self-esteem because the realistic appreciation of their talents and limitations would show a modicum of talent and a great deal of limitation. So, the logical conclusion of Kernberg's view is that a successful analysis for a person with few talents would be to have a negative self-image. And those with a great deal of talent would feel inflated because their ability warrants it, but they can only sustain their good feeling about themselves as long as their talents remain. As talented individuals age and their abilities erode, realistic appreciation for talents and limitations would lower self regard.

Defining self-esteem as talents and limitations puts the self in the same ontological category as any machine or instrument: it is valued for its function and loses its value when its productivity declines. With no role given to the experiencing subject, Kernberg's view of self-esteem, like all other major efforts to formulate this concept in analytic terms, recognizes no distinction between the self and material resources judged by their utility. Consequently, it is difficult to distinguish Kernberg's concept of self-esteem from the evaluation of robots, which are also assessed according to their abilities and limitations (Turkle, 2011).

The near imperceptibility of the reductionism and objectification that inheres in analytic conceptualizations of self-esteem shows the degree to which such objectifying tendencies are integrated into the American way of thinking. While there has been little questioning of Kernberg's criteria in the analytic literature, one sees the deleterious impact of assessing "talents and limitations" as patients become anxious about their intelligence, performance, net worth, professional status, talents, looks, and other attributes. Kernberg's concept constitutes a collusion with the cultural view of the self as a commodity like any other. Although few analysts would agree with such a commoditization of the self, defining self-esteem as the assessment of "talents and limitations" is tantamount to making the self a commodity with little demonstrable difference from instruments, machines, or robots. Such a view, of course, is antithetical to the psychoanalytic clinician who is interested in the way the patient experiences herself. The theory remains far from the practice when the culture of objectification infiltrates analytic thought.

Kernberg's view of healthy narcissism is an example of analytic theory failing to resist the cultural pressure to reify the self as a functional capacity. A self denuded of quantifiable measures is an experiencing self, a self evolving in and through its experience, wherever that may lead, none of which is measureable nor subject to an evaluation from outside of itself. This is the self that seeks only its own actualization, a self long ago conceived by the Romantic Movement that reemerged in nineteenth- and twentieth-century phenomenological and existential philosophy, and is now brought to fruition in contemporary psychoanalysis, the psychoanalysis of the experiencing subject. This way of conceiving the self is not simply a shift in content, but a different way of experiencing what it is to be a human being. To be human is to be in relation to the world in its horizon of possibilities, to be engaging the world and others with one's unique experience, an experiencing subject treating others as subjects. This is the psychoanalytic vision, and it does not fit the dominant trends of contemporary America.

It is this concept of the self as potential for ever expanding ways of being and relating that was utilized in the analysis of Herb. The analytic process was directed to the opening up of self experience in order to de-objectify the self and facilitate the development of a self based on experiential process. While it would be simplistic and one-sided to say that the distress in which Herb found himself was a "cultural product," the societal pressures to become a function, to reduce himself to a means of production, played an important role in the objectification of his experience. By adapting to his feeling of emptiness, fear of relationships, and dread of failure by a single-minded devotion to productivity, Herb was enacting the cultural ethic of productivity to the point of self reification. The fact that this pathological adaptation fits the American hegemonic values of objectification, quantification, and materialism made it almost imperceptible until Herb became dysfunctional. The invisibility of his suffering indicates that self reification is so deeply implicated in American life that it tends to be hidden in plain sight within a culture that assumes the overriding importance of what is material.

Conclusion

In this chapter we have seen the cultural level of objectification in the experience of the self. The logical conclusion of a culture that values materialism, objectivism, and quantification is the reification of self experience. Herb is one example of this cultural phenomenon. It is not just that the culture pressures children and adolescents to absorb its value system, but that the cultural paradigm becomes internalized to the point that the self becomes a reified entity.

The patient's relationship to herself is a cultural product. So, patients like Herb bear the imprint of the culture in their state of commoditization and the consequent objectification of their life divorced from experience. Needless to say, that does not provide a complete explanation because virtually everyone in the United States is exposed to the same value system. Herb's father's frequent failures and his mother's inability to manage her six children left him feeling inadequate, empty, and lonely during much of his childhood despite his large family. His effort to feel a sense of worth took the path of least resistance by identifying with and adopting the dominant American value system of productivity for which he received accelerated promotions and enjoyed an exceptional reputation for hard work and effectiveness. And, this *modus operandi* is so integrated into the value system of the culture that no one noticed the bitter truth that the more successful he became in conventional terms the more he solidified the split between his experience and his sense of self.

In Chapter Two we noted the dominant impact of the culture of quantification on psychological science, and in this chapter we saw how that same influence can operate on the individual psyche. Herb's case represents a paradigmatic representation of the way the materialist culture can dominate self formation to the point of psychic paralysis. But, the contemporary age consists of new levels of technology that promote even greater opportunities for the reification of human experience. We now turn to the newest form of cultural assault on the experiencing subject: the technological revolution of the twenty-first century.

10

SEARCHING FOR THE SELF IN A WORLD OF TECHNOLOGY

Jerold, a young and spectacularly successful businessman, was shocked to find himself in a state of hopelessness and despair. Having been anxious throughout his business career around almost every deal, he had come to expect anxiety, but after a recent bout of the flu, he found himself deeply depressed with no apparent precipitant. He had difficulty motivating himself to return to work and his normal anxiety had become paralyzing over an impending routine deal. After intensive analytic work, he came upon the realization that he had never liked business, but had always assumed it would be his career because it was the only vocational path valued in his family, especially by his father, a self-made wealthy real estate developer. After years of analytic exploration, Jerold had thoughts of giving up his business career, but he had no idea what else he might do, and his confusion was deeper than any particular life choice.

Patients like Jerold do not know what they want from life, what they value enough to pursue, and, what is even more disturbing to them, they have no idea how to find out. Now the problems faced by this young, bright, talented professional man would not appear to be related to technology in the way we ordinarily think about it. It is the thesis of this chapter that the not uncommon problematic sense of self in patients like Jerold is an index of a technological culture that threatens the very nature of human being, and that seeing this connection between modern technology and the fragile sense of self adds a crucial dimension to the analytic understanding and amelioration of problems in self formation.

On Human Being

As we saw beginning in Chapter Two and continuing throughout this work, the essence of being human is Being-in-the-world, relating to the world, not simply occupying its space (Heidegger, 1962/1927). Heidegger brought to light that in our relationship to the world, we bring forth its possibilities, and, in this process, we dis-cover who we are and who we can become. Essential to human being is reaching beyond the given, to the exploration and formation of new possibilities. It is a truism in cultural anthropology that culture is never static, but always changing. As we have seen, the human mode of relating is not static, but, in Heideggerean terms, "ek-static," moving beyond itself. To disclose and bring forth possibilities is distinctly human and, therefore, the transcendental is built into human experience. The realization of transcendental possibilities requires openness to unrealized potential. It will be argued in this chapter that modern technology, whatever its value in efficiency and production, has clouded this uniquely human relationship to the world and therefore contributed to the difficulty in establishing authentic selfhood endemic to so many of our patients and to the wider culture.

Even in our materialistic civilization the happiest people are those who have found something in the world that calls them forth, that provides what Joseph Campbell (1988) calls "bliss." Self-actualizing people show this passion for the joy of realizing their capacities and becoming themselves (Maslow, 1969). Optimal experience is "flow," the mental absorption in an activity that is inherently fulfilling (Csikszentmihalyi, 2008). In flow the person is at one with the activity and all implements used to complete it. The entrepreneur, musician, writer, scientist, chess player, scholar, or athlete performs optimally when there is no awareness of the instruments employed or of the outside world. We are most human when we are so in the world that we are not aware of it as separate. The spectacular popularity of concepts such as Campbell's notion of "finding your bliss" and Csikszentmihalyi's "flow" demonstrates the hunger for passion, authenticity, and meaning in contemporary culture.

Heidegger made the claim, astounding to many, that there is no tool when an instrument is working the way it is meant to perform. When the carpenter hammers well and effectively, there is no hammer, but when the hammer begins to break, when the head is shaky, the carpenter becomes aware of the hammer; it then makes its appearance as a hammer. The hammer when it is in optimal use fits into a person-world unity that brings forth some possibility in the world. It is "ready-to-hand," which means that it is not thought about nor represented in any way. Heidegger's concept of "ready-to-hand" reflects the experience of flow. In flow, all objects utilized, the computer, the chess pieces, the instrument, the power tools, are all "ready-to-hand." In this person-world unity, Csikszentmihalyi showed, people not only operate most fully and effectively, but also find the most fulfillment. When that unity is disrupted, as by the hammer beginning to break, then it becomes a hammer; it is now separated from the person using it and its use. The hammer now becomes "present-at-hand," which means it is viewed as a scientist or other observer would see it, as an object of observation, of curiosity.

In "flow," there are no concerns, no perturbations, only the task at hand. The questions and doubts of life disappear as the person engages the world. One cannot ask of a person in flow, do you think this is the right way to live? The person would look with amazement that the question is asked, and of course, it would not be. The fact that such a question strikes us as absurd shows that in flow we do not question our experience, our knowledge of how to live. The spirit of being flows through the self into the activity and all its parts, and that can happen only if we are drawn into the activity by its appeal, or as Heidegger would say, "called by the world." Without openness to what the world's possibilities are, the door stays closed.

The popularity of "flow" in contemporary culture suggests that the idea meets a need; that there is some lack in experiencing that many hope to fill by obtaining the state. Because the nature of flow is to feel a concentration of purpose, a oneness of mind, one is drawn to the conclusion that the miracles of modern life have resulted in a culture of distraction, a difficulty in maintaining concentration, in a world of easy, quick sources of gratification that operate all too easily as distractions.

The Technological World

The essence of modern technology was captured well by Heidegger (1977/1955) long before the computer revolution brought computers, the Internet, cell phones, and the iPad into our daily lives. While Heidegger was referring to the Industrial Revolution and its aftermath, his ontological grasp of the technological world seems apt today even as the specifics of technology have changed dramatically. He notes that the root of technology is *techne*, the Greek word that referred to knowing how to do, which, for the Greeks, applied to arts, such as poetry, as much as crafts, such as ship building (Aristotle, 350 BCE/1984. The person-world relationship throughout antiquity and into the sixteenth century at least was an organic unity. "Person" and "world" were regarded as two sides of a single relating. This relationship was characterized by "techne" to the degree that possibilities of the world were brought out by a craft. However, the transformation in the person-world relationship that began as long ago as the seventeenth century with the Cartesian splitting of subject and object led to the concept of "objects" in the sense of points of mass in homogenized space. Once this ontological revolution occurred, Heidegger argues, exploration of the world was no longer confined to bringing forth possibilities; the Earth became vulnerable to manipulation.

As a result, the concept of "techne" eventually shifted from knowing how to bring out the possibilities of the world to a manipulation of objects in homogeneous space, a "seizing upon" in the mode of "ordering." This manipulation of the Earth in lieu of appreciating and disclosing it separates person from world and defines the modern age. Unlike technologies of other ages, according to Heidegger, modern technology—again, referring to the Industrial Revolution—attacks nature in order to manipulate it in the mode of ordering, and thus nature became "standing reserve." Heidegger's fundamental point was that the origin of modern technology, the technology of the Industrial Revolution and beyond, is not any particular technological innovation, but the sundering of the person-world relationship. In this fundamental, ontological sense, Heidegger's meditations on modern technology apply as well to the current age of the Internet, cell phones, and social networking, as they do to the factory and the assembly line.

According to Heidegger, by treating nature as "standing reserve," a resource to be harnessed for some purpose, the Earth has been reduced from a dwelling to a source of energy and stockpiled resources. Whereas the techne of the ancients opened the world, the essence of modern technology is more about *cause* than opening. Instead of revealing the Earth's ever boundless possibilities, modern technology seeks to find a cause so that the Earth can be harnessed for some future use. For example, Heidegger argues that planting and harvesting bring out the nature of the Earth in a particular way, "disclosing" its possibilities for growing food, but scientific agriculture challenges the Earth by attempting to exploit its resources. In this mode of exploitation, things are then made according to arbitrary will (Feenberg, 2003).

Unique to modern technology, for Heidegger, is the adoption of "enframement," placing a "frame," a structured delimitation on the experience of the world, rather than being open to what it reveals to us. In this mode of being, everything becomes available for control. Heidegger did not deny the great value of technological advances; his purpose was to elucidate its hidden cost. The Industrial Revolution of the eighteenth century is a dramatic example of enframement, and our current information revolution, the age of "miracle and wonder" in Paul Simon's words, is but its most recent and awe-inspiring iteration.

Despite the exploitation of the Earth, Heidegger sees the greatest danger of modern technology to lie not in "enframement" per se, but seeing it as the *only* way of Being-in-the-world and thus applying it to human being. To adapt "enframement" to the human condition is to fit the person into a preconceived conceptual apparatus. The openness of human being is then stifled beneath an externally imposed structure, just as the Earth is reduced to what it can yield for someone's arbitrary will. Human being as "standing reserve" is a resource on call to be utilized when necessary, and Heidegger saw this objectified view of the person as so restrictive of the openness to the world that it threatened the very essence of the human way of being. The ultimate threat of technology, then, for Heidegger, is the enframement of human being which would constitute nothing less than the loss of what makes us distinctly human: our very Being-in-the-world. As the self becomes ever more saturated with technological imposition, it loses contact with its own experience and acts increasingly like an object in homogenized space. It is this loss of humanity that Heidegger regarded as the most dangerous threat of the new technological age.

Heidegger saw emerging from the Industrial Revolution a new entity, a person reduced to "standing reserve," a resource to be utilized for an external purpose, much like any other natural resources of the Earth, such as coal, copper, or magnesium. When the person becomes a resource, a capability for some purpose not of its own making or choosing, the human is objectified, thus losing its unique quality as human being. The experiencing subject disappears when the individual becomes only a means for ends imposed by unknown sources.

Now this outcome is not the inevitable result of technological advances, but it is a realistic possibility in a society that valorizes quantification, objectification, and materialism. Assessing the value of a culture by quantifiable production, such a society becomes enamored of the manipulation of nature and tends to make technology the very embodiment of reality. In the context of this value system, the objectification of the human process is a most fitting result. As we saw in Chapter Two, economists now have developed formulae for quantifying the value of human lives. In such a world, "enframement," rather than being one among many ways of relating to the world, dominates and severely constricts the person-world relationship. Technology fits the Zeitgeist so well that its infiltration into daily life occurs without question and with little attention to its cost except for a few intellectual critiques that are largely ignored (e.g., McDermott, 1969; Marcuse, 1964/1991; Turkle, 2004, 2011). The nature of human experiencing, of *being*, recedes ever further from daily life.

As we have seen in Chapter Two, the discipline that could be most expected to affirm human experiencing has chosen to adopt the ideology of the culture and thus deleted the experiencing subject from the study of the human process. By defining psychology as the "behavior of living organisms," psychology has all too willingly complied with and promoted the reduction of the person to observable behavior subject to the same "enframement" as the natural world. As an object in homogenous space, human behavior becomes one more resource to be utilized for an external end. This reduction of the person to an objectified entity in space "completes the circle" by reducing the final opposition to objectivism, the human process, to a commodity (Heidegger, 1959–1961/2001). With the enthusiastic cooperation of academic psychology, the contemporary age has now defined the very nature of all being, including the uniquely human way of being as a resource, "standing reserve" for something else, although the ultimate purpose is never known.

Applying Heidegger's view of modern technology as "enframement," a technological society may be defined as a social structure in which technology dominates the person-world relationship, even the way people experience themselves, typically with little notice given to this infiltration of the technological into the experience of self. Rather than an exploration of ways of being and relating, the human being is reduced to functions, a "standing reserve" of practical applications the purpose of which is often unknown and typically not owned by anyone. Like any other resource of nature, humanity becomes a link in what Maslow (1969) called a "means-means-means" way of existing.

As the human process is reduced to a source of productivity, human life is assessed by the same criteria as technology, rather than evaluating technology according to its ability to satisfy human experience. So, "dominance by technology" means that people are evaluated according to the technological criteria of efficiency and productivity, even if the purpose of the production is unknown and unquestioned. The technological society does not ask the purpose the technology is to serve. The unexamined assumption is that technological advance means improvement in the condition of humanity.

The Contemporary Technological World

Heidegger's concern about the cleavage between person and world is even more apposite to the contemporary world of technological saturation than the world of factories and production lines of Heidegger's acquaintance. The home computer interposed technology in daily living to a far greater degree than did industrial machinery, but at least in the age of the home computer, one must be in the location of the desktop to use it. Today's technological world is differentiated from other ages by its mobility and omnipresence. Now not only do laptop computers make computers omnipresent, but also handheld mobile devices, such as the iPhone, BlackBerry, and iPad, are constant companions. To borrow a phrase from Turkle (2011), it is this "tethering" to gadgetry that makes the current technological society unique. Text messaging and social networking go on continually: during meetings, while on the phone, writing, doing homework, shopping, waiting in line, listening to a lecture. In Heidegger's time technology was a major presence but it was not mobile; in today's culture of cell phones, iPads, and wireless communication, technology is a constant companion. It is this tethering to technological devices that defines the contemporary age of technology.

Continual connectivity was heralded as a means of increasing production, a value of the highest order in the postindustrial world. However, Turkle's (2011) comprehensive study of the impact of omnipresent technology on daily life tells a much more complex story. Turkle found that many white-collar workers express a feeling of suffocation at the expectation that they should be available continually with little respite from the demands of productivity, a tension felt even when not working. Business is conducted on evenings and weekends, and the expectation of continual availability of employees and service providers is not uncommon. Mobile technology has blurred the distinction between work and home life. And, of course, speed has become the highest priority. In a world shaped by Internet communication, rapid response is expected because technology makes it possible.

One subject of Turkle's (2011, p.165) study, whom she calls Diane, summarized the effect of technology on her work life this way, "I suppose I do my job better, but my job is my whole life. Or my whole life is my job. When I move from calendar, to address book, to e-mail, to text messages, I feel like a master of the universe; everything is so efficient. I am a maximizing machine. I am on my BlackBerry until two in the morning. I don't sleep well, but I still can't keep up with what is sent to me." The constant tension of this life is manifest despite Diane's belief that she is "master of the universe." That self-image is transparently empty coming from the mouth of someone who feels like a "maximizing machine" unable to keep up with the demands she is desperately attempting to meet.

The proof that the burden of performance of her machine-like existence outweighs any value ascribed to her technology-driven grandiosity lies in the fact that Diane suffers from insomnia and a hysterical loss of voice. Living with the constant tension of falling behind, Diane cannot relax enough to sleep. Even more tellingly, her life is not under her control; her self-image as master of the universe ironically applies only to what is demanded of her. It is as though she is a piece of machinery being run relentlessly even as it is being worn down. Her efficiency makes her feel like a "master," but she is a slave to high-speed demands that dominate her life. Not being able to influence how she is used, Diane has no voice, figuratively and now literally. Diane is a paradigmatic example of "enframement," a productive piece of an imposed structure with little regard for her experience.

As the above quote from Diane shows, the enhanced capabilities made possible by the wonders of mobile and cyberspace technology stimulate among some a feeling of exceptional power, an almost superhuman sense of oneself. But, this grandiosity applies to externally imposed expectations and therefore translates not into a good feeling for oneself, but into the fear of failing to keep pace, as we saw in the case

of Diane. My patient, Daniel, a lawyer who was a managing partner in a successful firm, put it this way, "I used to enjoy the creative part of the law, but now with
computers and iPhones, clients expect everything to be done immediately, and there
is no time for the creative part. I can't think. I can get much more work done more
quickly, but I am just churning it out; it is never enough. Clients expect everything
to be done immediately and 24/7 availability. I feel like a drone." What could be a
more clear expression of Heidegger's concern about technology? Heidegger's fear
that human being was becoming reduced to a machine-like source of productivity
has come closer to the reality in the contemporary world than it was in Heidegger's
precomputer society.

Turkle's subjects articulate what Jerold felt and enacted during his entire professional life. He was tethered to his mobile devices like any professional in Turkle's
study and very much imprisoned by the very technology that was supposed to make
life easier. Of course, the BlackBerry is not the cause of his depression; such a view
would be simplistic and superficial. The pressure of the modern world made possible by the Cartesian split has fostered the crystallization of Jerold's self into a
means of production. Once Jerold adopted that *modus operandi* he was vulnerable to
the demands of responding to the heightened expectations fostered by the world
of mobile technology. His BlackBerry and laptop computer did not create his over-
burdened life, but they made it possible and added a level of speed and heightened
expectations to his already overloaded life. Jerold's need to keep his mobile technological devices with him was a symptom of a worldview that sees people as behavioral
organisms of productivity, and the weight of that pressure expressed itself in his
depression. Jerold fell victim to what might be called the *productivity/grandiosity/empti-
ness* dynamic of the contemporary technological world.

The demand of productivity goes back at least to the Industrial Revolution, but the
assembly line, as dehumanizing as it can be, is left behind at the end of the workday.
Continual productivity was not even expected in the computer age of the 1980s;
the blurring of the boundary between work productivity and leisure time became a
common expectation in the current age of mobile devices. The spectacular capabilities of contemporary technology have made it possible, and the societal response
has been to seize upon that opportunity to accelerate work production and use it
to intrude on personal life. Family and personal existence are increasingly eroded
as mobile technology breaks down the boundaries between home and work life.
Another patient, Rebecca, an assiduous and seemingly tireless worker, slept with her
cell phone in anticipation of a work call in the middle of the night. Anxious about
the possibility of a problem occurring that she was not available to fix, she was not
able to fall into a restful sleep. Her exhaustion eventually resulted in her leaving the
job in a depressed state.

As a society, we have adopted the principle that all should be done as fast as
resources allow. When technology accelerates a process, the new speed becomes the
new standard. One is reminded of what the developmental psychologist Jean Piaget
used to call the "American question." Once a developmental process is discovered,
Piaget used to say, the Americans will ask if it can be done faster. The invention of

cyberspace has set a standard for speed that enslaves many people to the devices that were supposed to free them.

The result of these contemporary technological breakthroughs has been to facilitate a further widening of the gap between person and world that began in the Cartesian age and was accelerated by the Industrial Revolution. One telling example of this ominous trend in our current age of "tethered technology" is Turkle's observation that in the early days of cell phones, to answer a call in the middle of a conversation was considered rude, but within a few years, it was commonplace and acceptable. Mobile technology not only intercedes between people, it also takes priority whenever there is a conflict between human interaction and technological communication. The world can be seen only by peeking through the occasional holes in the glitter of technological brilliance, and one has to work to find the openings. Because technology is an assumed way of life, very few contemplate the existence of such openings, and fewer still seek them out. This situation is in stark contrast to the pretechnological world in which the person-world relationship did not have to be made conscious because it was assumed.

A dramatic example of the widening cleavage between person and world is the popularity of computer role-playing games, such as Ultima2, which allow people to live out parallel lives. Even more tellingly, Second Life is a virtual place rather than a game. One can create a life that, as the producers put it, "you can love." Turkle (2011) describes adults in mid-life who lead a second life on the Internet. They use the term "life-mix" to refer to the intertwining of their life and their simultaneous online life that is often preferred. What Turkle (2004) calls the "second self" enters into the creation of one's Avatar, which many take so seriously they prefer their Avatar life to the life they are living on Earth. The Avatar is treated as though one is living out its life, but the person remains hidden and thus protected from the blows of human interaction. For the devotees of the game, the degree of control they have of the Avatar life makes it preferable to their daily lives.

While people have always found means of escape from life's conflicts, in today's technological world two simultaneous lives can be lived. Some of Turkle's subjects are on Second Life all day, intermittently living both lives throughout a typical day. The "second life" removes such people from the world via a dissociated self, a regressive move analogous to the imaginary friends of young children. The need for such a "second life" is both an indictment of their current life and a defensive response to it that can only cause stagnation, an arrest in growth that is uniquely technological. Like the distractions of cell phones and iPads, the age of contemporary technology did not cause this type of dissatisfaction, but it did make possible a type of avoidance that simulates reality far better than any more typically avoidant defense and therefore is more seductive and likely to arrest growth.

The infiltration of mobile devices into virtually every aspect of daily life has been especially acute for young people. Some of the most basic human experiences can no longer be taken for granted. Turkle's research in the 1980s found children doing homework with the TV and music on, perhaps holding a video game in hand. While that scene might be disturbing to the parents of these children, it is a tranquil atmosphere compared to today's child who does homework, according to Turkle (2011, p.162), while "attending to Facebook, shopping, music, online games, texts, videos, calls, and instant messages." E-mail is not part of the package, says Turkle, because it is regarded as a technology of the past by the under-25 generation. The omnipresence of mobile devices has led to a pervasive distractibility among young people. They have difficulty maintaining concentration on a single activity as they juggle a myriad of activities while attempting to complete tasks such as schoolwork.

A commonly held myth is that by learning to manage a variety of tasks simultaneously, today's youth have developed a new competence: the ability to multitask. The dizzying array of simultaneous activities is defended on the basis that it promotes the ability to perform well on a variety of projects simultaneously. While mobile technology has created the grandiose illusion that we can perform many activities at one time without any loss of performance, the evidence emphatically and convincingly debunks this belief. There is an abundance of well-confirmed research showing that in multitasking all tasks are done at a subpar level (e.g., Ophir, Nass, & Wagner, 2009; Jackson, 2008). The reality is that doing several tasks simultaneously serves to degrade performance on each one.

Most tellingly, texting and instant messaging are no longer primarily practical activities; they have become a way of life, pervading virtually every way of being. Although the Internet began as a way to communicate practical information with alacrity, it quickly became a forum for gossip and social conversation, and, from there the Internet's spectacular communicative capabilities became a venue for social life and a popular source of meeting potential romantic partners. Turkle's (2011) research found that from a means of quick communication to achieve goals, the Internet has become the way adolescents contact and relate to each other. As a result, today's adolescent seems to feel unsure of what his experiences are outside of the magic of cyberspace communication. Adolescents report a sense of self so fragile that they cannot even be sure of the emotions they begin to feel without calling a friend to seek validation for their nascent affective states (Turkle, 2011, p.176–9). Often they send out a text or voice mail message in order to *have* a feeling.

Living lives of continual, for some almost nonstop, Internet contact, adolescents today commonly lack the ability to be alone and reflect on their states of mind. When feeling lonely, the adolescent uses texts and the instant messaging of brief telegraphic communications to feel connected. In the terse chatter of Internet communication, today's adolescent takes the sting out of his loneliness, but he is not engaged with the other. He gains neither the satisfaction of solitude, nor the enrichment of human connection. In Turkle's words, he is alone together.

The loneliness of so many of today's adolescents appears in their difficulty separating from their family of origin. Departure from the family home is a scary proposition that many of today's young people attempt to avoid, and cyberspace provides them with the opportunity. There is a tendency among many college freshmen to stay in continual contact with their parents (Turkle, 2011, p.173). Some newly departed adolescents make contact with home 15 times in one day. But, this contact consists primarily of texting. The texting and other brief communication used for this purpose do not constitute an emotional connection, and often the students do not even attempt a conversation. Their messages are typically the telegraphic style characteristic of texting. While not producing a human connection, the online communication or texting serves to create a distant sense of contact that takes the sting out of the loneliness. In this way, the adolescent makes contact without forming a meaningful bond. Once again, she is alone together.

This fragility of interpersonal life has resulted in a dramatic shift in the nature of relationships among today's youth. Now social networking and dating service websites have become well-established means for pursuing, finding, forming, and maintaining relationships. For many people it is the *primary* means for social interaction and meeting future partners. Approximately 100 million people use Facebook in the United States alone (Turkle, 2011). The average user has 130 "friends" in her list, sends out eight requests each month for new friends, visits the site 40 times every month for an average of 23 minutes per visit, and creates 90 pieces of content per month. As an aggregate, 30 billion pieces of content are shared every month on the site leading to a staggering 770 billion page views in a typical month. In a few years online communication has gone from a casual way of conversing to a primary method of social contact and interaction. "Being connected" once meant an emotional bond but now refers to available communication technology. People who rely on Facebook and online communication for their social world make contact, but they are alone.

Much online contact occurs through the Facebook profile that young people learn to manage in order to present themselves with an acceptable façade. A typical subject was a 14-year-old who agonized over her profile for days, worrying that she would not sound interesting (Turkle, 2011, p.180). She wondered what kind of personal life she should *say* she had. Ages 13 to 18 were once the years of experimenting with identifications; they are now the years of profile writing, which is to say, façade creation. Adolescents tend to see the profile as an opportunity to create a presentation to the world. One college senior warned Turkle away from anyone who claimed his Facebook profile was authentic. "You make a character," he told Turkle.

These well-constructed façades would not be of great concern if they were seen as acting, as playing with one's online identity. But, these online personas are taken seriously. The adolescents writing their profiles are fearful of being judged for the very preferences they indicate. Girls obsess over what pictures to use and whether to purchase special software to look better. Shrinking software makes girls look thinner. One student worked so hard to perfect his Facebook façade as cool and "in the know" that he dropped out of the online world. The profile is not a game; the carefully crafted image is who one *is* online, which for many is tantamount to their social existence. The seriousness with which the online self is taken is captured by a teen who said, "If Facebook is deleted, I am deleted." And the concocted persona is available to a public that peruses every preference listed. To be sure, concern about self presentation is an age-old affliction among adolescents and many adults as well, but to have that presentation documented in detail and available for public scrutiny is unique to this generation.

For similar reasons, young people prefer texting and other more distant modes of communication such as instant messaging to the telephone because they fear the spontaneity and open-endedness of conversation. Online communication protects from displays of emotion which many adolescents and young adults believe makes them vulnerable. One of Turkle's subjects learned of the sudden death of a friend by instant messaging and was grateful for being told online so she could "compose herself" and ensure no one would see her grief. She then proceeded to discuss her pain online where no one could see her. Fearing that the eyes of the world would see her as vulnerable, this subject carefully organized her grieving so that her affects would be hidden behind the Internet. "Composure" came first. Another high school student had to move when her parents separated, and one friend expressed her regret and sense of loss by texting her. Today's instant cyberspace connections provide a ready defense against emotional vulnerability.

One of Turkle's most dramatic findings is that this protectiveness has resulted in the inability to converse among many of today's youth. Turkle's high school sophomore subjects acknowledged that they were avoiding direct human interaction through the safety of the Internet. All agreed on staying away from telephone conversations, the very fabric of teen social life just two decades ago. They fear both the emotional revelation that might emerge spontaneously and the potential rejection if the other person wanted to end the call first. Texting is preferred because it provides greater control over the communication and less opportunity to feel rejected. One girl commented: "You wouldn't want to call because then you would have to get into a conversation. . . . It is almost always too prying, it takes too long, and it is impossible to say good-bye" (Turkle, 2011, p.200). Another summarized the feelings of the group by saying she does not "see the point" of a phone call because it is "too much recap and sharing of feelings. With a text . . . I have control over the conversation and control over what I say" (Turkle, 2011, p.190). This young woman went on to say she thought telephone conversations require "too much pressure" to sustain and are "too difficult" to end.

This comment crystallizes the feeling of many of today's adolescents that conversation is a burdensome, anxiety-ridden undertaking that is best avoided. As a result of such assiduous avoidance of spontaneous interaction, these young people simply do not know how to hold a conversation. One teenage boy with refreshing candor said he was not ready to talk on the phone, but at some point he might have to "force himself. . . . For later in life I'll need to learn how to have a conversation . . . rather than spending my life in awkward silence" (Turkle, 2011, p.201).

Turkle's findings show young people are using the Internet to stay away from the anxieties and vulnerabilities of direct emotional encounter. On the Internet one can ask someone for a date or break off a relationship without having to look into the eyes of the other or even hear their response. Internet communication has become a readily available means for maintaining the aloof, defensive stance adopted by many adolescents to defend against the vulnerability of emotional contact with others. One boy stated that in telephone conversations "too much might show" (Turkle, 2011, p.200). Cyberspace communication, because it tends to be brief, superficial, and does not require spontaneous responses, provides a ready means to circumvent the anxieties that bedevil adolescent interaction. One does not have to confront the spontaneous feelings of either intimacy or conflict when hiding behind the barrier of Internet space. That posture would not have serious consequences if it were used as a supplement to substantive dialogue. But, as a primary means of communication, emotional distance, superficiality, and inauthenticity characterize today's adolescent interactional style.

Reification of the Self

As we have seen, it is precisely in the interaction with another seen as an experiencing subject that the self grows and flourishes. The use of cyberspace as a means for forming relationships withdraws the nutrients young people need for the growth of the self and therefore impedes self development. The cost of using the Internet as a primary means of communication and relating is no less than the danger it presents to the capacity to engage in discourse with fellow human beings. And while most people would intuitively endorse the importance of conversation, few ponder the hard truth that dialogue is what makes us human and without the ability to converse, young people are in danger of losing their very humanity. Cut off from the world of meaningful human conversation, the individual is left in a solipsistic enclosure that remains static and feels empty. The adolescent will often attempt to fill this void by the stimulation of Internet games and activities, a strategy that ultimately only removes him ever further from the world of human relationships.

Joyce, a 20-year-old female patient, illustrates the dilemma of some of today's youth precisely because she was so exceptionally bright, talented, and creative that her inability to hold a serious conversation seemed strangely disconnected from who she was. This college student could write with sophistication well beyond her years, took sensitive photographs, and had a mature intellectual understanding of drama, cinematography, and literature. But, she could not discuss anything of an emotional nature without laughing. Her discussions with friends were almost entirely by texting and instant messaging with occasional brief e-mails. In the therapeutic process, when beginning to discuss any emotionally laden topic—the trauma of her parents' divorce, her mother's inability to take care of her, her mother's emotional dependency on her and difficulty allowing her to separate—Joyce laughed, insisting all those issues were "funny" or even "ridiculous." She could not feel the gravity of any of her struggles, even as she called them "weird" while laughing at the apparent absurdity of her anger, fear, and anxiety. Only highly intellectualized conversations about abstract topics were treated with any degree of seriousness.

It may be tempting to conclude that Joyce is simply defending against painful affects with her laughter, but there is more to the story. Joyce could not converse, and the expectation of doing so in therapy felt to her like an unrealistic demand. She was being asked to do something she had never done: communicate affects and viewpoints directly, a request she found alien. Her only serious communication taking place via cyberspace, this demand was beyond her. In psychotherapy, she laughed off all the painful experiences of her life that she was able to discuss on the Internet. Her experience of psychotherapy could have been described by Turkle's subject: "too personal," too much out of her control.

Joyce was unpracticed at even minimal conversation around anything save intellectual discourse. Cyberspace had offered her a ready defense, and having taken it, direct, meaningful human conversation was unknown to her. She was victimized by not only the traumas of her past, but also the technological dominance of a world that gave her little space in which to articulate the effects of her childhood pain.

The change in the way young people regard themselves and their fellow human beings can be seen in their attitude toward robots, one of the most sophisticated technological achievements of our age. In the early years of robots, when their performance was still somewhat crude, children tended to have doubts that robots could substitute for the human interaction they clearly preferred (Turkle, 2011). But, 20 years later the children were not so sure. Once robots could speak and express "caring" in response to distress, American youth became less sure that robots were poor substitutes for the human touch. If the robot can retrieve food and perform the necessary tasks, the children were likely to wonder, why not use a robot? Now both children and adults are much more likely to believe robots can meet the needs of elderly persons. The "human" element that mattered before seems to be vanishing.

The importance of this shift, Turkle notes, lies not in the capabilities of robots, which are far from being able to perform at a human level and not widely used, but in the transformation in the way humans are seen by young people. Identifying the person with observable performance, young people see the human as a specimen who performs tasks, and such a view blurs the distinction between human and robot. Despite limitations on the capabilities of robots, the subjects in Turkle's study saw themselves as machine-like, not clearly distinguishable from robots which they believe will eventually be able to do virtually everything people now do. The upshot is that there is a fast-growing tendency to see ourselves as machines (Turkle, 2004). Once we conceptualize the human as machine-like behavior without an experiential process, we no longer endow human experiencing with a unique value. If the robot can perform as we can, then the robot is substitutable for the person. This is what Turkle calls the "behaviorism" of our technological age.

While a behaviorist view of the person precedes contemporary technology, children did not always adopt this ideology. Turkle's investigations suggest that technological advances have had a significant influence on the way children and adolescents regard themselves and others. In Turkle's (2004) early work, many MIT and Harvard computer specialists tended to see their minds as computers, information processing organs, machines housed inside their bodies. At that time, such a mechanistic view of human being was found primarily among those who built computer systems. Today, however, this equation of people with their behavior has spread well beyond those who work in information processing. In fact, as we saw in Chapter Two, academic psychology does exactly that.

Vanishing from the minds of today's youth is the experiencing subject, the very being deleted by psychology textbooks. As the behavior of human-constructed machines achieves a degree of behavioral similarity to what people do, the importance of what is experienced has tended to disappear from the consciousness of young Americans who are not sure we are not robots, or at least they question whether there is a meaningful difference.

Two points are salient here. First, this weakening respect for the quality of the human experience is inconceivable apart from a technology-saturated environment. In a world of robots and tethered technological devices, machine simulating human behavior has become the icon for the well-functioning person. Rather than making machines to emulate the human process, we look at the machine as the model of what we should be. If the machine can do the job, no more questions are asked. As a result, many young people believe that robots are suitable to care for the elderly because they can perform all the necessary tasks, such as retrieving food and doing errands.

Second, the severing of the human subject from the world of objects in homogenous space disturbs the very nature of what it is to be human. Without being attuned to the world, the self cannot realize its possibilities. Whatever emanates from "standing reserve" is a resource to be used for some external purpose analogous to the Earth as a source of electrical power rather than a place to dwell. And further, without the ability to disclose the world, to open ourselves to its possibilities, desire becomes deracinated, a mere reaction to the assault of forcible imposition on being. Thus, lack of self is often hidden beneath highly functioning behavior until anxiety-driven lifelong patterns are no longer viable, as we saw with Jerold. At that point the long-hidden confusion about where and how one fits, who one wishes to be, even who one is, surfaces in the form of symptoms, such as depression. Typically, it is interference with the ability to produce that motivates such patients to seek help, rather than any questioning of the all-consuming need to produce. Jerold is representative of this type of patient, unaware of the relationship between his symptoms and the attempt to fill his emptiness with productivity. Like most such patients, Jerold wanted to be "patched up," to return to his previous level of production, but the depression he endured was a symptom of a life devoted to producing, and his substitution of productivity for self was an unconscious assumption he did not question.

Jerold was engaged in a lifelong struggle to please his father and be the favorite among four brothers. Never having given a moment's consideration to whether business would be a satisfying career, after 20 years in business he was shocked to find himself deeply depressed with no apparent precipitant. Analytic work revealed the power of his need to be the favorite of the idealized patriarch, but what is easily overlooked from an analytic perspective is that in his rush to success Jerold identified himself with his vocation, thus reifying his sense of self. In the analytic work motivated by his psychic collapse, it became clear Jerold was miserable in a career he found meaningless, an awareness that was beyond him until the paralysis and resulting analytic exploration to which it gave rise. As a resource for the project of making his father happy, Jerold was single-mindedly focused and unable to engage the world in any other way.

Viewing himself as a resource, Jerold was unable to imagine any process of becoming and saw no path for discovering a meaningful purpose once his misery was manifest. Seeing no possibility of movement, no fluidity in its states, a reified self does not contemplate alternatives to productivity. Or, to say this another way, the self as standing reserve is ossified, such that other ways of living cannot be imagined. Mitchell's (1993) observation that psychopathology is a failure of the imagination can be understood as a recognition that the reified self is the root of much psychopathology. It is not just that the patient feels hopeless; it is that the concept of an alternative does not exist.

Jerold's way of experiencing himself shows that the impact of technology goes deeper than the use of cell phones, computer games, and the Internet. As Turkle (2004) has shown, many people now think of their minds as computers. A generation of young people is moving away from personal responsibility by conceptualizing their minds as information processing machines for which they take little responsibility. This cultural phenomenon may explain the clinical observation of Fonagy et al. (2002) that many patients do not see their experience as psychological, that is, they do not see that their perception of the world is *theirs*, a product of their viewpoint, but rather, as a "thing" the same as any object in space, what they call "psychic equivalence." The purpose of the analytic process for the Fonagy group is to have the patient recognize that his experience is psychological. Relevant here is McDougall's (1996) observation, discussed in the last chapter, of the pervasiveness of alexithymia in today's patients. This form of reification of human experience may well be a manifestation of the technological culture in everyday living. Such a reductionism was unthinkable prior to the Cartesian revolution.

Needless to say, the technological culture has penetrated the family. The selective responsiveness of parenting figures often bear an enframement that closes off space in a preshaping, and to this degree the child becomes "standing reserve," a commodity that is to be productive in some fashion, but at a great distance from what it is to *be*. One need look no further than the plethora of materials on the market designed for accelerating the child's intellectual development to be convinced that children are increasingly being seen as resources. While the toy market has been declining for years, the only growing portion of the market is educational toys with sales of more than $3 billion in the United States alone. As products of the technological culture, parents participate in the enframement of their children, often with good intentions. While it is only natural for parents to want their children to succeed, if the child is only a resource, the enframement will define who he is, as happened with Jerold. The very fabric of human interaction has become so saturated with technological presuppositions that we are blind to their influence.

Furthermore, the sundering of the person-world relationship creates the expectation and belief among some that they do not need the world. The omnipotent illusion that one can control all is an effort to concoct a mirage to fill the void where the self should be. The idea of a self that establishes and organizes itself apart from the world is one of the myths of post-Enlightenment Western civilization, a myth that "inflates the subjectivity of the controller, a narcissistic degeneration of humanity" (Feenberg, 2003, p.328). This illusion is nurtured, but not created, by the ability to perform complex tasks by clicking buttons on a computer. The widely recognized "culture of narcissism" (Lasch, 1991) is not simply a society of indulgence; it is a burden of the technological world, an oppression that not infrequently results in a sense of failure when the reality of dependence on the world can no longer be denied. It is not by accident that the emergence of narcissism as a major problem is roughly coincident with the age of modern technology. One of the great ironies of our age is that as we are increasingly removed from our humanity, individual grandiosity has become more common and pronounced.

This is all by way of saying that the issue at the most fundamental, ontological level is the reification of the self. In a technological world, the self is standing reserve, and, therefore can be "seized upon" not just by others but also by oneself. In such a world the temptation to reify the self, or at minimum acquiesce in its reification, and the objectification of the other is almost irresistible. A growing number of the more computer knowledgeable among us believe their lives are determined by physical processes over which they have little control (Turkle, 2004). But, many others who would not agree with that view implicitly treat themselves and others as reified entities rather than experiential beings. Such unnoticed objectification of self and others ensures that our experience will be dominated by a technological mode of being, and that has the potential to do more harm than explicit comparisons of the human brain with computers. It would be naïve to think that modern technology can be somehow overcome or dismissed, but we can be aware of its impact and the pressure it puts on us to shape ourselves to fit a technology-dominated world. Without such awareness, we remain enslaved to the enframement dictated by the impersonal march of technological advance. But, with consciousness of this influence, it is possible to resist the pressure to reify the self and stay attuned to one's experience and open to the world's possibilities.

Heidegger Meets Winnicott on the Analytic Couch

So, Jerold, unhappy in business, desperately tried to use the analytic process to find more satisfying avenues of gainful employment, none of which seemed appealing. What would he like doing? What would work? He could not seem to know how to think about the question. The dilemma he now confronted was not simply that he had been in competition to please his father, but that his life had been built on a presupposition that his role was to be a resource, to be utilized as a commodity. Within that enframement, no vocational path could look appealing.

At first I tried to facilitate an answer by encouraging the search for alternative vocational routes. But, when I realized I was motivated by a fear that his prodigious intellect would go to waste, it occurred to me that I had been colluding in his assumption of himself as "standing reserve." It was then I began to convey to Jerold that underlying his competition with his brothers was an assumption that his aim in life was to produce. Attempting to free us both from the assumption that he needed to be a resource, I wanted the analytic space to be a "clearing" (Heidegger, 1927/1961) so he could be attuned to new possibilities. He would be depressed, I thought, as long as he was unable to be open enough to listen to where the world called him. I asked him to stay open, not to foreclose anything, but to see what appeared to him in the potential space we were now creating in the analytic dyad (Winnicott, 1971). Although this approach puzzled Jerold, in my view it is the pivotal analytic move because it kept open the potential space in which Jerold could listen to the call of the world, the negative capability Keats (1817/2005) recognized as so important for self discovery and creativity.

Jerold was skeptical, but after many sessions of excruciating analytic work, he began to think of vacations in Maine, the only times, he said, that he ever really felt he was anywhere he wanted to be. In fact, he went on to say, "Now that I think of it, although I never really noticed it before, being in the woods is the only time I feel at all like myself." This thought led to his depiction of idyllic times in wooded, rural areas, a peace he had allowed himself only rarely and had not regarded as a particularly important part of his life. When there, he was absorbed in the rural experience and thought of little else. It was only now in the analytic space that he realized the depth of these experiences and their unique ability to bring him alive. This is to say, those experiences became real for him in the potential space of the analytic relationship.

Without describing the ensuing process in detail, suffice it to say that Jerold used the analytic relationship to explore the meaning of these rural experiences. Eventually he came to the realization that they represented a distinctive way of being in his life that conflicted with the life he felt obliged to follow. He contemplated leaving business completely, but eventually realized the entrepreneurial creation of new ideas and products offered an intellectual challenge he would miss. It was not business itself that made his life so burdened, but the dominance it had gained over his life. He decided not to quit business to live a rural existence, but he did reshape his life, delegating much of the administration of his business to others while focusing on developing new ideas and creating more time for himself apart from the business world. He bought a farm, explored a myriad of activities there, and divided his life between business and farm living.

As he constructed this way of being, Jerold was surprised to see himself creating a life that did not fit a preconceived niche. He saw that he found not simply a new balance between vocation and other interests, but the ability to listen to his experience and use it as a guide. It was this capability of attuning himself to a world of much wider contour that opened his life. He found ever-new ways to engage his family life, conduct his business, and relate to friends and business associates. The ability to use the potential space in the analytic dyad began the tortuous journey to liberate himself from the imprisonment of existing only as a resource to ways of being that were in no way prescribed.

And this is the way the analytic process can be used to transcend the stifling nature of modern technology to create the self engaged with and open to the world in the face of whatever miracles and wonders are wrought by the latest technological gadgetry. When he left, Jerold said that the greatest benefit he derived from analysis was the ability to question assumptions and find a new way out of any dilemma by an engagement with his own experience. Able now to use his imagination, Jerold was no longer helpless and no longer a prisoner of a technological way of being.

11

CREATING A LIFE FROM TWO CULTURES

In the previous chapter we saw that the Cartesian separation of person and world provided the groundwork for our contemporary technological society, which, in turn, resulted in the penetration of the technological worldview into the very experience of the self. In this chapter another implication of the self-world cleavage is confronted: the divorce of the individual from the ethnic culture in which she finds her identity and home. The belief that the person can find her destiny, the realization of her possibilities, without influence from her ethnic and social background reverses the ancient wisdom known to Western civilization since Aristotle that self and community are interdependent and mutually defining. A self so conceived is cut off from the world now regarded as "external" and ethnicity then becomes divorced from individual experience. The present technological society, built on the value system of quantification, in its effort to reduce the subject of experience to an object in homogenized space has served to mask the interdigital relationship between self and ethnic community.

Within psychoanalysis, the historical emphasis on the "intrapsychic" and universal meanings followed the dominant Cartesian tendency to view the individual apart from social context and therefore diminished the importance of culture in understanding the individual. For many decades, psychoanalysis was equated to the study of the "internal world," the world of fantasy and dream that was supposed to be cut off from the social world. This theoretical prejudice was undoubtedly a major reason for the relative neglect of the role of ethnicity in the analytic process. While Freud did not regard culture as inherently implicated in individual desires, fantasies, or dreams, contemporary analytic theory emphasizing the self and its interdependence with other selves for its very existence ties the psychical to the ethnic and social culture in which the individual self grows and develops. So, with the self in the center of the analytic enterprise, ethnic and social identity becomes integral to analytic exploration.

Undoubtedly, a factor in the relative neglect of cultural influence is the demographic of the analytic patient population, which has been primarily white, affluent, well-educated professionals who shared their identity with the analyst. Under such conditions, it is easy to ignore or at least deemphasize the impact of culture. For example, Jerold, discussed in the last chapter, was an upper-middle-class, affluent, white male. As a member of the majority culture, there was no *apparent* reason to be conscious of his ethnicity or any such group identity in order to understand his depression.

While these factors are important in the historical neglect of race and ethnicity in the psychoanalytic dialogue, there is undoubtedly a deeper reason for the historical avoidance of ethnicity: Discussions of color and ethnic identity are in the United States likely to stir considerable anxiety, anger, and guilt (e.g., Bodnar, 2004; Leary, 1997b; Smith, 2006). The history of discrimination and racism is so brutal that it is difficult to even mention the topic without evoking an emotional reaction of some type. A white person often fears being accused of racism, or feels guilty at the mention of race, and a person of color not uncommonly wonders what the agenda is and what form of white racism might be lurking under any mention of racial or ethnic identity. And those are only a very few of the many possibilities. So, historically both parties in the analytic dyad have disavowed ethnicity even when it is a clear influence in the analytic relationship.

The quickly accelerating ethnic pluralism in the wider society and the growing ethnic diversity of the analytic patient population along with a very modest increase in analytic therapists of color has stimulated an increased awareness of this lacuna in analytic discourse (e.g., Dimen, 2000; Dalal, 2006; Leary, 2006; Smith, 2006). The implicit pact to not mention skin color and ethnic group has been breached in recent years by analysts who have brought ethnicity out of the analytic closet and into analytic discourse (e.g., Leary, 1997a, 1997b, 2000; Perez-Foster, 1996; Bodnar, 2004; Aggarwal, 2011). These groundbreaking discussions, having opened the door to the engagement of race, culture, and ethnicity in the analytic process, have emphasized the importance of culture and societal norms in defining the self (e.g., Benjamin, 1995; Layton, 2004, 2006; Dalal, 2011). This valuable and long overdue work demonstrates the influence of cultural values in the therapeutic relationship and the makeup of the self.

This chapter will explore the particular clinical issues presented by one group of people of color who live under the dual influence of the contemporary American world and the culture of their origin. I focus here on a group of American women of Asian descent who find themselves caught between the traditional ethnic culture of their family of origin and the wider American society to which they have been exposed by education, vocation, and social interaction.

Ethnicity in Psychoanalytic Therapy

The analytic exploration of ethnic identity has tended to focus on "cross cultural" psychotherapy, the therapeutic process that takes place between patient and therapist from different cultures (e.g., Leary, 1995, 1997b; Yi, 1998; Bodnar, 2004; Apprey, 2006; Aggarwal, 2011). In most cases, a white therapist treats a patient of color, and, in some, the reverse is the case, and of course there are discussions of analysts of color treating patients of color from a different ethnic group. A major theme of this work is the understanding of dissociative processes of both therapist and patient as they collude in the denial that their cultural backgrounds have an impact on their interaction. Bodnar (2004) argues that such a dissociation walls off a source of potentially transformative meaning. The purpose of this type of analytic exploration is to sensitize the therapist to the cultural influences on both parties to the dyad in order to overcome the mutual dissociation of ethnic identity that, if brought into the analytic dialogue, can be a useful source of therapeutic action.

This cultural sensitivity has alerted analytic therapists to the cultural assumptions and norms with which the therapist all too easily enters the consulting room. Most commentators in this area admonish the therapist to be aware of the cultural assumptions made by both parties in the therapeutic encounter especially if they differ from each other (e.g., Leary, 1997a, 2000). A fundamental tenet of this emerging psychoanalytic theory of ethnicity and race is that without consciousness of these assumptions the therapeutic couple is likely to replicate the unconscious cultural belief system of the therapist and miss the unique opportunity to use cultural differences in the service of transformative meaning (e.g., Bodnar, 2004; Layton, 2006).

What Layton calls *normative social unconscious processes* shape the analytic dialogue if these norms are not brought to consciousness. For example, class, racial, and gender hierarchies require splitting of independence from dependence, and it is this split that is psychically damaging rather than the dependence or independence itself. In this way, unconscious normative processes not only influence, but also may even define the analytic process outside of the awareness of both patient and analyst. For example, tethering dependence to the female and independence to the male splits the psyche, and fosters the use of narcissistic defenses to maintain the split. Layton notes that traits that can only flourish in tandem are split from each other, leaving the individual with profound narcissistic defenses. Identity categories based on splitting reify certain attributes while denying others, and this split in the psyche weakens the ability to function. So, it is the splitting of traits that can operate only in conjunction with each other, not the traits themselves, that creates the pathological outcome of normative unconscious processes. The key for the therapeutic process, for Layton, is making conscious such identity categories so they can be negotiated in the analytic relationship.

Therefore, it is crucial to this nascent psychoanalytic theory of race and ethnicity that analysts not fall into the trap of assuming what it means for any individual to belong to a cultural group. Critical to these discussions has been the linking of what is conventionally labeled a postmodern sensibility to race and ethnicity. Damage is done when the therapist, even with the best of intentions, presumes patient characteristics based on race or ethnicity. Leary (1997a, 2000) has been most convincing in arguing that race is not a given, not a fixed entity the meaning of which can be assumed, but a construction that can and does have widely different meanings to different patients of the same race or cultural background. She reports a case in which a clinic assigned a black patient to a black therapist on the assumption that the patient would prefer such racial matching although the patient herself never expressed such a preference. Leary believes that this stereotypical treatment of the patient was a serious roadblock to therapeutic progress. This type of assumption, Leary notes, amounts to a reification of race. Such stereotypes, whether of persons of color or white people, make unwarranted assumptions that certain attitudes are characteristic of a single ethnic group and therefore miss the patient's experience and replace it with reifications.

Nonetheless, it cannot be denied that race is a social reality. Even if one believes that race is purely a social construction, it remains a reality for both the member of any identified racial group and for those outside its borders. Consequently, Leary's conclusion is that racial and ethnic meanings constitute a dialectic between the social reality and individual meaning. Bodnar makes the point more broadly that identification with categories determined by social organizations of any type imposes a social meaning that has a tendency to calcify the individual. Nonetheless, roles such as "unemployed," "black," "poor," "Hispanic," and "blue collar," are social realities that have very real meaning. In Bodnar's view, awareness of the imposition of such roles makes possible the questioning of and confrontation with them required to achieve freedom from imposed social categories. Bodnar's conclusion accords with Leary's idea that the problem with racial, social, and cultural categories is not their existence, but their reification. The tendency in the culture at large to make assumptions about the attitudes, values, and traits of a single group makes ethnic identity one more self experience reified by the culture.

As Leary and Bodnar note, psychoanalysis has been guilty of the same hypostatization of ethnicity. Here we find a bright blue line separating classical and contemporary psychoanalysis at the juncture of culture and ethnic identity. The break from the past is that not only have race and ethnic identity become part of the analytic discourse, but also they are no longer viewed as reified entities, but rather as social realities subject to widely different meanings. In the terms of Fonagy et al. (2002), ethnicity must be *mentalized*, that is, seen as a psychological process, a way of perceiving, rather than "psychic equivalence," an entity with a determined meaning.

Although broached in somewhat different terms, we can see that a variety of analytic commentators on ethnic identity see the dangers of race, ethnicity, and culture to lie not in the existence of these categories, but in splitting them into simplistic binaries. Originating in the dominant American culture and its stereotypes, this splitting is passed through the family to the individual. The multicultural patient caught between the dominant culture and the ethnic group in which he was raised is particularly prone to this split. Needed here is a clinical strategy for patients who feel a sense of connection to two conflicting cultures, to one of which they are bound by filial and loyalty ties and to the other, by societal, cultural, and political connections and obligations.

While the "cross cultural" psychotherapy studies have opened the door to the exploration of race and ethnicity in the therapeutic interaction, such issues are but one type of psychotherapeutic dilemma emanating from the cultural diversity of contemporary American society. Attention to cross cultural psychotherapy is filling a lacuna in analytic thinking, but in today's world of rapidly growing ethnic diversity the cultural makeup of the population including those seeking therapy is far more complex than can be captured by a statement of the difference in cultural background between therapist and patient. In today's ethnically diverse population, many patients come to the consulting room possessing a "cross cultural" conflict of their own. Either immigrants or children of immigrants, such patients were raised in an ethnic minority family with varying degrees of involvement in a minority culture. Some grow up in a white community within which their family is a minority; others are raised in their own minority ethnic community within the hegemonic culture. To different degrees, these individuals bear imprints from both cultures.

Being influenced by two cultural groups is not problematic if the two cultures are synergistic, but when they are in conflict, as is common, the child grows up with pressures from competing value systems that can easily lead to unresolved identity conflict and symptom formation. This danger was well recognized in some Ancient Greek tragedies, the essence of which is the hero caught between cultures (Federici-Nebbiosi, 2006). The patients under discussion are raised with conflicting influences on basic values and ways of interpreting their experience and life expectations. This conflict puts the growing child and adult in a position of having to forge an identity among values and attitudes that are not easily reconcilable.

The Multicultural Patient

Most ethnic minority patients were either born in the United States or have lived here for many years, often being raised here, before seeking therapeutic help. With varying degrees of influence from the traditions of their ancestors and native lands, patients of color typically have a great deal of exposure to the culture of the United States, much of it in their formative years. The "multicultural patient" as used here means a patient whose formative influences are rooted in more than one culture. So, to say that such patients are of a different culture from their therapist, even if she is white, is only partly true. In most cases, it is more accurate to say that patients from ethnic minority backgrounds come from overlapping but different cultural backgrounds from the white therapist and often have an even more mixed combination of similarity and difference from therapists of color who may be from an ethnic or racial background different from the patient.

However, there is a caveat here, too. The dominant culture is experienced differently by people raised in a bicultural context from those who know only the hegemonic culture. That is to say, the person raised in an ethnic minority subculture reacts to the values and beliefs of the majority from a viewpoint steeped in an alternative worldview. Whatever attitudes, values, and beliefs of the mainstream culture are adopted by a multicultural individual have to be psychically housed alongside the values of the minority culture. So, the experience of American beliefs and practices cannot be assumed to be the same for the ethnic minority as for the white person. The former absorbs the dominant culture in conjunction with her ethnic culture thus producing a mixture of cultural identities that can be quite confusing and disorienting. Whatever anxieties the white patient has, they do not emanate from being identified as an outsider by the color of her skin. So, the analytic encounter of two such people involves overlapping but distinct cultural experiences.

The multicultural patient brings to analytic therapy a greater degree of conflict in values, self-representations, and identity formation than is likely to be found among other patients, and those conflicts are imbued with cultural assumptions. I focus here on one subgroup of American women of Asian background who are sensitive to pressure exerted by their culture of origin to adopt a compliant stance toward others, especially their family of origin. While this expectation of putting the needs of others before herself exists in varying degrees, in its most extreme form it becomes self abnegation or even collusion with one's own exploitation. This group is used here solely as an illustration of the treatment issues in multicultural patients and should by no means be taken to mean that all or even the majority of Asian American women possess this particular conflict. Many are not raised to be compliant, and of those who do experience such pressure, many do not acquiesce to it. The patients under discussion represent a subgroup of Asian American women who, even though they grew up in the United States, have been raised in a subculture that places the greatest value for women, even for women professionally trained, on doing service for the family. While promoting education for all children, in this subculture the parental expectation is for the girl to obey parental authority and adopt a service orientation to her parents even into her adulthood, an expectation not imposed upon male children.

But, of course, such women are part of the larger American society in which self determination is valued for both genders. To varying degrees, all these women have adopted these values and believe in their right to make decisions about their own lives, but that conviction conflicts with their loyalty to the principles on which they were raised. Because of the conflicting values of the two cultures, this group of patients is ideal for representing the treatment issues in the analytic therapy of patients caught between two cultures. Elucidating the dynamics of this particular group of patients draws out the therapeutic problems and issues raised by patients who are caught between two conflicting cultural value systems.

Feeling pressure from an early age to follow authority unquestioningly, many women in this group have difficulty combating pressure to be continually available to serve the family even if it feels wrong to acquiesce to it. Often the childhood of these patients includes vitriolic parental attacks for any suggestion of noncompliance with parental injunctions. Even as the patient becomes an adult, the unspoken assumption of the family is that she is to question neither these demands nor her obligation to fulfill them. This familial expectation becomes the "unthought known," a pattern known but not symbolized (Bollas, 1987). This group of patients feels a sense of loyalty to the family that leads them to submit to various degrees to familial expectations, accommodating to the wishes of others, often at the expense of their own desires and life goals.

The indication that this overt compliance does not bring psychic peace is the symptom picture, which may include anxiety, depression, relationship dysfunction, underachievement, and somatic complaints. Such reactions show that the patient has an aversive reaction to the demand for obeisance even as she enacts it repetitively. That is to say, the emergence of symptoms is an index that a motivation for agency and control opposing the need for pleasing others also has a powerful influence on the patient's psyche, however unconscious it may be. So, while the patient has the conscious belief that she has no choice but to acquiesce in others' requests, another voice struggles to speak out in silent rebellion against the passivity, but is able to expresses itself only in muted and indirect form. Unable to articulate her opposition directly, the young woman's desire and need for self determination are expressed in depression and other symptoms.

The longing for a sense of agency in opposition to compliance reflects a counter-vailing influence from the wider society, dominated by white culture but including many people of color, in which the patient was educated and socialized outside of the home. The values of autonomous choice making and feminism to which such women are exposed encourage opposition to blind acquiescence including the freedom to say "no" to one's parents. While this group of women is well aware that the implementation of these values is often spotty, or worse, in the culture that claims to live by them, the ethic of respect for all is the avowed standard. Even if it is an ideal, the American value system, whatever its drawbacks in application, in theory valorizes asserting control over one's life, becoming master of one's own destiny. Although the value of pursuing one's own destiny was largely confined to men until the 1960s wave of feminism, and in some areas continues to be a male-only virtue, girls raised since the 1960s, whether they identify overtly with feminism or not, have been exposed to a model of the female life as commanding choice equivalent to males. Women raised in a subculture that conflicts with the wider society in which it is embedded often can neither opt for one value system nor find a welcome reconciliation between them. They comply with the subculture on the surface, but express the other side of the conflict in symptomatic form.

The Therapeutic Interaction

Analytic inquiry into the compliant pattern can make conscious some of the dissatisfaction and frustration the patient feels over the lack of control over her own life. A key juncture of the therapeutic process is reached when the patient sees that she is harboring resentment just beneath her surface accommodation, a realization that provides incontrovertible evidence that she is in more conflict about the compliant pattern than she knew. Despite this awareness, when the therapeutic process focuses on the patient's pattern of compliance, the patient will often explain her behavior as the gender norm in her culture of origin. She feels she ought to collaborate with whatever is asked of her because that would be true to the culture in which she was raised and to which she continues to belong. However, that ethic is now in conscious conflict with the emerging anger at the disavowal of her desires. Resorting to a cultural value constitutes an avoidance of the patient's dissatisfaction with and growing anger at the cultural norm, an ideal that she now regards as problematic. So, the subcultural value of female accommodation reinvigorates the patient's ethnic identity, but at the same time operates as a defense against her growing conflict with that identity.

The idea that the patient should live her life with few choices of her own evokes anger at the value system on which she was raised, but that negative feeling toward her culture of origin leads to guilt and a sense of betrayal. Nonetheless, the anger constitutes a rebellion against what she comes to regard as a stifling subculture, despite the fact that it represents the ethnic heritage to which she still feels loyal. The anger and resentment, the rebellious rage at a culture that she feels costs her freedom, evokes a powerful sense of betrayal of her ethnic group that she feels is a minority fighting for its place in American society. The feeling of having betrayed one's community and its values is a more onerous guilt than the feeling of injuring one person. In addition, it issues in a fear that she may be enacting a cowardly accommodation to the dominant culture. This thought adds a sense of shame for not taking pride in the ethnic culture of one's community, childhood, and upbringing, especially when that group consists of recent immigrants who are battling for respect in the American melting pot that does not seem to melt very many. It is a haunting feeling, indeed, for such a patient to think she may be turning her back on the community that raised and provided her with practices and skills she uses for daily living. While her family and subculture of origin fight for respect and recognition on the stage of American life, such a patient fears that by adopting values of a white-dominated culture she is being disloyal to the culture with which she still strongly identifies.

Nonetheless, to accept the subcultural norm of compliance at the expense of one's own desires is to acquiesce in an unacceptably self-demeaning posture of helplessness. Once the patient realizes the cultural nature of the conflict, she is paralyzed by the burden of having to encounter distressing and paradoxically conflicting states of mind. Oscillating between the two cultures produces a confusion that often seems more disruptive, complex, and unresolvable than the symptoms for which she sought help.

The guilt and fear of betraying the culture of one's origin, the fear of feeling like a coward for accommodating to the more powerful culture, do battle with the feeling of not being respected, even exploited, and that any apology for mistreatment as a "culturally approved" pattern of behavior constitutes a betrayal of oneself. One sees these conflicting, often polarizing, positions, wax and wane as the patient becomes increasingly confused about who she is and what she believes.

For example, as the patient feels her subculture was imprisoning, she often begins to take steps toward psychic agency, opposing requests and demands from her ethnic group. The temptation is then strong to split off the ethnic culture as the bad object, but that evokes guilt and betrayal of cultural identity. My clinical experience has been that the patient reacts with intense anxiety to her new efforts at assertiveness. Beyond the guilt is a fear of being lonely, of burning bridges with kin on whom she had always felt she could rely, and being left all alone with neither community nor support. Nonetheless, those same kinship ties are enslaving, and the patient seeks the freedom to live without the burden they impose on her life. Returning to a life of self abnegation is not a possibility. Freedom has been tasted. The result is a seemingly irreconcilable conflict between ethnic identity and a growing sense of and need for agency derived from the values of the wider culture.

The therapist finds herself in a similarly perplexing dilemma. While therapists' reactions treating patients of different color inevitably vary widely, trying to engage the experience of a patient who possesses at least one set of unfamiliar cultural norms, the therapist is often unsure of what this different culture consists and what in the patient's behavior can be attributed to ethnic difference. And, even when it becomes clear that a pattern emanates from a cultural value, if that behavior is harmful, the analyst is left with the perplexing dilemma of having to confront a norm that may be a source of ethnic pride for the patient. The fact that behavior fits a subcultural norm does not end the story if it is implicated in the symptom picture.

The therapist is caught between, on the one hand, a fear of making assumptions that would impose his cultural beliefs on a person with a different set of cultural values, and, on the other hand, overlooking behavior that is pathological or abusive which can be hidden beneath the invocation of subcultural norms. How can the therapist be sure that she is not imposing a Western value on a patient who is simply living according to a different culture-bound value system? Is the therapist's temptation to encourage the patient to oppose familial expectations a function of the patient's dynamics or an inability to accept a different cultural value system? It is not for the therapist to judge the norms of the patient's subculture, so by dint of what can the therapist pursue an inquiry into the patient's compliance?

Whether the therapist is imposing an alien cultural value if he questions the patient's compliant way of being depends on the motive for such questioning. To the degree that the therapist reacts out of an aversive feeling that the patient's behavior is inherently strange and too far from what is regarded as the norm, it is based on the therapist's personal standard of familiarity. If, however, the patient's compliance leaves her helpless, unable to pursue her own desires, and depressed, the therapist's inquiry is beyond defensible; it is an imperative. For cultural reasons, the patient may feel compelled to follow filial dictates, but if the price is paid in symptoms such as helplessness, futility, and/or depression, the therapist would be remiss to accept the patient's compliance as an unquestioned subcultural norm. That is to say, symptoms justify the analyst's setting into question any culturally sanctioned way of operating. The patient's entrance into the consulting room does not put at issue all her convictions, but it does cede to the therapist the right to question any such belief or value involved in the emergence or maintenance of symptoms. As difficult as it may be to question the values of a culture to which one does not belong, the therapist cannot refuse to pursue a line of inquiry out of anxiety or the guilt of questioning the values of an ethnic group.

Understanding the conundrum from each perspective including the impact on both participants in the analytic dialogue sets the issues in high relief in the analytic space, but this emergence is rarely sufficient to find a way out of the conflict. The patient is made aware of the dilemma, but does not see a way out. A clinical strategy is needed to overcome the seemingly insurmountable dilemma that goes beyond the understanding of each side. Here again, as we have seen in other clinical impasses, the need is for a strategy of transcendence, a way to go beyond the positions on which the patient has been historically impaled and the analytic couple now find themselves. To demonstrate how this strategy works in the case of cultural conflict, let us turn to the analytic process with a patient who was trapped in this therapeutic problem.

Woman Trapped

We can see how these dynamics enter into analytic therapy with the multicultural patient by considering the therapeutic journey undertaken with Safia, a 38-year-old single Pakistani American woman, who had been depressed for two years before coming for a consultation. Not employed at the time of entering thrice weekly psychotherapy, Safia had held a high-level job with a large company for several years, but had finally quit two and one-half years before because she "could not take the stress." The youngest in a sibship of three, Safia came from an affluent suburban background. Both parents were Pakistani immigrant physicians who did well professionally and financially. At the point of entering therapy, her mother was retired and father about to do so. Her two brothers were financially successful, one a physician, the other in business, and both lived in other parts of the country. There was a large extended family, most of which lived out of town, but with whom the parents seemed to be in continual contact.

Safia was labeled the "difficult child" from an early age. She was considered a problem largely because she did not achieve academically as had her two older brothers. She went to a local college, but beginning in her sophomore year did not go to class and lied to her parents about her attendance. After she was forced to withdraw from college, she did very little, working only sporadically. One day her father informed her that he had enrolled her in medical school in Pakistan, and she was leaving the next day. She stayed with relatives and suffered through two years "hating every minute" until she returned home to her parents' chagrin. She eventually attended evening classes at a local university where she earned enough credits to enroll in a degree program, followed that with a Master of Arts, and shortly after, took an entry-level position with a large multinational corporation. Safia became consumed with the work, staying late, and working on weekends for which she was promoted several times and enjoyed a meteoric rise through the company. Safia described her former work life as demanding such constant availability that she slept with her BlackBerry and often was on the phone in the middle of the night trying to quell a crisis or meet a deadline the next day. Working almost around the clock, Safia slept little. After three years her exhaustion was so extreme she had to leave the company to relieve the stress. Although the company made clear it would welcome her back, Safia had lost her motivation and fell into a depression in which she remained at the point of entry into therapy.

Since leaving the job, she had not sought employment, and it appeared that she spent most of her time running errands and performing tasks for her parents, especially her mother. Although her mother was able-bodied and retired, she requested that Safia perform routine tasks for her on an almost daily basis. She asked Safia to go to the drugstore, shop, hardware store, or to secure any item, no matter how minor, that she might need. Although Safia fulfilled these requests without questioning them, her efforts were not appreciated by either parent. Her father constantly excoriated her for not doing enough for her parents or making mistakes in the errands she ran. She would fume and feel unfairly treated, but never overtly protested these vitriolic diatribes. Safia came under attack for being a bad daughter, selfish, and not fulfilling her obligations to the family. Nonetheless, Safia traveled to her parents' home daily to do their bidding, often subject to abusive criticism for her failure to fulfill some obligation correctly, and she often came to her sessions tired from the scurrying about to complete endless tasks and from the continual verbal sparring with her parents. When her two brothers visited, few requests were made of them. They joined the family chorus by accusing her of being too critical of her parents.

Early in the therapy, Safia went into detail around these events, and I noted that her exhaustion seemed to be similar to the state in which she described herself during her period of employment. At that point Safia explained how her job became so consuming. Once she had established a reputation as an effective worker, many people came to her with requests and assignments that were not in her purview, but she did them anyway. In part, she was flattered by the confidence others, including senior executives, placed in her, but more important was her inability to refuse a request. In a repetition of her family pattern, she simply never took seriously the option of setting limits on what she could do no matter how far outside her job description it was. Ultimately, she had more tasks to perform than she could manage and was frantic as deadlines approached. Overworked and exhausted from lack of sleep, Safia found that the only escape from these imprisoning demands was to terminate her employment.

Therapeutic Process

As might be expected, Safia's need to comply with what she regarded as my expectation of a "good patient" was paramount in her relationship with me. After an extended period of impeccable attendance, Safia began to oversleep on occasion and miss sessions. She was so anxious about whether she was meeting the standards of a good patient that when she overslept the session she felt a burdensome guilt and avoided calling me. I asked if she might be reacting to the demands she felt therapy placed upon her as she had ultimately enacted her anger at her company by quitting. But, Safia had no access to the negative side of meeting expectations. Her oversleeping was due to "exhaustion," and her explanation for quitting the job was that the "stress" was too much.

Despite not working and with an abundance of apparent free time, Safia felt that her life was not her own. Many of her therapy sessions were consumed with complaints about the treatment she was receiving from the entire family, which demanded her continual availability to them, but she never once suggested that she had the option of noncompliance. When I asked why not, she explained to me that she could not say "no" to her parents' demands without incurring their wrath and suffering the accusation of being an ingrate. Their expectations of her, Safia went on to explain, were part of the Pakistani culture in which she was raised and educated. I asked if she had feared retribution if she refused to fulfill an expectation on her job even if it was outside her job description. She was surprised at the question, but responded unhesitatingly in the affirmative even though she had never before noticed this dynamic.

Safia acknowledged resentment of her parents, especially her mother, for expecting her to do for them what they are fully capable of doing on their own. She also began to voice displeasure at the way her parents' demands were consuming her time to the point that she felt her life was being taken from her. In one conversation, her mother acknowledged that she asked Safia to do so much for her because she "did not want to be bothered." This rare moment of candor along with Safia's increasing awareness of the suffocation she felt at the ever-mounting parental demands for her time resulted in Safia's becoming consciously angry at her parents. I emphasized to her that the escalating anger was due to the awareness of how little control she was able to exercise over her life. I then went on to say that her feeling of helplessness and the immobilizing depression were directly related to her compliance with endless requests, many of which she knew the parents could do themselves, and the familial expectation that it was her role to serve the parents while her brothers did not. Safia responded curtly, "That is cultural." For Safia "cultural" seemed to represent a satisfactory explanation admitting of no further discussion.

Caught off guard by the decisiveness of the statement, I felt I was being told not to trespass upon another's culture. This strong stance was the first time Safia had shown any degree of noncooperation with me or the process. I felt that any probing of her pattern of compliance would be an ethnocentric devaluation of another way of life. Fearful of offending her ethnic group, I withdrew from questioning the practices of her subculture. I felt stymied, but the therapy sessions continued to be filled with expressions of her dissatisfaction and exhaustion in response to her parents' endless demands she felt constrained to meet.

At this point, the transference was taking shape in two primary forms. In the first, she was asking me to bear witness to her victimization at the hands of what she regarded as her cold, exploitive parents. I noted that she seemed to want me to hear and encode the unfair demands she felt her parents placed upon her. Safia agreed, saying that she needed someone to listen and acknowledge the validity of her complaints and the injustice of her parents' treatment of her because her entire extended family believed that she was the bad, ungrateful child who balked at doing her duty. She felt that I understood the hardship the family placed upon her in a way that no one in her family would ever see. At times she burst into tears sobbing that no matter how hard she tried, she felt "all alone" in the family. On the one hand, she lost control of her life by trying to please her parents who were critical of her irrespective of the demands she fulfilled, and, on the other, felt isolated as the black sheep who did not fit.

Safia experienced considerable relief in being able to discuss the constant demands placed upon her to someone who listened and seemed to understand the impact on her life. Nonetheless, she never questioned whether she should do anything differently. She saw me as the outsider who could empathize in a way her ethnic group could never do. While one might be able to justify the inference that I was the benign father she never had, I did not represent any significant individual from her background. The more powerful reaction to me was as a representative of the *cultural background* of her youth, the outside world different from and even critical of the subculture that her parents used to justify casting her in a submissive role. The outside world had given Safia at least the awareness that alternatives were out there, and I was its current iteration. The complexity of this case is demonstrated in the fact that Safia's strongest response to me in this phase of the analysis was her projection onto me of a *cultural* representation, an outsider who offered a different, freer, if not well-defined, open-minded outlook, just as the dominant culture had represented a more liberated role for the female in her formative years. Safia's view of me as a benign figure who represented a different approach, an alternative worldview, constitutes a *cultural transference*. The culture I represented made a deeper impression on her than how she saw me as an individual.

In this period my role seemed to be confined to that of a receptive audience, and there was a certain degree of gratification in the recognition that I could offer a perspective different from her family, focused on her experience, rather than the norm to which she was expected to fit. I felt that in a limited sense I was the benign parent she had always coveted. Nonetheless, despite the relief it brought Safia to have me in this role, I found myself having a number of disturbing reactions. While I maintained a consistently empathic stance toward Safia's helplessness, I was not doing anything about it. I was the audience to her unhappiness, but not the agent of its transformation. I found myself feeling a mounting frustration with my passive role.

I was operating on the basis that the only way to not become the insensitive white male who did not respect traditional cultures was to refuse to question the effects of Safia's passive stance. Unable to question the passivity that I believed to be implicated in Safia's depression, I felt that my therapeutic leverage had been stripped and a growing helplessness eventually led to anger, resentment, and a sense of paralysis. A strong tension arose between my role as therapist in which I felt free to pursue any line of inquiry I deemed of ultimate benefit to the patient and my fear of imposing my white American values on a woman of color.

It was then that I realized my refusal to question Safia's cultural attitudes and roles, although based on the realistic fear that she might be offended, had been an unwitting collusion with Safia's belief that she was helpless in the face of the customs of her subculture. Clearly I was prone to think this way because I seemed to adopt the attitude quite easily, although unconsciously. My refusal to inquire into her passivity put me in an ironically passive position. Unable to act for fear that I might offend, I shared Safia's paralysis. Rather than help her become more inquisitive and agentic, I had adopted the helpless stance toward Safia's culture that had made her unable to author her life. What I had regarded as my empathy for her plight was, in fact, a collusion with Safia's passive stance toward her subculture norms including a previously unsayable gender role that constrained the analytic discourse to the point of paralysis.

Convinced that I had colluded with Safia's cultural assumptions and having fallen into a therapeutically untenable position, I began to violate my vow of silence. This active stance precipitated the second major transference constellation. Timorously, I told her that I knew she did not want me to question the principles of her culture, and that I also feared imposing my values on her cultural customs, but that I also believed it is my obligation to speak about anything I judged to be doing her harm. I indicated that I felt there was a strong connection between her pattern of compliance, helplessness, and depression. Safia responded with a puzzled, but knowing look, as if she could see that I made some sense, but repeated her belief that she was following a role defined by her culture. When I then asked how she felt about my questioning the norm she regarded as "cultural," she said that she was skeptical of my motives because I might not appreciate the importance to her of a culture I did not understand, and the fact that I seemed to be aware of the consequences she was paying for her compliance only redoubled her suspiciousness of my ability to respect the customs of her culture. She went on to say that she found me threatening and perplexing because I was able to understand the deleterious impact of her subculture precisely because my cultural stance was outside her culture of origin. The two perceptions were born of the same cloth, but Safia had split them, experiencing me as either representative of the outside, part of a benign culture that offered her opportunities, or as the representative of an ethnocentric white culture who could not have any valid concerns about her culture of origin.

My insistence on exploring the connection between Safia's compliant pattern that was tied to her subcultural role and her symptoms ushered in a period of concentration on Safia's second transference constellation. Now she saw me as an outsider who, despite seeing the damaging effects of what she regarded as inviolate cultural norms and offering her what she regarded as support and validation not available from her closest ethnic connections, was suspect as someone who might dismiss her cultural background as an antiquated, misogynist, even oppressive minority culture and seek to erase its influence on her psyche. In the first transference perception, I was a breath of fresh air, someone who listened to her suffering; and in the second, a potential toxin that might destroy a major part of not only her heritage, but also her current identity. Safia acknowledged that she had refused to allow any discussion of her subculture because she feared I would blame it for her depression and pressure her to disown her ethnic identity. Thus, the stonewall of refusal to allow probing of the role of her subculture in her depression emanated from a strong transference perception that I would not be able to see the downside of her culture in broader context and therefore I would dismiss it as a pathogen.

Safia had projected onto me the negative side of her split view of her subculture: her ethnic group as a bad object steeped in an attitude of male dominance. But, at a deeper level the problem that made it seem irresolvable was her splitting the subculture into two opposite images. After pointing out that she perceived me as representing her ethnic group as either "all good" or "all bad," I said that she believed when I saw its flaws, I would dismiss it, and when I detected its strengths, I would miss the pain it caused her. Safia was startled by this comment, but felt it made sense of her confused feelings about her culture of origin, and, in this way, helped dissipate some of her anxiety. The therapeutic process oscillated between her view of me as benign or malignant, understanding or dismissive. Safia could not combine those contradictory attributions into a single-person perception.

In Safia's primary transference I represented the hegemonic white society, sometimes for better, other times, for worse. In this role, I was an embodiment of her fears that the intolerant white culture would, if given the chance, mutilate, if not annihilate, all traditional minorities. That fear was the basis of her stonewall refusal to allow discussion of subcultural norms. What bears emphasis here is that the therapeutic process had been stalled and threatened to be stalemated by our shared reification of her ethnic culture. Fearful of becoming part of an intolerant, hegemonic culture that could not respect the customs of a different way of life, I had refused to challenge the values of Safia's subculture. However, to end the discourse here, as we both had seemed to do, would have reenacted the passivity of Safia's life while assuming the "subculture" of Safia's upbringing was a finalized entity, a reified structure impervious to the exigencies of a human process. Safia regarded it that way, and I had colluded in that unstated assumption by my silence around it.

Our shared reified perception of her culture constituted a *cultural transference—countertransference* pattern that had become the primary obstacle to the progress of the analysis. As we have seen, the analytic literature on race contains valuable warnings to the therapist to avoid stereotypical notions of ethnicity and race. What has been given much less attention is the problem of the *patient's* experience of *her* ethnicity as just such a reification. This not uncommon feature of multicultural individuals is at the root of the dilemma in which Safia found herself. She was ensnared in a pattern of compliance that was handed down as though it was the inviolable Pakistani culture through her parents. However, neither she nor her parents saw that the way her parents' conceptualized her role constituted a decision to apply Pakistani culture selectively. Not seen as a decision, the rigid role into which Safia was fit amounted to a reification of a paternalistic attitude toward women in a wider society with a broad spectrum of attitudes toward gender roles.

I now put strong emphasis on my new understanding that Safia's apparent stonewall defense against any questioning of her ethnic background had been based not only on her suspicion of me as a white male, but also on a projection of her own view of the culture as an ossified, unbending imposed set of rules. I noted to her that the result of that perception was her belief that I had either a totally accepting or totally rejecting attitude toward her culture. Safia saw that she had been viewing her cultural beliefs and practices as a reified structure with no flexibility. Important in this regard was her realization that I was, indeed, making the connection between the passivity to which her subculture had been binding her and her depression, but not otherwise questioning the value of her ethnic background to her development.

Safia was ensnared in a pattern of compliance that was handed down under the banner of "Pakistani culture" as a matter of faith through her parents. As we have seen, the analytic literature on race contains valuable warnings to the therapist to avoid stereotypical notions of ethnicity and race in favor of engaging each patient's experience of the racial or ethnic group to which she is societally assigned (e.g., Leary, 1997a, 1997b, 2006; Holmes, 1997; Altman, 2006; Dalal, 2006). What has been given much less attention is the tendency of many patients to experience their own ethnicity as just such a reification. This *self reification,* not uncommon among multiculturally trapped individuals, is at the root of the dilemma in which Safia found herself. When I emphasized to her that she possessed a concept of her subculture as an unbending set of injunctions, Safia began to question whether there was more potential flexibility in her connection to the culture than she had seen.

This new awareness led to a discussion of the family's relationship to traditional Pakistani culture. The irony is that the Pakistani culture supposedly passed down in pristine form by Safia's parents was very different from the subculture in which she was raised. In traditional Pakistani society women are trained to obey their husbands and although routinely beaten and brutalized, they typically do not leave the marriage because divorce is shameful (globalvoicesonline.org/2010). The culture that was passed down by Safia's immigrant parents to her appeared to be an uncompromising injunction that the female role is to comply with male strictures at the penalty of disloyalty and betrayal of the Pakistani tradition.

However, there are some powerful caveats that render questionable the attitude toward women that Safia and her parents attributed to Pakistani culture. Safia was not Pakistani, she was Pakistani American, born here and raised in an affluent, mostly white suburban environment. Although her parents were immigrants, they had lived in the United States for most of their lives and were well acculturated in many respects. They wore American clothes, belonged to exclusive American clubs, and their lifestyles were generally indistinguishable from their white neighbors except that they often spoke their native language at home. Furthermore, the demands placed upon Safia came more from her mother than her father. In the traditional culture, the woman is expected to be subservient to the male: her father until she is married and then to her husband (Country Profile, 2005). Safia's mother ignored this tradition of Pakistani culture even as she insisted the traditional norms were the basis of the family expectations of an unmarried daughter.

One of the few vestiges of the native culture was their choice to interpret traditional Pakistani culture to mean that Safia's role in life was to serve them. Neither Safia nor her parents had seen that the way her parents' conceptualized her role constituted a decision to apply traditional Pakistani culture in a highly selective fashion. The rigid role into which the parents attempted to fit Safia amounted to a stereotypical reification of a paternalistic attitude toward women in the context of a society with a broad spectrum of attitudes toward gender roles. The compliant female became an ensconced and unquestioned component of the parental prescription for Safia in seeming obliviousness to the society in which the family lived.

At this juncture, I put great emphasis on Safia's equation of any questioning of her cultural customs with loss of her identity and betrayal of her ethnic roots. I added that both of us felt the analytic space had been suffocated by this rigid perception. I then brought into the analytic dialogue the fact that her parents had found their own way of becoming Pakistani American, but had not offered her the same opportunity. This comment evoked a deeper anger toward her parents than Safia had heretofore experienced, and she launched into a litany of complaints about the unfairness and imprisoning upbringing she experienced. Complaints about her parents were familiar, but now she used the anger to play with the possibility of opposition, of making her own decisions without betraying her ethnic roots. She became determined to free herself of the need to please, but she was adamant that I was not to nudge her toward an American or any other identity. She then said that she now realized she had "overslept" appointments as her protest against my expectation of multiple analytic visits per week and intense analytic work, much like her parents' demands to do work for them. Although she conceded that the two types of work had different motives, she felt it was essential to her growth to do the analysis in her way.

Accordingly, Safia began to assert herself with me as she had never done with her parents by insisting on changes in her analytic schedule, staying silent for long periods, making assessments of how much analytic work she could tolerate in a given session, and titrating the amount of insight and affect she could tolerate in a given session. In one analytic hour, she said very little, just rested peacefully, saying that was what she needed to do. Safia had taken control of the analytic space and sessions to use as she saw fit. I felt rebuffed, challenged, and delighted for her, almost simultaneously. Against her new independence, at times I felt my analytic authority was being challenged by her exercise of freedom that defied the rules of analytic custom. At times I wanted to tell her to "get control of herself" and act like I expected analytic patients to act. At other times, I felt I was witnessing a former prisoner whom I had helped to escape enjoying her newfound freedom. I winced more than once, at times in anger, as she either said little or talked so much I had little chance to reply. But, ultimately I saw her use of the analytic space as her way of achieving the agency I had coveted for her from the beginning. So, whether I winced or reveled in her new ways of being, I affirmed her self expression as the exercise of a new agentic capacity.

The greatest test of Safia's newfound freedom was in relationship to her family. Safia began to tell her family that she would only spend a certain amount of time helping them or be available only until a predetermined hour. While Safia felt a surge of freedom and a huge relief in being able to enforce requirements of her own, she set these limits with a great deal of trepidation. As she began to assert her desires and often refused to accede to others, Safia no longer felt like herself. Refusing family requests felt relieving, but it also led to a strange, uncanny feeling, as though she had lost her anchor in the world. Her *modus operandus* having been removed, she began to feel her identity slipping away. Safia felt lost. Who was she?

The price for the move away from her pattern of accommodation to others was becoming palpable. In gaining control over her life, Safia looked at her ethnic origin as a bad object, a source of exploitation and pain. As angry as she was, the feeling that she was turning her back on the culture that had formed her felt like a betrayal, a caving in to the dominant white culture. No sooner did Safia begin to exercise agency than she felt guilty and isolated. Nonetheless, she believed in her right to assertiveness that the Pakistani identity of her parents' interpretation would deny her. When I inquired about her tie to her culture of origin, Safia championed the importance of the extended family and the traditions that made her feel at home. She felt that if she continued to oppose the values of her ethnic heritage, she would suffer a loss of belonging, a disruption to her identity. She was already feeling her ethnic connection slipping away, but she did not experience the dominant culture as her home. Fearing we were back to square one, I felt helpless and frustrated. We were both lost, without seeing any options to move, in an analytically closed space.

I failed to see any solution to this conundrum until I realized that Safia and I were at a juncture of closed therapeutic space much like the earlier stalemate when I fell speechless out of fear of cultural imposition. The logjam began to come undone when I realized that the source of the paralysis was not different from the previous stalemate. I had been implicitly colluding in Safia's belief that her culture of origin had to be split off for her to become an agentic woman who made free decisions.

As I realized that the stalled therapeutic progress was due largely to the splitting of images of cultural identity shared implicitly by Safia and me, I began opening the

176

space by emphasizing that we had both assumed a binary opposition between her split self images, but, in fact, she held strong convictions from both cultures. I made clear that I knew her desire for agency was embedded in the dominant culture, her need for identification with tradition was to be found in her culture of origin, and she assumed that she could not have both. When she repeated her claim that Pakistani culture did not allow female agency, I noted that she was treating the culture as a monolith, an either/or in which one adopted all its values or was guilty of rejecting the culture. I repeated that her family violated the traditional cultural norms in some important respects, and in fact the obedient female role appeared to be the only aspect of traditional culture her family felt obliged to follow. To claim that she had to disavow all agency to sustain her connection with her ethnic heritage was to reify her subculture and use it to avoid confronting difficult cultural and personal identity conflicts.

The therapeutic space was reopened by the recognition that Safia's culture of origin was an ongoing interpretative process, not the stereotyped reification she had been brought up to believe. Safia was invited to consider options not previously taken, ways of interpreting her culture and defining her role within it. In this way, the therapeutic space was reopened to possibility by the ambiguity of options not taken, rather than closed off by understanding or conclusion. In this context Safia began to explore ways of remaining connected to her culture that fit her value of self determination. Proud of the culture that valued tradition and family ties and gave her a sense of identity and belonging, she maintained continuity with her ethnic background and remained loyal to her family and many of its customary culinary and domestic practices, but she did not allow that continuity to affect the assertion of her will and desire. Safia was fully aware that she was fashioning a sense of self from previously split off parts of her self. She had brought together her need for assertiveness and Pakistani tradition.

The principle that the analyst should never assume how the minority patient experiences her subculture has never been more applicable than in the therapeutic process with Safia. During the course of the analytic process, she shifted her cultural identity from the narrowly stereotyped Pakistani woman to a newly created Pakistani American with a membership of one, a one composed of a mixture of elements from each culture.

Conclusion

The critical transformational experience for Safia came in her recognition that her concept of Pakistani culture and especially the female role were subject to interpretation, that is, that they were alive only as subjects of human experience. Jettisoning the stereotyped image of the Pakistani woman imposed on her in her formative years, Safia came to see the Pakistani woman as someone honoring family and tradition who may take those values in any of a variety of directions and combine them with other ideas and values. Such a view is consonant with Heidegger's (1968) concept of a "thing." Any "thing" for Heidegger, following Husserl, has an essence that consists of potential to be formed, experienced, and interpreted in a variety of ways, as a tree can be a specimen for botany, potential lumber, a source of shade, or an object of beauty. Safia adopted such a view of the Pakistani woman by following Pakistani traditions in food, values, many customs, and religion, but not in her role as woman and professional. She fashioned her own version of being Pakistani and female.

The essence, then, of Safia's psychopathology was her self reification. The paralysis she suffered in her life, which we call depression in conventional terms, was a direct product of this imposition of rigidity. Her parents bequeathed her a straight-jacket existence that served their interests. So, while Safia was caught between two cultures, it would miss the essence of her dynamics to formulate her issues as a conflict between two cultures. What paralyzed her was the conflict between reified roles that led her to believe her choices were either/or. It was only after she experienced the analytic space as open and then both cultures as ongoing experiences of the members of the culture that she could begin to extricate herself from what had seemed like an irresolvable paralysis. At the end of the therapeutic process, she was living with both subcultures, but their differences were no longer immobilizing because she was free to experience and adopt the attributes of each to fashion a newly created self. And that is where the therapeutic action was: in the freedom to utilize and experience subcultures, to make those cultures one's own, and in that process create a new self.

In this sense, Safia's dilemma had an ontological similarity to the paralyzing conflict in which Jerold found himself, as discussed in the previous chapter. As Jerold had an unreflective reified conception of himself as a producer of wealth, so Safia had adopted a reified conception of herself as a passive woman fulfilling the demands of others. Although living in different cultures, the depression suffered by each was rooted in self reification. It was the inability to see oneself as an experiencing subject able to interpret, appropriate, or refuse the givens of the social and cultural worlds that froze both into behavior patterns not of their choosing. The freeing experience for both was the recognition that they were interpreting their role in life according to a constricting canon. Once they began to use their own experience as their guide, both were able to create new ways of being.

It is conventional to look at the therapeutic action in cases such as these as the establishment of a sense of agency. However, if we ponder what it means to lack agency, it becomes clear that the creation of agency is more complicated than it would appear. Jerold was a highly active individual who was quite resourceful and able to create business opportunities. The issue for Jerold was not simply that he was doing something he did not like, but that he had been unable to use his experience as guide. His sense of self had been perverted into a frozen behavioral mechanism. And here we see the same dilemma suffered by Safia who was unhappy in her role as family "gopher" but could not use that experience to transform her life into her own ways of being. In fact, she barely paid attention to her own experience. Having an imposed identity to which she gave little thought, Safia treated herself and her role as a given, what Fonagy et al. (2002) calls "psychic equivalence," as though her essence had been decided for her.

178

So, agency implies utilizing one's experience to discover how to be and belong in the world. The roles in which Jerold and Safia were encased were not modes of being in the world, but activities imposed upon them. In this regard, it is irrelevant that Jerold had been successful in business for 20 years, or that Safia had enjoyed a meteoric rise in her company. In neither case was the motivation an authentic expression of the patient. So, both cases demonstrate the importance of becoming a subject of one's own experience. And that means interpreting societal strictures rather than submitting to their imposition. That does not mean one cannot adopt societal practices; it means that such practices must be chosen on the basis of experience. So, the therapeutic action for Safia was her transformation into a subject whose experience became a guide to her interpretation of the two cultures in which she lived.

12

CONCLUSION

The Psychoanalytic Vision

Psychoanalysis is under heavy attack from the dominant Anglo-American culture and its iteration in the social sciences, including its own parent disciplines, academic psychology and psychiatry. The splitting of person from world and the resulting scientistic belief that one can objectify the human process have increased their dominion over the human sciences in American academia. The pressure on psychoanalysis to show it is a natural science, or at least shares its methods, has been felt by psychoanalysis since its inception. Freud (1895a, 1938) took great pains to categorize the field he created as a natural science like any other, but acknowledged that his case studies often read more like novels than scientific experiments. This tension has permeated the history of psychoanalysis as some have argued that analysis is an objective science differing only in content from the others (e.g., Rubenstein, 1976, 1980; Bachrach, 1989), while theorists in the other camp have argued that psychoanalysis cannot be judged on the criteria of empirical sciences because its subject matter is human experience and therefore can be judged only by criteria befitting the experiential process. In recent years, with technological advances, especially in communication, and ever mounting pressure from insurance companies to use only quick-fix solutions, the mental health field is turning increasingly to so-called evidence-based treatment, which is not an unbiased look at evidence, but a selective use of some evidence while ignoring other data to reach predetermined conclusions (Shedler, 2010). Clinical psychology and psychiatric training programs have drastically cut back or eliminated psychoanalytic input from their curricula. Many in the fields of psychology and psychiatry consider psychoanalysis to be outmoded and even dead. The pressure on psychoanalysis has never been greater to demonstrate objectivist methods or fold up shop.

These relentless attacks have given the psychoanalytic world a choice decisive for its self understanding and place in the world of ideas. The field can either defend itself on the basis that it is a natural science, or it can assert itself as a discipline of the subjective with its own methods and criteria of truth and effectiveness. We saw in Chapter Two that the criticisms of psychoanalysis for its lack of "scientific" status are derived from the scientism of the contemporary age, that is, the fallacy that only disciplines that mimic the methods of the natural sciences can make a legitimate knowledge claim. Furthermore, the very essence of psychoanalysis is engagement of the patient's subjectivity. The history of the field is a history of increasing recognition of the invaluable role of the subjective in therapeutic action. From his earliest psychoanalytic work, Freud (1895b) saw that the mutative impact of analytic insight required the patient to have an affective response, and the role of affect has only increased as analysts have found that the effectiveness of an interpretation is a function of the intensity with which the patient experiences it. At this juncture of analytic history, every analytic school, from the most classical to the most contemporary relational, shares the view that unless the patient can experience the analyst's offering with feeling it is neither confirmed nor useful. The key role of experiencing, the criterion of the patient's affect, has led psychoanalysis down the path toward a science of the subjective, sometimes against the wishes of many of its practitioners.

The Reification of Analytic Concepts

As we have seen, the nature of the psyche as *consciousness of* and human experience as Being-in-the-world gives us the basis for understanding psychic events of any type as ways of relating to the world. The pivotal step here is discarding the reductionism that privileges perception and views many psychic events as distorted forms of perception. Each psychic act is a way of being in itself. Dreaming, for example, is not a misperception, but a way of being in the world that has a unique dramaturgical poignancy. Once analytic theory is denuded of its reifying and reductionist elements, the theory and practice are freed to appreciate and understand every form of experience for itself. As a science of the subjective, psychoanalysis engages human being in all its topographic levels and transcendental possibilities. This mission is founded on the phenomenological finding that human being is uniquely characterized by *relating* to the world, rather than occupying a point in space.

From the theoretical viewpoint, the grasp of the human process as Being-in-the-world spawns a rich variety of clinical and theoretical implications, some of which have been brought out in various chapters of this book. Perhaps the most fundamental change called forth by this new philosophical foundation is the erasure of the distinction between inside and outside. Fantasies and dreams are ways of Being-in-the-world as much as perceptions. To designate one as "inside" and the other "outside" is to cut off the individual from the world and then attempt to reunite what should never have been split. The fact that we are so influenced by the measurement view of reality shows the powerful influence of culture in all we do. As Beings-in-the-world our sense of self is imbued with the culture that we are born into. Granted the degree of cultural influence varies widely with the culture and individual predilection, the sense of self is always related to the culture, even if the relationship is overt rejection. To oppose a cultural belief is to be taking a stand in response to it. This Aristotelian concept has been lost to psychoanalysis due to the historical focus on the "intrapsychic" and the corresponding tendency to universalize psychological findings. As analysis builds a new foundation on the uniquely human way of being, the reciprocal nature of culture and self becomes a topic of psychoanalytic understanding and the values of the culture become central to the understanding of the self.

The history of psychoanalysis shows a deep ambivalence toward the nature of the subjective, which is, on the one hand, promoted as the very essence of the analytic enterprise, and, on the other, covered by a veil of objectivist concepts intended to fit analysis into the natural sciences. The latter, as we have seen, is a concession to the hegemonic culture for which analysis has paid the price of diluting and in some cases even deforming the nature of experience. Objectivist concepts have no role in a science of the subjective, but they have been allowed into analytic discourse largely so the field can claim kinship to the natural sciences. This ambivalent analytic self concept has slowed the ability of psychoanalysis to make its maximal contribution to the culture as a counterforce to the objectification of human being. Once analytic thought is denuded of its reifying and reductionist tendencies, we have a science of the subjective, a rare bastion of subjectivity ready to affirm the human experience in opposition to the technological world of contemporary America.

Psychoanalysis will be most free to achieve its mission as a science of the subjective by ridding itself of the objectifying influences of the culture. We have seen that some analytic concepts and thinking about the process fall prey to the devilish societal encroachment on individual experience. To reify the psyche with psychological processes turned into entities is counterproductive to the analytic mission of understanding the patient's experiential world. Whatever is imposed or imported from somewhere other than the patient's experience constitutes a counterforce to the evolution of the patient's transcendental possibilities.

A science of the subjective shifts the foundation of the analytic process away from theoretical constructs such as a drive, ego, or object representation, which divide the psyche into reified entities, as well as theoretical abstractions, such as relational matrix or nonlinear dynamic systems theory, that likewise detract from the personal nature of experience. Commensurate with that warning, the development of the science of human experiencing requires the elimination of spatialized concepts so often used in common discourse as well as psychoanalytic theory. From the early days of the field, it was the use of spatialized metaphors for the psychical that reified experience into a group of mechanisms and rigid conceptualizations. The seat of repression was regarded as "the unconscious" as though there was a "place" for all that was not conscious. Moreover, "the unconscious" was spoken of as though it had its own mind, as in "the unconscious plays tricks." Later "the id" was expected to do battle with "the ego." This type of conceptualizing makes separate parts of the mind into anthropomorphic entities operating on their own and thus becomes another form of reification and avoidance of the experiencing subject. What I have proposed in these pages is an analytic account of human experience that attempts to stay faithful to humanity as Being-in-the-world while maintaining the depth of dynamic understanding.

The reality of unconscious mental processes, fantasies, dreams, and free associations, is not disputed by founding psychoanalysis on Being-in-the-world. What changes is the ontological status of unconscious psychic acts and all psychical phenomena. Rather than an entity, "the unconscious," unconscious psychical acts refer to the topographic level of a mental event.

These reconceptualizations reflect the fact that experience is not spatial, but temporal. We know the psyche not through any perception of a thing in space, but through its temporal continuity. I know who I am because I experience myself as the same at different points of time, and others know me by connecting their experiences of me temporally. The temporality of being matters for analytic theory because it reformulates the nature of self and opens up the temporal for analytic exploration in a new way. Temporality cannot be "spatialized," so it lends itself to experience and offers protection against reification. By maintaining a consistent approach to the self as temporal rather than spatial, the process is more likely to adhere to the patient's experience in its temporal flow rather than being waylaid by abstractions. Immersed in the patient's experience, the therapist finds the importance of futurity and is able to engage all the patient's temporal modalities.

The analytic view of self-esteem is a good example of the tendency of analysts to adopt the culture of objectification unconsciously and collude with the dominant culture in opposition to the subjective perspective of analysis. There is no greater testimony to the power of the hegemonic culture than to see its objectifying influence in the discipline that is most theoretically opposed to it.

One recalls here Heidegger's (1955/1977) concept of modern technology as transformation into resource, as has been done first to the Earth, and now to humankind. The analytic concepts of self-esteem all fit into this view of the person as resource by conceptualizing self-esteem as a calibration toward goal fulfillment. Unwittingly, the psychoanalytic conceptualizations of self-esteem have advanced, rather than combatted, the objectification of human being, and in this way have interfered with the analytic mission of engaging and expanding the subjective. Perhaps some surreptitious societal influence is inevitable, but where it occurs, it needs to be combatted as anti-analytic discourse if psychoanalysis is to realize its potential as a science of the subjective. That is why I have characterized the contemporary analyst as Camus's rebel, refusing to be determined by historical circumstance.

A New Beginning

From a clinical perspective, psychoanalysis is returning to a new beginning and then moving forward to bring out the full implications of its concentration on the subjective. The importance of living in accordance with one's experience cannot be overstated. Beginning with Winnicott (1965), the paradigm shifted for many analysts to the expression or derailment of self potential, what I have called the "expressivist turn" in psychoanalysis. Once the realization of the self became the crux of the developmental process, ways of being came into analytic focus. The analytic lens was pointed to the degree of authenticity of self expression.

The Heideggerean interpretation of human being as Being-in-the-world is well aligned with the dual pillars of Winnicott's theory: the maturational process and the facilitating environment. Heidegger's authentic expression of oneself is the maturational process and the environment can facilitate the expression of being or impinge on it.

This Winnicottian stimulated view of analysis constitutes an analytic version of the Romantic-inspired "expressivist turn" that was so pivotal for the humanities in the early nineteenth century (Taylor, 1989). The purpose of life is to realize our potential in all arenas, to become, as Nietzsche once said, who we are. The corollary is that to the degree the person is unable to author her own life, suffering is inevitable, although the form it assumes varies widely. Like the reaction of the Romantic Movement to neoclassicism, psychoanalysis has transformed itself from helping the patient fit into a preconceived model of mind to bringing out the unique potential of the individual patient.

While Taylor (1992) is concerned that self expression must be tempered with empathy to ensure that it does not become a licentiousness, the contemporary analytic view of the self has no problematic narcissism requiring neutralization. As we have seen (see Chapters Three and Four), self expression, the realization of one's potential, is possible only if an other sees this potential and the child sees the other as a subject. Self realization does not mean a narcissistic indulgence because the self can come to fruition only in the context of the other who is seen as a separate subjectivity. The subjectivity of the other being implicated in the very sense of self, the realization of self potential is inherently intertwined with the recognition and appreciation of the other's subjectivity. Self realization takes place only within the interpersonal world where "interpersonal" means the recognition of and respect for the other's subjectivity. This is the basis for an ethic for modernity that psychoanalysis can uniquely provide.

With the expressivist turn, as the analytic purpose shifts to the creation of new ways of being, transcendence is brought into analytic theory and practice. Granted many practitioners do not use the word, but the effort to stimulate new ways of being puts the analyst in the position of detecting new possibilities in who the patient is and helping to bring them to fruition. All of this is predicated on grasping the psychical as lived experience, not a manifestation of another reality to which it can be reduced.

Self Reification

Conceiving human experience as Being-in-the-world sensitizes the analyst to the reification of human experience and its subtle manifestation as the patient's reification of her own experience. Psychopathology is often rooted in such reifications which are easily overlooked without a special sensitivity to the nature of human experiencing. A critical component of the therapeutic process consists of helping the patient overcome the reified limits within which she lives her life. To some degree, each patient discussed in this book hypostasized her own experience in a way that ensnared her in an imprisoning constriction of interactional patterns from which no escape could be seen. We saw Jerold regard himself as a commodity whose job on Earth was to produce wealth. Herb treated himself as a piece of machinery whose sole function was to produce good numbers for his firm. Rebecca conceived of herself as a resource to be utilized by whoever saw fit to deploy her for a purpose of their own. Safia saw herself as a cultural icon of passivity, a stereotyped passive female consigned from birth to serve others by dint of her culture and gender. Although from different cultures and leading sharply different lifestyles, these patients suffered from reifying their experience and then feeling imprisoned by the reification. In every case of psychopathology, the configurational patterns were not only dysfunctional, but also reified structures that choked off possibilities resulting in a loss of freedom and a feeling of fatedness. A critical component of the analyst's role, then, is to shift the patient's ontological view of her psychic states from reification to psychic process.

This reifying process is the objectifying materialism of the culture applied to the individual psyche. The pressure in the society to hypostasize anything that claims ontological status can be seen in the way patients experience themselves as commodities or pieces in a machine of production. When the dominant values of materialism, objectivism, and quantification saturate the self experience, the individual becomes impaled on an ossified sense of self. It is not that these values are inherently destructive; to the contrary, they play an essential role in understanding the world of natural objects. It is their application to human being that reifies human experience into a rigid structure which is taken as a given. Anglo-American culture pressures the individual to treat himself as a commodity, as we saw in Herb, Jerold, Sarah, and others. Although Safia was part of a subculture, she felt a similar reification in the servile role passed to her by her family from their self-serving interpretation of their ethnic background. We might say that the degree to which the individual applies the objectifying tendencies of the culture to himself, he is likely to become ensconced in resilient pathological patterns.

It follows that the aim of analysis includes the liberation of the patient from the reifying structure in which he is imprisoned. Fonagy et al. (2002) have taken a significant step in this direction with their emphasis on "mentalization" of psychic processes, but therapeutic action requires the creation of new ways of being, and for that reason the analytic therapist needs to see beyond the immediacy of the patient's experience to its transcendental possibilities. The view of the patient, then, goes beyond the historical and the present to the patient's futurity, the possibilities for who he might be.

A decisive break from the past is the recognition that bringing to awareness unconscious processes is not the end, but a step along the path to the creation of new ways of being and relating. Awareness shakes the foundation of previously held assumptions, and it thus opens the analytic space to modes of engagement that transcend the historical patterns. A continually expanding experiential process is opened to the patient, the clinical implications of which are continuing to emerge. The analyst's role is to open the space so the patient can play with possibilities to create new ways of being. The word "play" is key here because it is in play that one can find what is most uniquely one's own. In words that could have been written by Winnicott, Frederich Schiller (1794/2004, p.107) put it this way: "Man only plays when he is in the fullest sense of the word a human being, and he is only fully a human being when he plays."

Psychoanalysis as a Worldview

As the analytic therapist helps the patient de-objectify, or "mentalize," self reification, he adopts a posture and clinical strategy that stands in direct opposition to the culture of objectification that pressures the patient to commodify himself. The attitude adopted by the analyst is not just a clinical approach to the patient, but a stance toward the world, or, simply put, a worldview. To treat the patient as a subject whose experience is taken seriously in its immediacy as well as its potential assumes a belief in both the subjective and the transcendental, in contrast to the dominant culture which avoids the subjective in favor of the productive capacity of the individual. That is, the therapist is not simply adopting a technical strategy; he is bringing to the analytic setting a worldview that regards people as subjectivities pregnant with possibilities, subjective beings who can be understood in their immediacy and transcendental possibilities. The analyst engages the patient with a worldview that gives pride of place to the experiencing subject seen as a potential of ever expanding possibilities.

The psychoanalytic perspective regards all clinical phenomena as emanating from an experiencing subject who endows the world with meaning. Kierkegaard (1854–1855/1968) once asked, "In all of Christendom is there a single Christian?" Even if the answer is "no" that did not deter Kierkegaard from his belief in the Christian religion, which is an idea of great spiritual importance to him whether or not anyone is successfully practicing it. How many analysts in their daily practice completely eschew reification and objectification is an open question, but given the tendency of analytic theory to reify concepts, it is likely that many analysts hypostasize at least some psychological processes. But, that does not damage the idea that inspires analysis. What defines analysis as a unique worldview is its commitment to understanding the patient's individual experience on its own terms, as it is experienced, and what its possibilities may be, wherever that may lead. This is the ideal toward which analysis aims, albeit analysts are undoubtedly imperfect in achieving it. It is this idea that defines the analytic vision and makes analysis a unique viewpoint in contemporary culture. No other discipline, therapeutic or otherwise, can claim to pursue the world of human experience in all its depth and complexity, in its immanence as well as its transcendental possibilities, as analysis does.

Freed from dominant self reifying tendencies, the successfully analyzed individual has a new sensitivity to the realization of latent potential. This ability to transcend self boundaries in itself defines a new way of being that affects future experiences.

This adherence to immeasurable human subjectivity as the essence of human existence situates psychoanalysis in rebellious opposition to the dominant culture that pressures the individual to objectify himself. In offering a contrasting viewpoint that regards experiencing as the key to human existence, psychoanalysis becomes an alternative worldview that places the highest value not on any measurable outcome, but on the realization of potential based on awareness and expansion of experience. That is the psychoanalytic vision.

Psychoanalysis has become a worldview not so much because its practitioners aspire to become philosophers as because the opposition of the hegemonic culture has forced upon the field an outlook on the person and her relationship to the world distinct from the culture in which it resides. We might say that psychoanalysis has become a worldview despite itself. Many analysts to this day do not see, and do not wish to see, their craft as an oppositional subculture, and that is undoubtedly why the discipline continues to deploy reified concepts that do not fit the everyday practice of understanding the other's experience. But, if analysis is to pursue what makes it unique, if, that is, it is to achieve its destiny as a science of the subjective, then a consistent language of subjectivity is required. The consistent pursuit of human subjectivity without preconceptions of who the person is expected to be sets analytic science in direct contrast with the dominant beliefs and epistemology of the culture. The belief that human being, or *Da-sein*, Being-in-the-world, is a uniquely human way of being that can be engaged, understood, and any particular form transcended, is the psychoanalytic vision undiluted with biases from the dominant culture.

If we are right that the commoditization of people in widespread, we must be prepared to see many, perhaps the majority, of citizens feeling deflated and dissatisfied about who they are. In fact, this is what we do find, as we saw in Chapter Nine. While there are undoubtedly many factors responsible for the pervasive emotional distress in American society, its widespread nature suggests that something is amiss in the culture. Therapists commonly see people who have become depressed and even despairing because their productivity fails to fulfill an image to which they are bound. We need not puzzle over the high rates of depression and other emotional disorders in a society that reduces people to objects in points of space to be manipulated as any other object. We have seen that patients such as Jerold and Herb had regarded themselves as commodities whose function was to fulfill a productivity quota. One would expect a high incidence of depression and other emotional disruption among those who fail to meet the test of productivity. This cultural value system, then, is implicated in the patient's symptoms so that awareness of the cultural is inherent in the analytic way of knowing.

That psychoanalysis affirms itself as the science of the subjective is especially important today precisely because the areas in which human experiencing is valued are shrinking to virtual insignificance in our technologically dominated society. The movement to apply the technological concept of resource to human being is accelerating rapidly. As Turkle (2011) has found, many young people view themselves as computer brains, a reflection of the growing societal tendency to reduce the human experience to material processes, like neurological events. The spectacular growth of the neurosciences is one further reflection of our rapid movement toward a technological view of people. In such a world, there is an urgent need for a discipline of the subjective.

The analytic process is designed to accomplish the very opposite of what technology has wrought in its application to human being. We have seen in this book the stories of several people who as a result of gaining insight into unconscious meaning and motivation shifted how they viewed their experience from a reified assumption to a psychological process. This transformation permitted transcendence of their old patterns by finding new possibilities embedded within them. Herb, Jerold, Safia, and others saw they had reified psychological constructions into rigid structures of an unbending "reality" that did not have the reality status they had accorded it. When each of these patients experienced himself or herself both in the immediate and transcendent modes of experience, when consciousness and unconscious processes became accessible, the experiential world expanded and became enriching in its own right. All these patients became aware that their experience contained unexplored possibilities from which they could create new ways of being. This acute sensitivity to one's own experience becomes a way of living, and at that point both human being and the uniqueness of the individual's own created ways of being are appreciated as expressions of the human spirit. Evaluation of one's life does not arise under these conditions. It is not that Herb, Jerold, and Safia felt they had achieved a standard that gave them a more positive feeling about themselves, but rather that living in accordance with their experience in its transcendental possibilities obviated the need for evaluative standards. There is no assessment applicable to a life lived in accordance with one's experience.

This is not to say that all unconscious processes are ever brought to awareness, nor is that possible. There will always be new motivations and meanings to be uncovered and transformed, but it is precisely the ability to discover possibilities in the thicket of existence and transform them into new ways of being that marks a successful analysis. The person who is able to do this puts confidence in the fiber of his own experiential process in contrast to those whose esteem is derived from the meeting of standards. The etymological root "with faith" captures the belief in one's experiential process that becomes the guiding light of his life. We have seen this faith in experience emerge in Safia's confrontation with her parents, Herb's learning to broaden his sense of self, Jerold's abandonment of his family's commodification, Rebecca's willingness to assert herself, and Sarah's ability to accept the limits of relationships. In each case, the patient relied on immanent experience and transcendental possibilities as life guides. Because their directives for action now came from their own experience, they learned to parlay their transcendence of a core conflict into the creation of new ways of being for their lives. It is this ability to expand awareness, to find and articulate new possibilities for one's life, that may be the most lasting and useful impact of analytic therapy.

Ultimately, we all have to rely on what our experience tells us, and the greater our awareness, the more reliable it is as a guide and the greater is our ability to act according to our desires and values, overcome conflicts, and continually create ways of being of our own. In psychoanalytic therapy, one hopes the patient will become aware of the subtleties of her experience, the moment-to-moment experiential shifts and emotional ebbs and flows. When that happens, the patient becomes attuned to her psychic states and the life lived is an expression of experience in the interpersonal world. Belief in one's ability to find creative solutions to emotional dilemmas means that obstacles do not become barriers. The resurgent confidence of Safia, Sarah, Jerold, Herb, and all the others in this book is a function of their belief they can use their creative capacities to transcend the rigid patterns that impale so much human progress. In the end, it is not as much who I have become as knowing I can move beyond who I am to who I have never been.

It is this attunement and excitement in articulating one's experience that brings a stable sense of appreciation for the human process as it unfolds. And that is the psychoanalytic vision.

And so it is that a field that began with the positivist mission to make the psyche into a natural science achieves its full potential and makes its greatest contribution on a societal as well as individual level as a science of the subjective. And that is the psychoanalytic vision.

REFERENCES

Aggarwal, N. (2011). Intersubjectivity, transference, and the cultural third. *Contemporary Psychoanalysis, 47*, 204–223.

Allgood-Merton, B., Lewinsohn, P. M., & Hops, H. (1990). Sex differences and adolescent depression. *Journal of Abnormal Psychology, 99*, 55–63.

Altman, N. (2006). Whiteness. *Psychoanalytic Quarterly, 75*, 45–72.

Apprey, M. (2006). Difference and the awakening of wounds in intercultural psychoanalysis. *Psychoanalytic Quarterly, 75*, 73–93.

Arendt, H. (1959). *The origins of totalitarianism*. New York: Benediction Books.

——— (1963). *Eichmann in Jerusalem: A report on the banality of evil*. New York: Penguin.

Aristotle. (1984). *The politics*. Chicago: University of Chicago Press. (Original work published 350 BCE)

Arlow, J., & Brenner, C. (1964). *Structural concepts and psychoanalytic theory*. New York: International Universities Press.

Aron, L. (1996). *A meeting of minds*. Hillsdale, NJ: The Analytic Press.

Arvidsson, A., Bauwens, M., & Peitersen, N. (2008). Crisis of value and the ethical economy. *Journal of Future Studies, 12*(4), 9–20.

Ashenfelter, O. (2002). Researchers tally the value of human life. *News at Princeton*. http://www.princeton.edu/main/news/archive/S01/11/87I80/index.xml

Attie, I., & Brooks-Gunn, J. (1989). The development of eating problems in adolescent girls: A longitudinal study. *Developmental Psychology, 25*, 70–79.

Bacal, H. (1985). Optimal responsiveness and the therapeutic process. In A. Goldberg (Ed.), *Progress in self psychology* (Vol. 1, pp. 202–226). New York: Guilford Press.

——— (1988). Reflections on "optimum frustration." In A. Goldberg (Ed.), *Progress in self psychology* (Vol. 4, pp. 127–131). New York: Guilford Press.

Bacal, H., & Newman, K. (1990). *Theories of object relations: Bridges to self psychology*. New York: Columbia University Press.

Bachrach, H. M. (1989). On specifying the scientific methodology of psychoanalysis. *Psychoanalytic Inquiry, 9*, 282–304.

Balint, M. (1968). *The basic fault*. London: Tavistock.

Baron, J., & Norman, M. F. (1992). SATs, achievement tests, and high school class rank as predictors of college performance. *Educational and Psychological Measurement, 52*(4), 1047–1055.

Barzun, J. (1943). *Romanticism and the modern ego*. New York: Little, Brown & Co.

Basch, M. (1977). Development psychology and explanatory theory in psychoanalysis. *The Annual of Psychoanalysis, 5*, 229–263.

———— (1983). Empathic understanding: A review of the concept and some theoretical considerations. *Journal of the American Psychoanalytic Association, 30,* 101–126.

———— (1985). Interpretation toward a developmental model. *Progress in Self Psychology, 1,* 33–42.

———— (1988). *Doing psychotherapy.* New York: Basic Books.

———— (1990). Further thoughts on empathic understanding. *Progress in Self Psychology, 6,* 3–10.

Beauchamp, T., & Childress, J. (2001). *Principles of biomedical ethics.* Oxford: Oxford University Press.

Beebe, B., & Lachmann, F. (2002). *Infant research and adult treatment.* Hillsdale, NJ: The Analytic Press.

Beiser, F. (2003). *The romantic imperative: The concept of early German romanticism.* Cambridge, MA: Harvard University Press.

Beland, H. (1994). Validation in the clinical process: Four settings for objectification of the subjectivity of understanding. *International Journal of Psychoanalysis, 74,* 1141–1158.

Benjamin, J. (1995). *Like subjects, love objects.* New Haven, CT: Yale University Press.

———— (1997). *The shadow of the other.* New York: Routledge.

———— (2004). Beyond doer and done to: An intersubjective view of thirdness. *Psychoanalytic Quarterly, 73,* 5–46.

Bergson, H. (2010). *Time and free will.* Charleston, SC: Nabu Press. (Original work published 1910)

Bettelheim, B. (1950). *Love is not enough: The treatment of the emotionally disturbed child.* Glencoe, IL: The Free Press.

———— (1984). *Freud and man's soul.* New York: Alfred A. Knopf.

Binswanger, L. (1957). *Sigmund Freud: Reminiscences of a friendship.* New York: Grune & Stratton. (Original work published 1955)

Bion, W. R. (1957). Differentiation of the psychotic from the non-psychotic personalities. *International Journal of Psychoanalysis, 38,* 266–275.

———— (1962). *Learning from experience.* London: Tavistock.

———— (1970). *Attention and interpretation.* London: Tavistock.

———— (1995). *Attention and interpretation.* London: Tavistock. (Original work published 1970)

Blum, H. P. (2010). Object relations in clinical psychoanalysis. *International Journal of Psychoanalysis, 4,* 973–976.

Bodnar, S. (2004). Remember where you come from: Dissociative processes in multicultural individuals. *Psychoanalytic Dialogues, 14,* 581–603.

Bollas, C. (1987). *The shadow of the object.* New York: Columbia University Press.

———— (1989). *Forces of destiny.* London: Free Association Books.

———— (1992). *Being a character.* London: Routledge.

———— (2005). *I have heard the mermaids singing.* London: Free Association Books.

Bolognini, S. (2001). Empathy and the unconscious. *Psychoanalytic Quarterly, 70,* 447–471.

———— (2004). *Psychoanalytic empathy.* London: Free Association Books.

———— (2009). The complex nature of psychoanalytic empathy: A theoretical and clinical exploration. *Fort Da, 15,* 35–56.

Bonime, W. (1989). *Collaborative psychoanalysis: Anxiety, depression, dreams, and personality change.* Teaneck, NJ: Farleigh Dickinson University Press.

Boss, M. (1977). *"I dreamt last night . . ."* New York: John Wiley & Sons.

Bowlby, J. (1988). *A secure base: Parent-child attachment and healthy human development.* London: Routledge.

Brandchaft, B. (2007). Systems of pathological accommodation and change in analysis. *Psychoanalytic Psychology, 24,* 667–687.

Brenner, C. (1971). The psychoanalytic concept of aggression. *International Journal of Psycho-Analysis, 52*, 137–144.

————— (1976). *Psychoanalytic technique and psychic conflict.* New York: International Universities Press.

Breuer, J., & Freud, S. (1895). *Studies on hysteria.* New York: Hogarth Press.

Bromberg, P. (1998). *Standing in the spaces.* Hillsdale, NJ: The Analytic Press.

Bronowski, J. (1965). *Science and human values.* New York: Harper.

Busch, F. (1995). *The ego at the center of clinical technique.* New York: Aronson.

————— (2005). Conflict theory/Trauma theory. *Psychoanalytic Quarterly, 74*, 27–45.

Busch, F. N., Milrod, B. L., Rudden, M., Shapiro, T., Singer, M., Aronson, A., & Roiphe, J. (1999). Oedipal dynamics in panic disorder. *Journal of the American Psychoanalytic Association, 47*(3), 773–790.

Callahan, D. (2004). *The cheating culture: Why more Americans are doing wrong to get ahead.* Tequesta, FL: Mariner.

Campbell, J. (1988). Joseph Campbell and the power of the myth. *Interview with Bill Moyers.* Episode 3: The first storytellers.

Camus, A. (1992). *The rebel: An essay on man in revolt.* New York: Vintage. (Original work published 1951)

Casement, P. (1985). *Learning from the patient.* New York: Guilford Press.

Chomsky, N. (1975). *The logical structure of linguistic theory.* New York: Plenum.

Country Profile: Pakistan. (2005). Library of Congress, Research Division.

Csikszentmihalyi, M. (2008). *Flow: The psychology of optimal experience.* New York: HarperCollins.

Curtis, H. C. (1985). Clinical perspectives on self psychology. *Psychoanalytic Quarterly, 54*, 339–378.

Dalal, F. (2006). Racism: Processes of detachment, dehumanization, and hatred. *Psychoanalytic Quarterly, 75*, 131–161.

————— (2011). *Thought paralysis: The virtues of discrimination.* London: Karnac.

Davis, C., & Katzman, M. (1999). Acculturation as perfection: A study of the psychological correlates of eating problems in Chinese male and female students living in the United States. *The International Journal of Eating Disorders, 25*(1), 65–70.

Davoine, F. (2007). Reply to commentaries. *Psychoanalytic Dialogues, 17*, 671–682.

de Graaf, J., Waan, D., & Naylor, T. (2005). *Affluenza: The all consuming epidemic.* London: Berrett-Koehler.

Demos, E. V. (1991). Affect and the development of the self: A new frontier. In A. Goldberg (Ed.), *Frontiers in self psychology: Progress in self psychology* (Vol. 3, pp. 27–53). Hillsdale, NJ: The Analytic Press.

————— (1992). The early organization of the psyche. In J. Barron, M. Eagle, & D. Wolitzky (Eds.), *Interface of psychoanalysis and psychology* (pp. 200–233). Washington, DC: The American Psychological Association.

Diener, E., Sandvik, E., Seidlitz, L., & Diener, M. (1993). The relationship between income and subjective well-being: Relative or absolute? *Social Indicators Research, 28*, 195–223.

Dilthey, W. (1900). The development of hermeneutics. In R. A. Makreel & F. Rodi (Eds.), *Wilhem Dilthey: Selected works* (Vol. 1). Princeton, NJ: Princeton University Press.

Dimen, M. (2000). The body as Rorschach. *Studies in Gender and Sexuality, 1*, 9–39.

Donaghue, N., & Broderick, P. (2011). "What you look like is such a big factor": Girls' own reflections about the appearance culture in an all-girls' school. *Feminism & Psychology, 21*, 299–316.

Edelman, G. (1987). *Neural Darwinism.* New York: Basic Books.

Eigen, M. (1993a). *The electrified tightrope*. Northvale, NJ: Aronson.

———— (1993b). *The psychotic core*. London: Karnac.

———— (2005). Healing longing in the midst of damage. *Psychoanalytic Dialogues*, *15*, 169–183.

Eisenstein, P. (2007). Devouring holes: Darren Aronofsy's *Requiem for a dream* and the tectonics of psychoanalysis. *International Journal of Zizek Studies*, *1*(3), 1–23.

Elise, D. (2007). The black man and the mermaid: Desire and disruption in the analytic relationship. *Psychoanalytic Dialogues*, *17*, 791–809.

Erikson, E. (1994). *Identity: Youth and crisis*. New York: W. W. Norton. (Original work published 1968)

Esen, E. (2010). Academic achievement of American and Turkish students. *Human Architecture: journal of the sociology of self knowledge*, *8*(1), 125–140.

Fairbairn, W. R. D. (1958). On the nature and aims of psychoanalytic treatment. *International Journal of Psychoanalysis*, *39*, 374–385.

Federici-Nebbiosi, S. (2006). "Earth, speak to me, grass speak to me!" Trauma, tragedy, and the crash between cultures in Medea. *Psychoanalytic Dialogues*, *16*, 465–480.

Feenberg, A. (2003). Modernity theory and technological studies. In T. Misa, P. Brey, & A. Feenberg (Eds.), *Modernity and technology* (pp. 1–33). Cambridge, MA: MIT Press.

Feiner, K., & Kiersky, S. (1994). Empathy: A common ground. *Psychoanalytic Dialogues*, *4*, 425–440.

Ferenczi, S. (1931). Child-analysis in the analysis of adults. *International Journal of Psychoanalysis*, *12*, 468–482.

———— (1945). Notes and fragments. *International Journal of Psychoanalysis*, *30*, 231–242. (Original work published 1930–1932)

Fichte, J. (1848). *The vocation of man*. London: Chapman.

Fonagy, P. (2000). Attachment and borderline personality disorder. *Journal of the American Psychoanalytic Association*, *48*, 1129–1146.

Fonagy, P., Gergely, G., Jurist, E., & Target, M. (2002). *Mentalization, affect regulation, and the self*. New York: Other Press.

Fosshage, J. (1988). Dream interpretation revisited. *Progress in Self Psychology*, *3*, 161–175.

———— (1991). Beyond the basic rule. In A. Goldberg (Ed.), *The evolution of self psychology, progress in self psychology* (Vol. 7, pp. 64–71). Hillsdale, NJ: The Analytic Press.

Foucault, M. (1980). *Power/knowledge: Selected interviews and other writings*. New York: Pantheon Books.

French, T., & Fromm, E. (1964). *Dream interpretation: A new approach*. New York: Basic Books.

Freud, A. (1936). *The ego and the mechanisms of defense*. New York: International Universities Press.

Freud, S. (1895a). Project for a scientific psychology. In J. Strachey (Ed. & Trans.), *The standard edition of the complete psychological works of Sigmund Freud* (Vol. 1, pp. 283–397). London: Hogarth Press.

———— (1895b). Psychotherapy of hysteria, chapter 4. In J. Strachey (Ed. & Trans.), *The standard edition of the complete psychological works of Sigmund Freud* (Vol. 2, pp. 253–305). London: Hogarth Press.

———— (1898). Sexuality in the etiology of the neuroses. In J. Strachey (Ed. & Trans.), *The standard edition of the complete psychological works of Sigmund Freud* (Vol. 3, pp. 263–285). London: Hogarth Press.

———— (1900). The interpretation of dreams. In J. Strachey (Ed. & Trans.), *The standard edition of the complete psychological works of Sigmund Freud* (Vols. 3–4). London: Hogarth Press.

——— (1906). My views on the part played by sexuality in the aetiology of the neuroses. In J. Strachey (Ed. & Trans.), *The standard edition of the complete psychological works of Sigmund Freud* (Vol. 7, pp. 271–279). London: Hogarth Press.

——— (1910). "Wild" psycho-analysis. In J. Strachey (Ed. & Trans.), *The standard edition of the complete psychological works of Sigmund Freud* (Vol. 11, pp. 219–228). London: Hogarth Press.

——— (1912). Recommendations to physicians practicing psycho-analysis. In J. Strachey (Ed. & Trans.), *The standard edition of the complete psychological works of Sigmund Freud* (Vol. 12, pp. 109–121). London: Hogarth Press.

——— (1914). On narcissism. In J. Strachey (Ed. & Trans.), *The standard edition of the complete psychological works of Sigmund Freud* (Vol. 14, pp. 73–104). London: Hogarth Press.

——— (1915). Instincts and their vicissitudes. In J. Strachey (Ed. & Trans.), *The standard edition of the complete psychological works of Sigmund Freud* (Vol. 14, pp. 111–140). London: Hogarth Press.

——— (1916–1917). Introductory lectures on psychoanalysis. In J. Strachey (Ed. & Trans.), *The standard edition of the complete psychological works of Sigmund Freud* (Vol. 17, pp. 7–124). London: Hogarth Press.

——— (1917). From the history of an infantile neurosis. In J. Strachey (Ed. & Trans.), *The standard edition of the complete psychological works of Sigmund Freud* (Vol. 17, pp. 1–124). London: Hogarth Press.

——— (1923). The ego and the id. In J. Strachey (Ed. & Trans.), *The standard edition of the complete psychological works of Sigmund Freud* (Vol. 19, pp. 1–66). London: Hogarth Press.

——— (1924). Neurosis and psychosis. In J. Strachey (Ed. & Trans.), *The standard edition of the complete psychological works of Sigmund Freud* (Vol. 19, pp. 147–154). London: Hogarth Press.

——— (1926). Symptom, inhibition, and anxiety. In J. Strachey (Ed. & Trans.), *The standard edition of the complete psychological works of Sigmund Freud* (Vol. 20, pp. 75–176). London: Hogarth Press.

——— (1930). Civilization and its discontents. In J. Strachey (Ed. & Trans.), *The standard edition of the complete psychological works of Sigmund Freud* (Vol. 21, pp. 57–146). London: Hogarth Press.

——— (1938). An outline of psychoanalysis. In J. Strachey (Ed. & Trans.), *The standard edition of the complete psychological works of Sigmund Freud* (Vol. 23, pp. 141–208). London: Hogarth Press.

Fromm, E. (1947). *Man for himself: An inquiry into the psychology of ethics.* Greenwich, CT: Fawcett.

Gardner, H. (1983). *Frames of mind: The theory of multiple intelligences.* New York: Basic Books.

Garner, D., & Garfinkel, P. (1980). Socio-cultural factors in the development of anorexia nervosa. *Psychological Medicine, 10,* 647–656.

Gedo, J. (1981). *Beyond interpretation: Toward a revised theory of psychoanalysis.* London: Routledge.

Gedo, J., & Goldberg, A. (1976). *Models of the mind: A psychoanalytic theory.* Chicago: University of Chicago Press.

Gellner, A. (2005). America may be at the peak of latest materialistic cycle/Supersize homes, gigantic SUVs afflict a nation. http://www.sfgate.com/homeandgarden/article/America-may-be-at-the-peak-of-latest-2565873.php

Ghent, E. (2002). Wish, need, drive: Motive in the light of dynamic systems theory and Edelman's selectionist theory. *Psychoanalytic Dialogues, 12,* 763–808.

Gill, M. (1981). *The analysis of the transference. Vol. 1.* New York: International Universities Press.

——— (1994). *Psychoanalysis in transition.* Hillsdale, NJ: The Analytic Press.

Goldberg, A. (1988). *A fresh look at psychoanalysis: The view from self psychology.* Hillsdale, NJ: The Analytic Press.

———— (1999). *Being of two minds: The vertical split in psychoanalysis and psychotherapy*. Hillsdale, NJ: The Analytic Press.

Gray, P. (1973). Technique and the ego's capacity for viewing intrapsychic activity. *Journal of the American Psychoanalytic Association, 21*, 474–494.

———— (1982). Developmental lag in the evolution of technique for the psychoanalysis of neurotic conflict. *Journal of the American Psychoanalytic Association, 30*, 621–656.

———— (1990). The nature of therapeutic action in psychoanalysis. *Journal of the American Psychoanalytic Association, 38*, 1083–1097.

———— (1995). Undoing the lag in the technique of conflict and defense analysis. *Psychoanalytic Study of the Child, 51*, 87–101.

Green, A. (1975). The analyst, symbolization, and absence. *Journal of the International Psychoanalytic Association, 56*, 1–22.

———— (2008). Freud's concept of temporality: Differences with current ideas. *International Journal of Psychoanalysis, 89*, 1029–1039.

Greenberg, R. (1989). The concept of the self-state dream, revisited. *Progress in Self Psychology, 5*, 25–32.

Greenberg, R., & Pearlman, C. (1978). If Freud only knew: A reconsideration of psychoanalytic dream theory. *International Review of Psychoanalysis, 5*, 71–75.

Greenberg, R., Pearlman, C., Schwartz, W., & Youkilis, H. (1983). Memory, emotion, and REM sleep. *Journal of Abnormal Psychology, 92*, 378–381.

Greenspan, G. H., & Pollack, S. I. (1980). *Course of life*. Washington, DC: US Government Printing Office.

Greenspan, S. & Pollock, G. (Eds.). (1991). *The course of life: Volumes I–VII*. Madison, CT: International Universities Press.

Grossmark, R. (2007). The edge of chaos: Enactment, disruption, and emergence in group psychotherapy. *Psychoanalytic Dialogues, 17*, 479–499.

Grotstein, J. (1977). *Splitting and projective identification*. New York: Aronson.

Grunbaum, A. (1984). *The foundations of psychoanalysis: A philosophical critique*. Berkeley, CA: University of California Press.

———— (1993). *Validation in the clinical theory of psychoanalysis: A study in the philosophy of psychoanalysis*. New York: International Universities Press.

Harrison, K., & Cantor, J. (1997). The relationship between eating disorders and the media. *Journal of Communication, 47*(1), 40–67.

Hartmann, H., Kris, E., & Loewenstein, R. M. (1946). Comments on the formation of psychic structure. *The Psychoanalytic Study of the Child, 2*, 11–38.

Hebb, D. (1955). Drives and the CNS. *The Psychological Review, 62*, 243–254.

Heidegger, M. (1961). *Being and time*. New York: Harper & Row. (Original work published 1927)

———— (1962). *Being and time*. New York: Harper & Row. (original work published 1927)

———— (1968). *What is called thinking?* New York: Harper & Row. (original work published 1954)

———— (1977). The questions concerning technology. In W. Lovitt (Trans.), *The question concerning technology and other essays* (pp. 3–35). New York: Harper. (Original work published 1955)

———— (2001). *Zollikon seminars*. Evanston, IL: Northwestern University Press. (Original work published 1959–1961)

Hesse, H. (1999). *Demian*. New York: Harper. (Original work published 1919)

Hoffman, I. (2002). *Ritual and spontaneity in the psychoanalytic process*. Hillsdale, NJ: The Analytic Press.

Holmes, D. E. (1997). The analyst in the inner city: Review of Altman. *Journal of the American Psychoanalytic Association, 6*, 446–448.

Holmes, J. (2006). *Ideas in psychoanalysis: Narcissism*. London: Totem Books.

Hook, S. (1960). *Psychoanalysis, scientific method, and philosophy*. New York: New York University Press.

Husserl, E. (1913). *Ideas: Introduction to pure phenomenology*. New York: Springer.

——— (1964). *The phenomenology of internal time consciousness*. Bloomington: Indiana University Press. (Original work published 1905)

Jackson, M. (2008). *Distracted: The erosion of attention and the coming dark age*. New York: Prometheus.

Johnson, S. (2012). *London: A poem*. Charleston, SC: Nabu Press. (Original work published 1738)

Joseph, B. (1971). A clinical contribution to the analysis of a perversion. In M. Feldman & E. Spillius (Eds.), *Psychic equilibrium and psychic change* (pp. 51–66). London: Routledge.

——— (1985). Transference and the total situation. *International Journal of Psychoanalysis, 66*, 447–54.

——— (1992). Psychic change: some perspectives. *International Journal of Psychoanalysis, 73*, 237–43.

Kahneman, D., & Deaton, A. (2010). High income improves evaluation of life, but not emotional well being. *Proceedings of the National Academy of Sciences*, September 6.

Kalat, J. (2007). *Introduction to psychology* (9th ed.). New York: Wadsworth.

Keats, J. (2005). Letter to brother, December 21, 1817. In D. Wu (Ed.), *Romanticism: An anthology*, (3rd ed., p. 1351). New York: Blackwell. (Original work published 1817)

Kernberg, O. (1975). *Borderline conditions and pathological narcissism*. Northvale, NJ: Aronson.

——— (1976). *Object relations theory and clinical psychoanalysis*. Northvale, NJ: Aronson.

——— (1984). *Severe personality disorders*. New Haven, CT: Yale University Press.

——— (1988). Object relations theory in clinical practice. *Psychoanalytic Quarterly, 57*, 481–504.

Kernberg, O., Selzer, M., Koenigsberg, H., Carr, A., and Appelbaum, A. (1989). *Psychodynamic psychotherapy of borderline patients*. New York: Basic Books.

Khan, M. (1963). The concept of the cumulative trauma. In *The privacy of the self* (pp. 42–58). New York: International Universities Press.

——— (1974). *The privacy of the self*. New York: International Universities Press.

——— (1989). Beyond the dreaming experience. In *Hidden selves: Between practice and theory in psychoanalysis* (pp. –). London: Karnac.

Kierkegaard, S. (1968). *Attack on Christendom*. Princeton, NJ: Princeton University Press. (Original work published 1854–1855)

——— (1985). *Philosophical fragments/Johannes Climacus*. Princeton, NJ: Princeton University Press. (Original work published 1849)

Klein, M. (1937). *Love, hate, and reparation*. London: Hogarth.

——— (1940). Mourning and its relation to manic-depressive states. *International Journal of Psychoanalysis, 21*, 125–133.

——— (1945). The Oedipus complex in the light of early anxieties. *International Journal of Psychoanalysis, 26*, 11–33.

——— (1957). Envy and gratitude. In *Envy and gratitude and other works, 1946–1963*. New York: Delta.

Kohlberg, L. (1981). *Essays on moral development: Vol. 1. The philosophy of moral development*. San Francisco, CA: Harper & Row.

Kohut, H. (1959). Introspection, empathy, and psychoanalysis: An examination of the relationship between mode of observation and theory. *Journal of the American Psychoanalytic Association, 7*, 459–483.

Kohut, H. (1971). *The analysis of the self*. New York: International Universities Press.

———— (1977). *The restoration of the self*. New York: International Universities Press.

———— (1984). *How does analysis cure?* Chicago: University of Chicago Press.

Kohut, H., & Wolf, E. S. (1978). The disorders of the self and their treatment: An outline. *The International Journal of Psychoanalysis*, *59*, 413–425.

Krause, S. (2008). *Civil passions: Moral sentiment and democratic deliberations*. Princeton, NJ: Princeton University Press.

Lacan, J. (1970). *Les ecrits*. New York: [Publisher].

———— (1977a). *Les ecrits: A selection*. New York: W. W. Norton.

———— (1977b). The field and function of speech and language in psychoanalysis. In *Les ecrits* (pp. 30–114). New York: W. W. Norton.

Lachmann, F., & Beebe, B. (1992). Representations and selfobject transferences: A developmental perspective. *Progress in Self Psychology*, *8*(1), 3–15.

Lakoff, G., & Johnson, M. (2003). *Metaphors we live by*. Chicago: University of Chicago Press.

Laplanche, J. (1985). *Life and death in psychoanalysis*. Baltimore, MD: Johns Hopkins University Press. (original work published 1970)

Larmore, C. (1996). *The romantic legacy*. New York: Columbia University Press.

Lasch, C. (1991). *The rhetoric of science in psychiatry*. New York: Walter de Gruyter.

Layton, L. (2004). *Who's that girl? Who's that boy?* Hillsdale, NJ: The Analytic Press.

———— (2006). Racial identities, racial enactments, and normative unconscious processes. *Psychoanalytic Quarterly*, *75*, 237–269.

Lear, J. (1998). *Open-minded: Working out the logic of the soul*. Cambridge, MA: Harvard University Press.

———— (2011). *A case for irony*. Cambridge, MA: Harvard University Press.

Leary, K. (1995). "Interpreting in the dark": Race and ethnicity in psychoanalytic psychotherapy. *Psychoanalytic Psychology*, *12*, 127–140.

———— (1997a). Race in psychoanalytic space. *Gender and Psychoanalysis*, *2*, 157–172.

———— (1997b). Race, self-disclosure, and "forbidden talk": Race and ethnicity in contemporary clinical practice. *Psychoanalytic Quarterly*, *66*, 163–189.

———— (2000). Racial enactments in dynamic treatment. *Psychoanalytic Dialogues*, *10*, 639–653.

———— (2006). In the eye of the storm. *Psychoanalytic Quarterly*, *75*, 345–363.

Levy, S. T. (1985). Empathy and psychoanalytic technique. *Journal of the American Psychoanalytic Association*, *33*, 353–378.

Lewin, B. (1946). Sleep, the mouth, and the dream screen. *Psychoanalytic Quarterly*, *15*, 419–434.

Lewinsohn, P. M., Rohde, P., Klein, D., & Seeley, J. R. (1993). Natural course of adolescent major depressive disorder: I. continuity into young adulthood. *Journal of the American Academy of Child and Adolescent Psychiatry*, *38*(1), 56–63.

Little, M. (1977). *Transference neurosis and transference psychosis*. Northvale, NJ: Aronson.

Loewald, H. (1960). The therapeutic action of psychoanalysis. *International Journal of Psychoanalysis*, *41*, 16–33.

Loewald, H. W. (1962a). The superego and the ego-ideal. *International Journal of Psychoanalysis*, *43*, 264–268.

———— (1962b). Superego and time. In *Papers on psychoanalysis* (pp. 43–53). New Haven, CT: Yale University Press.

———— (1972). The experience of time. *Psychoanalytic Study of the Child*, *27*, 401–410.

Loewenstein, R. (1950). Autonomous ego development during the phallic phase. *The Psychoanalytic Study of the Child*, *5*, 47–52.

Lyubomirsky, S., Sheldon, K., & Schkade, D. (2005). Pursuing happiness: The architecture of sustainable change. *Review of General Psychology*, *9*, 111–131.

Mahler, M. S. (1975). On the current status of infantile neurosis. *Journal of the American Psychoanalytic Association*, *23*, 327–333.

Mahler, M. S., Pine, F. and Bergman, A. (1975). The psychological birth of the human infant. New York: Basic Books.

Mann, T. (1941). Freud's position in the history of modern culture. *Psychoanalytic Review*, *28*, 91–116.

Marcuse, H. (1991). *One-dimensional man: Studies in the ideology of advanced industrial society*. Boston, MA: Beacon Press. (Original work published 1964)

Maslow, A. (1969). *Toward a psychology of being*. New York: Wiley.

Matte-Blanco, I. (1975). *The unconscious as infinite sets: An essay on bi-logic*. London: Karnac.

——— (1998). *The unconscious as infinite sets: An essay in bi-logic*. London: Karnac.

McCarthy, M. (1990). The thin ideal, depression, eating disorders, and women. *Behavioral Research Therapy*, *28*(3), 205–215.

McCreary, D. R., & Sasse, D. K. (2000). An exploration of the drive for muscularity in adolescent boys and girls. *Journal of American College Health*, *48*, 297–304.

McDermott, J. (1969). Technology: The opiate of the intellectuals. *New York Review of Books*, July 31, 25–34.

McDougall, J. (1996). *Theatres of the mind*. London: Free Association Books.

Mendelsohn, R. (1990). *The manifest dream and its use in therapy*. Northvale, NJ: Aronson.

Merleau-Ponty, M. (1985). The experience of others. *Review of Existential Psychiatry and Psychology*, *18*, 33–63.

Mitchell, S. (1988). *Relational concepts in psychoanalysis: An integration*. Cambridge, MA: Harvard University Press.

——— (1993). *Hope and dread in psychoanalysis*. New York: Basic Books.

——— (1997). *Influence and autonomy in psychoanalysis*. Hillsdale, NJ: The Analytic Press.

Modell, A. (1990). *Other times, other realities*. Cambridge, MA: Harvard University Press.

——— (2003). *Imagination and the meaningful brain*. Cambridge, MA: MIT Press.

Morgan, C., Weis, J., Schopler, J., and King R. (2005). *Introduction to Psychology*. 7th Ed. New York: Tata Mc Graw-Hill.

Munn, N. (1969). *Introduction to psychology*. New York: Houghton-Mifflin.

Nafisi, A. (2003). The saving power of literature. Chicago Humanities Festival, Chicago, IL, November 9.

Neumark-Sztainer, D., Croll, J., Story, M., Hannan, P., French, S., & Perry, C. (2002). Ethnic/racial differences in weight-related concerns and behaviors among adolescent girls and boys: Findings from Project EAT. *Journal of Psychosomatic Research*, *53*(5), 963–974.

Neumark-Sztainer, D., Story, M., & Faibisch, L. (1998). Perceived stigmatization among overweight African-American and Caucasian adolescent girls. *Journal of Adolescent Health*, *23*(5), 264–270.

Newman, D. L., Moffitt, T. E., Caspi, A., Magdol, L., Silva, P. A., & Stanton, W. R. (1996). Psychiatric disorder in a birth cohort young adults: Prevalence, comorbidity, clinical significance, and new case incidence from ages 11–21. *Journal of Consulting and Clinical Psychology*, *64*, 552–562.

Nolen-Hoeksema, S., & Girgus, J. S. (1994). The emergence of gender differences in depression during adolescence. *Psychological Bulletin*, *115*, 424–443.

Novalis. (1997). *Philosophical writings*. Albany: State University of New York Press. (Original work published 1797–1799).

Ogden, T. (1990). Internal object relations. In *Matrix of the mind* (pp. 99–130) Northvale, NJ: Aronson.

——— (1994). *Subjects of analysis*. Northvale, NJ: Aronson.

——— (2001). *Conversations on the frontier of dreaming*. Northvale, NJ: Aronson.

Ohring, R., Graber, J., & Brooks-Gunn, J. (2002). Girls' recurrent and concurrent body dissatisfaction: Correlates and consequences over 8 years. *The International Journal of Eating Disorders*, *31*, 401–415.

Ophir, E., Nass, C., & Wagner, A. D. (2009). Cognitive control in multitaskers. *Proceedings of the Academy of Sciences of the United States of America*, *106*, 15583–15587.

Ornstein, A. (1990). Selfobject transferences and the process of working through. *Progress in Self Psychology*, *6*(5), 41–58.

Parker, S., Nichter, M., Nichter, M., Vuckovic, N., Sims, C., & Ritenbaugh, C. (1995). Body image and weight concerns among African American and white adolescent females: Differences that make a difference. *Human Organization*, *54*, 103–114.

Pearlman, C. (1982). Sleep structure variation. In W. Webb (Ed.), *Biological rhythms, sleep and performance* (pp. 143–173). New York: Wiley.

Peltz, R. (2005). The manic society. *Psychoanalytic Dialogues*, *15*, 347–366.

Perez-Foster, R. M. (1996). What is multicultural perspective for psychoanalysis? In R. M. Foster, M. Moskowitz, & R. A. Javier (Eds.), *Reaching across boundaries of culture and class: Widening the scope of psychotherapy* (pp. 3–20). New York: Aronson.

Phillips, A. (1998). *The beast in the nursery: On curiosity and other appetites*. New York: Vintage Press.

Pontalis, J. (1974). Dream as an object. *International Review of Psychoanalysis*, *1*, 125–133.

Pope, A. (2008). *Essay on criticism*. Hong Kong: Forgotten Books. (Original work published 1709)

Popper, K. (1962). *Open society and its enemies*, Vol. 1. London: Routledge.

——— (1963). *Conjectures and refutations*. New York: Basic Books.

Pulver, S. & Renik, O. (1984). The clinical use of the manifest dream. *Journal of the American Psychoanalytic Association*, *32*, 157–162.

Putnam, H. (1990). *Realism with a human face*. Cambridge, MA: Harvard.

Racker, H. (1960). *Transference and countertransference*. New York: International Universities Press.

——— (1968). *Transference and countertransference*. New York: International Universities Press.

Rangell, L. (1982). The self in psychoanalytic theory. *Journal of the American Psychoanalytic Association*, *30*, 863–891.

Rapaport, D. (1951). The autonomy of the ego. In M. Gill (Ed.), *The collected papers of David Rapaport* (pp. 357–367). New York: Basic Books.

——— (1957). The theory of ego autonomy: A generalization. In M. Gill (Ed.), *The collected papers of David Rapaport* (pp. 722–744). New York: Basic Books.

——— (1960). The structure of psychoanalytic theory. *Psychological Issues*, *2*(2), 1–158.

Reiser, M. F. (1999). Memory, empathy, and interactive dimensions of psychoanalytic process. *Journal of the American Psychoanalytic Association*, *47*, 485–501.

Ricouer, P. (1950). *Freedom and nature*. Evanston, IL: Northwestern University Press.

——— (1984). *Time and narrative*. Chicago: University of Chicago Press.

Riker, J. (2010). *Why it is good to be good: Ethics, Kohut's self psychology, and modern society*. New York: Aronson.

Ringstrom, P. A. (2007). Scenes that write themselves: Improvisational moments in relational psychoanalysis. *Psychoanalytic Dialogues*, *17*, 69–99.

Robbins, M. (2004). Another look at dreaming. *Journal of the American Psychoanalytic Association*, *52*, 355–386.

Rodin, J., Silberstein, L., & Striegel-Moore, R. (1984). Women and weight: A normative discontent. *Nebraska Symposium on Motivation, 32*, 267–307.

Rosen, J. (1990). Body-image disturbances in eating disorders. In T. Cash & T. Pruzinsky (Eds.), *Body images: Development, deviance, and change* (pp. 190–214). New York: Guilford Press.

Rosenfeld, H. (1987). *Impasse and interpretation: Therapeutic and anti-therapeutic factors in the treatment of psychotic, borderline, and neurotic patients.* London: Tavistock.

Rubenstein, B. (1976). On the possibility of a strictly clinical psychoanalytic theory: An essay on the philosophy of psychoanalysis. In P. Holzman & M. Gill (Eds.), *Psychology and metapsychology: Psychoanalytic essays in honor of George Klein* (pp. 229–264). New York: International Universities Press.

———— (1980). The problem of confirmation in clinical psychoanalysis. *Journal of the American Psychoanalytic Association, 28*, 397–417.

Sander, L. (1975). Infant and caretaking environment. In E. J. Anthony (Ed.), *Explorations in child psychiatry* (pp. 129–165). New York: Plenum.

———— (2000). Where are we going in the field of infant mental health? *Infant Mental Health Journal, 21*, 1–18.

Sartre, J. P. (1993). *Being and nothingness.* Washington, DC: Washington Square Press. (Original work published 1943)

Schafer, R. (1981). *A new language for psychoanalysis.* New Haven, CT: Yale University Press.

———— (1992). *Retelling a life.* New York: Basic Books.

Schiller, F. (2004). *On the aesthetic education of man.* Mineola, NY: Dover Books. (Original work published 1794)

Schlegel, F. (1991). *Philosophical fragments.* Minneapolis: University of Minnesota Press. (Original work published 1798–1801)

Schumacher, J. (2001). Dead zone: Criticism of American materialism. *New Internationalist Magazine.*

Schutz, A. (1974). *The phenomenology of the social world.* G. Walsh and F. Lenhert (Trans.). Evanston, IL: Northwestern University Press. (Original work published 1932)

Schwaber, E. (1990). Interpretation and the therapeutic action of psychoanalysis. *International Journal of Psychoanalysis, 71*, 229–240.

———— (1992). Psychoanalytic theory and its relationship to clinical work. *Journal of the American Psychoanalytic Association, 40*, 1039–1057.

———— (2005). The struggle to listen: Continuing reflections, lingering paradoxes, and some thoughts on the recovery of memories. *Journal of the American Psychoanalytic Association, 53*, 789–810.

Scriven, M. (1962). Frontiers of psychology: Psychoanalysis and parapsychology. In R. G. Colodny (Ed.), *Frontiers of science and philosophy* (pp. 78–129). Pittsburgh, PA: University of Pittsburgh Press.

Seeley, C. (2006). Teaching to the test. *NCTM News Bulletin, The National Council of Teachers of Mathematics.*

Segal, H. (1982). Early infantile development as reflected in the psychoanalytical process: Steps in integration. *International Journal of Psychoanalysis, 63*, 15–22.

———— (1983). Some clinical implications of Melanie Klein's work. *International Journal of Psychoanalysis, 64*, 269–276.

Seligman, M. (1995). The effectiveness of psychotherapy: The Consumer Reports study. *The American Psychologist, 50*, 965–974.

Shafer, R. (1980). Action language and the psychology of the self. *The Annual of Psychoanalysis, 8*, 83–92.

Schafer, R. (1983). *The analytic attitude*. New York: Basic Books.

Shapiro, S. (1985). Archaic self object transferences and the analysis of a case of male homosexuality. *Progress in Self Psychology, 1*, 164–177.

Shedler, J. (2010). The efficacy of psychodynamic psychotherapy. *American Psychologist, 65*(2), 98–109.

Shelley, P. (1820). *Prometheus unbound*. London: C and J Ollier.

Shultz, M. & Zedeck, S. (2008). Identification, development, and validation of predictors for successful lawyering, Report of University of California Berkeley School of Law. (unpublished)

Smith, H. (2006). Invisible racism. *Psychoanalytic Quarterly, 75*, 3–19.

Soldz, S. (2010). Psychologists defying torture: The challenge and the path ahead. In A. Harris & S. Botticelli (Eds.), *First do no harm: Paradoxical encounters of psychoanalysis, warmaking, and resistance* (pp. 67–105). London: Routledge.

Spring, B. (2007). Evidence based practice in clinical psychology: What it is, why it matters, what you need to know. *Journal of Clinical Psychology, 63*(7), 611–631.

Sroufe, A. (2000). Early relationships and the development of children. *Infant Mental Health Journal, 21*(1–2), 67–74.

Steiner, J. (1993). *Psychic retreats: Pathological organizations in psychotic, neurotic, and borderline states*. London: Routledge.

Stern, D. (2004). *The present moment in psychotherapy and everyday life*. New York: W. W. Norton.

———— (2010). *Partners in thought*. New York: Routledge.

Stern, Da. (1985). *The interpersonal world of the infant*. New York: Basic Books.

Stern, Do. (1997). *Unformulated experience: From dissociation to imagination in psychoanalysis*. Hillsdale, NJ: The Analytic Press.

Stern, D., Sandler, F., Nahum, J., Harrison, A., Ruth-Lyon, K., Morgan, A., Bruschweilerstern, N., & Trolnick, E. (1998). Non-interpretive mechanisms in psychoanalytic therapy: The "something more" than interpretation. *International Journal of Psychoanalysis, 79*, 903–921.

Stice, E., & Bearman, S. (2001). Body-image and eating disturbances prospectively predict increases in depressive symptoms in adolescent girls: A growth curve analysis. *Developmental Psychology, 37*(5), 597–607.

Stoljar, M. (1997). Introduction. In Novalis (Au.), *Philosophical writings*. Albany: State University of New York Press.

Stolorow, R., & Atwood, G. (1982). Psychoanalytic phenomenology of the dream. *The Annual of Psychoanalysis, 10*, 205–220.

Strawson, P. F. (1959). *Individuals*. London: Routledge.

Strenger, C. (1998). *Individuality: The impossible project. Psychoanalysis and self creation*. Madison, CT: International Universities Press.

Striegel-Moore, R., Silberstein, L., & Rodin, J. (1986). Toward an understanding of risk factors for bulimia. *American Psychologist, 41*(3), 246–263.

Sugarman, A. (1995). Psychoanalysis: Treatment of deficit or conflict? *Psychoanalytic Psychology, 12*, 55–70.

———— (2006). Mentalization, insightfulness, and therapeutic action. *International Journal of Psychoanalysis, 87*, 965–987.

Sullivan, H. S. (1953). *The interpersonal theory of psychiatry*. New York: W. W. Norton.

Summers, F. (1996). Existential guilt: An object relations concept. *Contemporary Psychoanalysis, 32*(1), 43–63.

———— (1999). *Transcending the self: an object relations model of psychoanalytic therapy*. Hillsdale, NJ: The Analytic Press.

———— (2000). The analyst's vision of the patient and therapeutic action. *Psychoanalytic Psychology*, *17*(3), 547–565.

———— (2003). The future as intrinsic to the psyche and psychoanalytic therapy. *Contemporary Psychoanalysis*, *39*(1), 335–353.

———— (2005a). *Self creation: Psychoanalytic therapy and the art of the possible*. Hillsdale, NJ: The Analytic Press.

———— (2005b). Discovery and creation in the psychoanalytic process. In J. Mills (Ed.), *Interpersonal and relational perspectives in psychoanalysis* (pp. 131–152). New York: Aronson.

———— (2006). Freud's relevance for contemporary psychoanalytic technique. *Psychoanalytic Psychology*, *23*(2), 327–339.

———— (2007). When one and one makes one . . . well, almost. *Contemporary Psychoanalysis*, *43*(4), 638–665.

———— (2010). Violence in American foreign policy: A psychoanalytic approach. In A. Harris & S. Botticelli (Eds.), *First do no harm: Paradoxical encounters of psychoanalysis, warmaking, and resistance* (pp. 153–174). London: Routledge.

———— (2012). Creating new ways of being. *Psychoanalytic Dialogues*, *21*(2), 1–19.

Taylor, C. (1989). *Sources of the self: Making of the modern identity*. Cambridge, MA: Harvard University Press.

———— (1992). Heidegger, language, and ecology. In H. Dreyfus & H. Hall (Eds.), *Heidegger: A critical reader* (pp. 247–269). Cambridge, MA: Blackwell.

Thompson, C. (1964). *Interpersonal psychoanalysis: The collected papers of Clara Thompson*. M. R. Green (Ed.). New York: Basic Books.

Thompson, J., & Stice, E. (2001). Thin-ideal internalization: Mounting evidence for a new risk factor for body image disturbance and eating pathology. *Current Directions in Psychological Science*, *10*(5), 181–183.

Thorndike, E. L. (1918). The nature, purposes, and general methods of measurements of educational products. In G. M. Whipple (Ed.), *The seventeenth yearbook of the National Society for Study of Education. Part II. The measurement of educational products*. Bloomington, IL: Public School Publishing Co.

Tolpin, M. (2002). Doing psychoanalysis of normal development: Forward edge transferences. *Progress in Self Psychology*, *18*, 167–190.

Tomkins, S. (1962). *Affect imagery consciousness: Volume I, The positive affects*. London: Tavistock.

———— (1978). Script theory: Differential magnification of affects. Nebraska Symposium on Motivation 1978, R. A. Deinstbier. Lincoln: University of Nebraska Press.

———— (1987). Script theory. In J. Arnoff, I. Rabin, & R. Zucker (Eds.), *The emergence of personality*. New York: Springer.

———— (1991). *Affect imagery consciousness: Vol. 3. The negative affects: Anger and fear*. New York: Springer.

Torrance, E. P. (2003). *Reflections on emerging insights on the educational psychology of creativity*. Cresskill, NJ: Hampton Press.

Turkle, S. (2004). Always-on/Always-on-you: The tethered self. In J. Katz (Ed.), *Handbook of mobile communications*. Cambridge, MA: MIT Press.

———— (2011). *Alone together*. New York: Basic Books.

Turner, J. (1988). Wordsworth and Winnicott in the area of play. *International Review of Psychoanalysis*, *15*, 481–496.

Wallerstein, R. (1992). *The common ground of psychoanalysis*. Northvale, NJ: Aronson.

Wampold, B. E. (2007). Psychotherapy: The humanistic (and effective) treatment. *American Psychologist*, *62*, 857–873.

Wilkerson, R. (1997). Existential-phenomenology and dreams. Part of the ED dream education series electric dreams, *4*(6).

Williams, M. H. (2010). *The aesthetic development*. London: Karnac.

Winnicott, D. W. (1960). Ego distortion in terms of true and false self. In *The maturational processes and the facilitating environment* (pp. 140–152). New York: International Universities Press.

———— (1962). The theory of the parent-infant relationship: Further remarks. *International Journal of Psychoanalysis*, *43*, 238–239.

———— (1965). *Maturational processes and the facilitating environment*. New York: International Universities Press.

———— (1971). *Playing and reality*. London: Routledge.

———— (1974). Fear of breakdown. *International Review of Psychoanalysis*, *1*, 103–107.

Wordsworth, W. (2010). *Ode: Intimations of immortality from recollection of early childhood memories*. Whitefish, MT: Kessinger Books. (Original work published 1843)

Yi, K. Y. (1998). Transference and race: An intersubjective conceptualization. *Psychoanalytic Psychology*, *15*, 245–261.

INDEX